Cockburn Sums Up
An Autobiography

Cockburn Sums Up

An Autobiography

Claud Cockburn

Quartet Books

London Melbourne New York

Published by Quartet Books Limited 1981
A member of the Namara Group
27 Goodge Street, London W1P 1FD

Some parts of this book first published in three volumes:
In Time of Trouble published by Rupert Hart-Davis 1956
Crossing the Line published by MacGibbon & Kee 1958
View from the West published by MacGibbon & Kee 1961
Revised edition (*I Claud*) published by Penguin Books 1967

Foreword copyright © Graham Greene 1981

ISBN 0 7043 2266 8

Typeset for Quartet Books Limited by Trendsetter
Photoset Limited, Brentwood, Essex

Printed in Great Britain by Litho at The Anchor Press
and bound by William Brendon & Son Limited,
both of Tiptree, Essex

Contents

Foreword

IF I were asked who are the two greatest journalists of the twentieth century, my answer would be G. K. Chesterton and Claud Cockburn. Both are more than journalists: both produced at least one novel which will be rediscovered with delight, I believe, in every generation – *The Man Who was Thursday* and *Ballantyne's Folly*. Both are manic characters, writing with what some sad fellows may find even an excess of high spirits. Perhaps Claud Cockburn will prove to have been more influential, for he discovered the influence that can be wielded by a mimeographed news sheet. *The Week* anticipated ironically enough, considering that Cockburn was himself then a Communist, the Samizdat publication in East Europe. Finally, if only to show that I have had my manic moments too, I would like to salute the only man with whom I have ever gone barrel-organing. The memory of that three-day escapade is still fresh after nearly sixty years.

Graham Greene

*If God lived on earth,
people would break his
windows*

1 War Games

In our little house, the question was whether the war would break out first, or the revolution. This was around 1910.

There were war scares every year, all justified. There was the greatest surge of industrial unrest ever seen. There was a crime wave. The young were demoralized. In 1911, without any help from Television or the Cinema or the Comics, some Yorkshire schoolboys, irked by discipline, set upon an unpopular teacher and murdered him.

Naturally, alongside those who viewed with alarm, there were those who thought things would probably work out all right. Prophets of doom and Pollyannas, Dr Pangloss and Calamity Jane, all lived near us in Hertfordshire in those years, and I well remember being taken to call on them all, on fine afternoons, in the open landau, for a treat.

At home the consensus was that the war would come before the revolution.

This, as can be seen from the newspaper files, was not the most general view.

At our house, however, people thought war was not any nicer than revolution, but more natural.

It was in 1910 that my father desired me to stop playing French and English with my toy soldiers and play Germans and English instead. That was a bother, for there was a character, on a white horse, who was Napoleon – in fact, a double Napoleon; because he was dead Napoleon who fought Waterloo, and also alive, getting ready to attack the Chiltern Hills where we lived. It was awkward changing him into an almost unheard-of Marshal von Moltke.

Guests came to lunch and talked about the coming German

invasion. On Sundays, when my sister and I lunched in the dining-room instead of the nursery, we heard about it. It spoiled afternoon walks on the hills with Nanny, who until then had kept us happy learning the names of the small wild flowers growing there. I thought Uhlans with lances and flat-topped helmets might come charging over the hill any afternoon now. It was frightening, and a harassing responsibility, since Nanny and my sister had no notion of the danger. It was impossible to explain to them fully about the Uhlans, and one had to keep a keen watch all the time. Nanny was no longer a security. (An earlier Nanny had herself been frightened on our walks. She was Chinese, from the Mongolian border, and she thought there were tigers in the Chilterns.)

One night, at hay-making time, when the farm carts trundled home late, I lay awake in the dusk and trembled. Evidently they had come, and their endless gun-carriages were rolling up the lane. My sister said to go to sleep; it was all right because we had a British soldier staying in the house. This was Uncle Philip, a half-pay Major of Hussars whose hands had been partially paralysed as a result of some accident at polo.

His presence that night was a comfort. But his conversation was often alarming, particularly after he had been playing the War Game.

In the garden there was a big shed or small barn, and inside the shed was the War Game. It was played on a table a good deal bigger, as I recall, than a billiard table, and was strategically scientific. So much so, indeed, that the game was used for instructional purposes at the Staff College. Each team of players had so many guns of different calibre, so many divisions of troops, so many battleships, cruisers and other instruments of war. You threw dice, and operated your forces according to the value of the throw. Even so, the possible moves were regulated by rules of extreme realism.

The Game sometimes took three whole days to complete, and it always over-excited Uncle Philip. The time he thought he had caught the Japanese Admiral cheating he almost had a fit – not because the Japanese really was cheating, as it turned out, but because of the way he proved he was not cheating.

The Admiral and some other Japanese officers, on some sort of goodwill mission to Britain, had come to lunch and afterwards played the War Game. As I understand it, they captured from the British team – made up of my father, two uncles and a cousin on leave from the Indian Army – a troopship. It was a Japanese cruiser which made the capture, and, at his next move, the Admiral had this cruiser move the full number of squares which his throw of the dice would normally have allowed it. Uncle Philip accused him of stealthily breaking the rules. He should have deducted from the value of his throw the time it would have taken to transfer and accommodate the captured soldiers before sinking the troopship. He found the proper description of this cruiser in *Jane's Fighting Ships* and demonstrated that it would have taken a long time – even in calm weather – to get the prisoners settled aboard.

The Admiral said, 'But we threw the prisoners overboard.' He refused to retract his move.

Uncle Philip hurled the dice-box through the window of the shed and came storming up to the house. Even in the nursery could be heard his curdling account of the massacre on the destroyer.

'Sea full of sharks, of course. Our men absolutely helpless. Pushed over the side at the point of the bayonet. Damned cruiser forging ahead through water thickening with blood as the sharks got them.'

Even when the Japanese fought on the British side in the First World War Uncle Philip warned us not to trust them.

His imagination was powerful and made holes in the walls of reality. He used to shout up at the nursery for someone to come and hold his walking-stick upright at a certain point on the lawn while he paced off some distances. These were the measurements of the gunroom of the shooting lodge he was going to build on the estate he was going to buy in Argyllshire when he had won £20,000 in the Calcutta Sweep. Sometimes he would come to the conclusion that he had made this gunroom too small – barely room to swing a cat. Angrily he would start pacing again, and often find that this time the place was too large. 'I don't want a thing the size of a barn, do I?' he would shout.

Once, some years earlier, his imagination functioned so powerfully that it pushed half the British Fleet about. That was at Queen Victoria's Diamond Jubilee in 1897, when the Fleet was drawn up for review at Spithead in the greatest assembly of naval power anyone had ever seen. Uncle Philip and my father were invited by the Admiral commanding one of the squadrons to lunch with him on his flagship. An attaché of the Admiral Commander-in-Chief was also among those present.

Half-way through lunch Uncle Philip began to develop an idea. Here, he said, was the whole British Fleet gathered at Spithead, without steam up, immobile. Across there, was Cherbourg. (At that time, the war, when it came, was going to be against the

French.) Well, suppose one night – tonight, for instance – some passionately Anglophobe commander of a French torpedo-boat were to get the notion of dashing across the Channel in the dark and tearing between the lines of the great ships, loosing off torpedoes. The ships helpless, without steam up. In twenty minutes, half of them sinking. In an hour, Britain's power reduced to the level of Portugal's. By dawn, the Solent strewn with the wreckage of an Empire. Before noon, mobs crazed with triumph and wine sweeping along the Paris boulevards, yelling for the *coup de grâce*.

He spoke of this, my uncle said, not as an idle speculation, but because he happened to have recalled, on his way to this lunch, that in point of fact a French officer, just mad enough to carry out such a project, was at this moment in command of a torpedo-boat at Cherbourg. (His voice, as he said this, compelled a closer attention by the Admiral and the attaché of the Commander-in-Chief.)

Certainly, he said, he had met the man himself, a Captain Moret, a Gascon. Hot-blooded, hating the English for all the ordinary French reasons, and for another reason, too: his only sister – a young and beautiful girl, Uncle Philip believed – had been seduced and brutally abandoned by an English Lieutenant, name of Hoadley, or Hoathly, at Toulon. A fanatic, this Moret. Had a trick of gesturing with his cigar – like this (Uncle Philip sketched the gesture) – as he, Moret, expatiated on his favourite theory, the theory of the under-rated powers of the torpedo-boat as the guerrilla of the sea.

'And there,' said Uncle Philip, in a slightly eerie silence, 'he is.' He nodded ominously in the direction of Cherbourg.

On the way back to Cowes in the Admiral's launch, my father upbraided Uncle Philip. A nice exhibition he had made of himself – a mere Major of Hussars, lecturing a lot of Admirals and Captains on how to run their business. Also they had undoubtedly seen through this yarn, realized that this Moret was a figment of Uncle Philip's imagination, invented half-way through the fish course. Then, and during the remainder of the afternoon and early evening, Uncle Philip was abashed, contrite. After dinner that evening they walked by the sea, taking a final look at the Fleet in the summer dusk. Silently my uncle pointed at the far-flung line. Every second ship in the line was getting up steam.

People told Uncle Philip that if he would employ his gift of the gab in a practical way, not spend it all in conversation, but take to writing, he would make a fortune – like Stanley Weyman or some-one of that kind. It seemed a good idea, and while waiting for the Calcutta Sweep to pay off, he wrote, and published at the rate of about one a year, a number of historical romances. They included *Love in Armour, A Gendarme of the King, The Black Cuirassier*, and *A Rose of Dauphiny*. It was unfortunate from a financial point of view that he had a loving reverence for French history, which he supposed the library subscribers shared. The historical details of his stories were to him both fascinating and sacred. He refused to adjust by a hair's-breadth – in aid of suspense, romance, or pace of action – anything whatsoever, from an arquebus to a cardinal's mistress. Once you were past the title, you were on a conducted tour of a somewhat chilly and overcrowded museum.

However, he did make enough out of these books to feel justified in buying a motor-car in the days when that was a daring and extravagant thing to do. He reasoned that since the Sweep would ultimately provide a motor-car as a matter of course, it was foolish to spend the time not having a motor-car just because the draw was still nine months off.

He was not its possessor for long. He was superstitious. The car was of a make called Alldays. He showed it to my father. My father was against motor-cars. Some people of his age were against them because they went too fast. My father disliked them because they did not go fast enough. He took the view that if people were to take the trouble to give up horses and carriages and go about in these intricate affairs instead, it was only reasonable that the machines, in return, should get them to wherever they wanted to be in almost no time – a negligible, unnoticeable time. The fact that even with one of these vaunted motor-cars you still took hours and hours to get from, say, London to Edinburgh, struck him as disgusting and more or less fraudulent. Later he felt the same way about aeroplanes. He was thus not enthusiastic about Uncle Philip's motor-car and when he saw the maker's name on the bonnet, he unkindly murmured the quotation, 'All days run to the grave.'

Uncle Philip took fright and sold the car immediately at a heavy loss.

The theoretical basis of Uncle Philip's belief that war was coming soon was quite simple. He thought any government which supposed itself to have a reasonable advantage in armaments and manpower over its neighbours or rivals would go for them as soon as it was convinced that this was the case and provided the weather was suitable for the type of campaign its armies preferred. In this view he had the concurrence of my Uncle Frank, my father's elder brother, who in other respects was so different from Uncle Philip that he might have been brought up on a different planet. But he did enjoy the War Game, finding it more sensible than cards, and even made, in collaboration with Uncle Philip, some suggestions for changes in the rules which were sent to the Staff College, or whatever the strategic institution was that used the Game, and I believe adopted there.

He was a banker and a Canadian, and he took, uninhibitedly, the view that the world was a jungle, and civilization a fine but flimsy tent which anyone would be a fool either not to enjoy or to treat as a secure residence. Compared to the rest of the family he was rich. Enormously so, I thought at the time, for there seemed to be nothing he could not afford, and I was told once that he actually had a lot more than Uncle Philip would have if he drew the winning ticket in the Sweep (which he never did).

During those years, when we were moving about southern England looking, my father kept assuring me, for somewhere to settle down permanently, Uncle Frank was a frequent visitor, fleeting, but as impressive as a big firework.

His headquarters were at Montreal, but the place where he felt at home was Mexico. He spent a lot of time there, helping to organize some kind of revolution or counter-revolution – nominally in the interests of the bank, but mainly because that was the kind of work he liked. The details were never fully revealed to us. This was due partly to discretion, partly to the fact that the precise lines and objectives of the undertaking – which once had been a quite simple business of violently overthrowing the government – had become year by year increasingly complex and uncertain.

Nobody seemed to know just whose side anyone was on, which generals and politicians and rival financiers and concessionaires were good – that is to say, pro-Uncle Frank – and which bad. Not, I think, that he cared much about that. He enjoyed a colourful kind of plotting for its own sake, regardless of the monotonous aims of the fogies back in Montreal.

People would say, 'But I thought So-and-So was the man you were supporting? Wasn't he the one who was so good and was going to save the country?' And Uncle Frank would say vaguely that that had been before that business when Whatsisname shot up the bunch of Thingummies that time in Vera Cruz. There would follow a story full of sunshine and pistols and oil – very exciting and even intelligible, as far as it went, like a single battle-scene from a Shakespearian drama.

It seemed to be wonderful to have a job where that sort of thing was your business, and you were praised for your hard work doing it. The banking business attracted me a good deal – a banker, evidently, was something between Long John Silver and the Scarlet Pimpernel, and rich, too, and respected. The clerk at the local branch of the London, County, Westminster and Parr's became a figure of romance. I made up stories about his secret life.

Uncle Frank proclaimed himself a 'reactionary'. This piece of news went around among the neighbours and was applauded. They were deep-blue Conservatives, but already nervous of calling themselves, uncompromisingly, 'reactionaries'. Yet they found it comforting when someone else was unashamed to do so. My mother, active in the Women's Conservative Association and the Primrose League, did not care for the word at all. A devout and serious Christian, she was often bothered by what she read of socialists because she could not, instantly and absolutely, see where they were so wrong. To her horrified ear, they kept sounding as though they had ideas rather like Christ's.

This hesitancy of mind ashamed her. She felt it to be a kind of betrayal of Mr Bonar Law and Lord Balfour. She would steady herself by thinking about the atheistic opinions of socialists in France.

Uncle Frank was, in his way, more disturbing, as a fellow-traveller in the Conservative caravan, than the Christian-looking socialists roaming the desert. He treated all politics as some kind of sordid Mexican brawl about money and land, and took for granted that anyone pretending to a different attitude was merely practising a cunning hypocrisy, deceiving simpletons for the sake of votes. To listen to talk about patriotism, the good of the community, progress and the imperial idea, except when the words came from a platform for a special political purpose, bored him shockingly.

He was in constant fear of having people bore him, and carried antidotes about. He was a big man, and his clothes bagged on him under the weight of financial reviews, stock-market reports and similar documents which were in some of the pockets, and fat little volumes of Homer or Herodotus which he carried in others. He must have had an idea that when he wished to abstract himself from company he became, by virtue of his wish, invisible. He would go to some local gathering and, at tea or after dinner, slide a paper or book on to his knee so as to read it while people were talking to him. 'I don't think anyone noticed,' he would say afterwards.

His period of popularity among the local gentry as a visiting imperial lion from the Great Dominion did not endure. He was taken to some garden party held in the Conservative interest, and there introduced by the Vicar to a young barrister who had political ambitions and was popular for his renderings of 'Yip-I-Addy-I-Ay'. This person said to him, 'I must say, Mr Cockburn, I do admire your courage – I hear you are not afraid to call yourself a reactionary.' He then, according to my father, who was present, neighed.

Uncle Frank, who had been in a trance, looking at the back view of the village church and meditating on episodes of the Trojan War, or the current price of hogs in Chicago, or whatever it was, took a moment to focus on this remark, and the musical barrister filled the pause by stating that he himself was a bit of a reactionary, too.

Uncle Frank shouted his approval. 'You're absolutely right,' he said; 'everything since ancient Greece has been a mistake. Of course the real trouble is Christianity, don't you agree? My idea of a real, dangerous damn fool is the Emperor Constantine. What an ass!'

My father remarked gently that the Vicar quite possibly did not agree with him. Uncle Frank, when he was talking to one person, often forgot that anyone else was present, and he now turned to the Vicar, with an apologetic bow. 'I don't,' he said, 'mean to say a word against Christianity as a religion. It's fine. But it's unsuitable.'

'Unsuitable?' said the Vicar.

'To the human race,' said Uncle Frank. 'That's where Constantine was a damn fool. Another hundred years of steady persecution and they'd have had the Christians licked. They could have got right back. After all,' he said to the Vicar, 'as a God there wasn't much wrong with Zeus.'

The story went around that he had sworn at the Vicar and insulted the Church of England, but he was not there to hear it, for next morning he succumbed, once again, to what my father referred to as 'Frank's deplorable weakness for this fellow Aitken'. He went off to London to see Sir William Maxwell Aitken, afterwards Lord Beaverbrook, who had lately embarked on the English stage of his career and of whom my uncle had been a financial associate, and later a close friend, in Canada.

Uncle Frank, when he was in England, liked to go and talk about money, and imperial politics, and – on occasion – religion and poetry with Rudyard Kipling and Bonar Law and Lord Beaverbrook at Beaverbrook's Surrey home. One day, when he was planning such a visit, my father said to him that if he went from our house to Lord Beaverbrook's, he need not bother himself to return. Thereafter, when he wanted to make such a visit, Uncle Frank pretended he was only going to London for a couple of days on business. But since he needed an intermediary who could forward urgent cables to him if necessary, he had to take me into his confidence.

'It's a pity,' he said, 'your father should feel this way about Max. Your father,' he added sadly, 'doesn't understand about Max.'

Though he found such an association shocking, my father felt sorry for Uncle Frank, considering that he should be pitied rather than censured.

'No doubt,' he would say in extenuation of his brother's choice of friends, 'a banker has to associate a good deal with financiers and people of that kind. Naturally. Your Uncle Frank has had a hard life, you know. You see, ever since he was a young man, he has had to deal with *money*.'

This, to his mind, melancholy fact, explained a great deal. It explained why his brother, of whom he was very fond, should have developed a view of life which seemed to my father lacking in delicacy and understanding of reality.

Each of them had been initially propelled along their widely divergent roads by the same force – namely the high principles of my grandfather, a younger son of Lord Cockburn, the great Scottish Advocate and Judge who shone so brightly in the Golden Age of Edinburgh society. The adults surrounding my grandfather's youth were gay, civilized and earnest. They would not have understood how, later, earnestness became a term of disdain, and was supposed to be incompatible with gaiety. They took life, as the saying goes, seriously. To take it any other way would have been, in them, a sign of despair.

When my grandfather was about fourteen he liked to make explosions by pouring gunpowder out of a horn into the kitchen furnace. Then his hand slipped, the whole of the gunpowder slid down the stone funnel into the furnace, and the explosion blew off his right arm. It was a horrid disaster to which relatives near and far reacted immediately and in the same way: before the week was out he received from uncles, aunts and cousins all over Scotland eleven separate presents of writing-desks, to encourage him to lose no time in learning to write with his left hand.

He learned not only to write but to drive a carriage and pair in a dashing manner. He went to India in the service of the old East India Company, lived in an oriental splendour which caused remark even in those unbridled days, became a Judge in the Administration of the new Indian Empire, and retired to Edinburgh intending to spend the remainder of his days in reasonably rich comfort. He lived, in fact, well, and was astonished at the comment of the son of some Rajah who came to visit him. The young man had seen my grandfather only with the trappings of a high British official in India. After what in Edinburgh was esteemed a rather magnificent dinner, the Indian asked permission to pose an indiscreet question. 'Sir,' he said, 'after your life in India, is it not irksome to exist in this state of indigent obscurity?'

Later, the indigence became, comparatively speaking, a fact. The cost of living rose. So did the number of relatives who for various reasons had to be supported by grandfather. Many of them were young women, more or less distant cousins whose parents had left them penniless. It might, even then, have been possible for them to support themselves by some kind of work, but they said, 'Our dear mother would not have liked it,' and that, in the circumstances of the time, was undeniably true. In the end, grandfather had to get a second house in Edinburgh to put some of them in. Seeking to ease the financial strain, he took his own immediate family to Bonn, on the Rhine, which was cheaper and warmer.

Frank, eldest male among seven children, was to go to work – in Canada, because friends said it was a fine place for a young man, particularly a Scotsman. Arrangements were made to get him, for a start, a good job in an engineering concern there. It was a new and prosperous concern and prospects were said to be fine. Just before he sailed, it was discovered that the managing director of this firm was a friend of an intimate friend of grandfather. The mutual friend had actually written to him asking him to keep a favourable eye on Uncle Frank. My grandfather was appalled. He felt at once that this necessitated a change in the carefully laid plans. As he pointed out to Uncle Frank, there was now, as a result of this deplorable turn of events, a distinct possibility that this director in Canada would feel obliged to show special consideration and favour to the lad – advance his interests by various means, give him preferential treatment. This would be morally wrong. In the circumstances, the only proper course was for Frank to write, withdrawing from the job in the engineering firm, and – on landing in Canada – simply do the best he could. That was how he happened to start working for a moribund bank at Quebec. He worked sixteen or seventeen hours a day and ate only at breakfast-time. Late at night he drank cocoa, which he tried to make more interesting and long-lasting by each night decorating the cocoa-jug with elaborately painted Greek verses and proverbs. The largest inscription he made on the jug was the Greek text of 'For the night cometh when no man can work' –

Nux gar erchetai, etc. Years later, the jug stood prominent on the study mantelshelf in his big house in Montreal, and was referred to by the staff – bidden to treat it reverently – as 'the Nuxgar Jug'.

The period of penury and cocoa did not, in fact, last very long. Thousands of miles from Bonn, and exhilarated by the atmosphere of Canadian business, Uncle Frank soon pushed his way out of the torpid bank for which he had originally gone to work and into the Bank of Montreal which was booming and brimming with opportunity. But at Bonn, in the meantime, another crisis had occurred.

For more than a year it had been understood that my father was to enter the Indian Civil Service, an ambition which had been his since he was fifteen. Indeed, to a young man brought up on Plutarch's *Lives* and the history of Rome, the Indian Civil Service in those days seemed to offer limitless scope for the realization of boyhood dreams – a subcontinent to be organized and governed, power to be exercised over millions of people, a game with whole kingdoms and principalities on the board.

At that time the examination for the Indian Civil Service was the most rigorous and the most highly competitive in existence – the prospects and prizes of that Service attracted hundreds of the brilliant and the ambitious. The age limits within which candidates were eligible were such that you could make, if necessary, three attempts in three successive years. Almost nobody expected to be among the winners at his first attempt, which was regarded chiefly as a trial run, a way of getting, so to speak, to know the course. If you did fairly well then, you could make your serious attempt next year.

My father at his first attempt failed by only two places. It was considered a spectacular achievement. His success at the second attempt seemed certain. But, perhaps made over-confident by this achievement, he was rash enough, in the course of a theological discussion with grandfather at Bonn, to disclose that under the influence of German philosophy he had become an atheist.

Grandfather was distressed, but felt that his first duty was to the Indians, whom he had so long helped to govern, and to the British Empire in India. He still had some influence at the India Office and with the government of India. He travelled to London, saw influential and authoritative friends holding power in that branch of government and disclosed the unpleasant situation which had arisen. It was obviously monstrous, inadmissible, that an avowed atheist should get into the Indian Civil Service, particularly as the young man concerned was evidently of exceptional ability and might quickly rise to a position of power and importance. Grandfather

11

believed strongly in the value of the Christian religion as an ideological instrument of imperial rule. An atheist in such a position
might cause havoc and wreckage. He therefore desired those in
authority to take whatever steps were necessary to ensure that,
however brilliantly he might perform in the examination, my father
should not be admitted to the Service.

He then returned to Bonn and reported his actions to my father,
who knew quite enough about the working of what is nowadays
called 'The Old Boy Net' to realize that as things now stood he had
considerably less chance of entering the Indian Civil Service than
he did of entering the Church of England and becoming a bishop.
Enough strings had been pulled in London to keep an Archangel
out of Delhi if he were caught disbelieving in the Thirty-Nine
Articles.

He was bitter about the way things had turned out and wished he
had kept his mouth shut about atheism. But he liked and admired
people who knew their own minds and had convictions upon which
they really acted, and he did not quarrel with grandfather.

'After all,' he said to me long afterwards, 'a person ought to carry
his beliefs to their logical conclusions. I think I should have been
rather dismayed if father had done anything else. It would have
seemed so feeble. Given his opinions on religion and government,
it was the only sensible thing for him to do.'

'He might,' I said, 'at least have tried to convert you.'

'But you see,' said my father, 'he took for granted that everyone
else's views were as unshakeable as his own. And he would have
thought, too, that I might be tempted to make a false pretence of
conversion – which would have been bad for my moral character;
and then, later, when I was Lieutenant-Governor, I might have
come out in my true colours and started massacring the missionaries,
or forced them to give readings from Feuerbach from their pulpits.'

It was, however, clear that life at home had reached an *impasse*,
and, not wishing to take any further chances with grandfather's
convictions, my father sold all his books and all except one suit of
clothes and disappeared to London. When his family next heard
from him, he had secretly sat for, and passed, his entrance examination for the Eastern Consular Service, which was then a kind of
half-way house between the Diplomatic Service – for which you
needed a lot of money – and the ordinary Consular Service which
dealt mainly with commercial affairs and was confined to Europe
and the western hemisphere. The point about the Eastern Consular
Service was that it functioned east of Singapore, and that it was

possible to pass from it into regular diplomatic service in the Far East.

He went to China and never left it until he was thirty years old. From his nineteenth to his twenty-second year he was British Vice-Consul at the then awfully remote city of Chungking. It was the most isolated British agency in Asia. The city had three hundred thousand inhabitants and was the pivotal point of trade along the Yangtze between central China and the south-east. But foreign trade was officially barred. In the whole of those four years he saw only half a dozen Europeans – none of them, he remarked with satisfaction, 'unduly obtrusive'. Since there was almost no trade, there was no tiresome routine work. His duties, in fact, were vague. He was simply an outpost. His life was full and happy, gay and studious by turns. There were at Chungking excellent professors of philosophy, poetry and calligraphy. The political intrigues in which as British agent he became involved were intricate, dangerous and delightful. Once a month he conducted a public exercise in imperialism.

At that time it was forbidden for foreigners to reside on or even visit that part of Chungking lying on the right bank of the Yangtze. Rightly, the Chinese believed that if you gave the foreigners an inch they would take an ell. Once a month my father – designing to establish precedents and break down this ban – used to send a formal notification to the Governor, who resided on the right bank, that the British Vice-Consul proposed to call on him on a certain date. The Governor, not wishing to make a formal breach of relations, always acceded. On the day fixed, my father was trans-ported across the river, and was met on the opposite bank by the Governor's litter, with a heavy guard of soldiers. The steep streets to the Governor's residence were lined with furiously hostile crowds – their natural hatred of the intruder encouraged and stimulated when necessary by agents of the Governor. They pelted the litter with stones. Every couple of hundred yards the litter was halted while the soldiers battled with the populace.

At the Governor's residence the Governor entertained the Vice-Consul and they talked for a couple of hours. At some point during the conversation, the Vice-Consul took occasion to remark with satisfaction that it was now evidently the policy of the Imperial Government to permit an Englishman to visit the right bank of the river at Chungking. At some other point the Governor would take occasion to express his satisfaction that in this single instance it had been possible for the Imperial authorities to suspend for a few hours the inviolable rule against the presence of foreigners on the right bank, and that the efficiency of the troops had sufficed to curb, on this particular day, the profound indignation of the people.

The parting ceremony was also a somewhat elaborate manoeuvre, it being necessary for the Vice-Consul to take his leave in words carrying the general sense of *au revoir*, whereas the Governor must give to his courteous parting remarks the unmistakable nuance of an *adieu*. Then came the progress back to the river with stoning, battles and occasional bloodshed.

When I was a little boy I thought it must have been a very grand feeling to be carried thus in a magnificent litter, an outpost of Empire with hostile thousands roaring for one's blood. 'Didn't you,' I asked my father, 'feel grand and triumphant?'

'A little, sometimes,' he said. 'But then I tried, too, to remember that to those people I didn't look grand at all. I reminded myself that to them I was physically an evil-smelling monkey, and in character and status a vulgar barbarian thief trying to break into China. An excellent spiritual exercise.'

Much later, when I was sixteen or so, I bothered him with another sort of question.

'Were you always absolutely sure it was a good thing to try to extend British power in China?'

'Absolutely.'

'But you don't much like English people. You prefer Chinese.'

'Hang it, I like some English people.'

'Not many.'

'True.'

'You don't care for their attitude to life. You know they bore you to death. Secretly, everything they say seems to you platitudinous or else untrue.'

'A lot of Chinese are awfully silly, too.'

'And you spent more than half your life working to help the English dominate the Chinese.'

'It's nothing to do with people. It's a question of realizing an idea.'

'"The Imperial idea"?'

'I hope you're not getting that deplorable habit of picking phrases out of newspapers and using them without knowing what they mean. A good thing to do is to read two pages of the *New Oxford Dictionary* every day. You get the exact derivations of all words and their differing shades of meaning at different periods. An excellent habit.'

'You seem to be changing the subject.'

'Let's play a game of chess.'

He seemed unaware of any contradiction in his attitude. He did not care to argue about it. He did say once that talking to me about it was like trying to explain music to a deaf child. It was tedious to make clear to a person who did not grasp it immediately how one could deplore almost every material and spiritual manifestation of the Empire and still dedicate oneself to its expansion and consolidation as the highest Good.

Between leaving Bonn and retiring, he spent more than thirty years in China and Korea, and less than that number of months in England. Except for the countryside in spring-time, he did not care much for anything about England. About the personalities and forces – political, financial, commercial – which motivated and directed the imperial machine, he had, as they say, no illusions. He found them comical, subjects for savage ribaldry. Or pathetic. Or sordid. And often simply ignoble. The machine, on the other hand – that was admirable and good: a fine bit of work, satisfactory and even inspiring to tend. Perhaps his reference to music was the clue. He was listening, perhaps, to some strange symphony. The rest was as irrelevant as would be the fact that the composer took dope and the conductor lived on the immoral earnings of women.

Just before the nationalist outbreak of 1900 my father went briefly to England, married and returned with my mother in time to be besieged in the legation quarter by the Boxers. Because of the official acceptance of reports that the legations had fallen and the besieged all been killed, he had the pleasure of reading his own obituary notice in the newspapers. He had always been in grave trouble with the finance-controllers in London on account of his heavy and ingeniously contrived over-spending of a special 'entertainment' allowance. He wrote to the Foreign Office, noting with pleasure that these difficulties were not mentioned in the obituary notices, based on official information, and were therefore evidently recognized as of a trivial nature. Dr Morrison, the famous China correspondent of *The Times*, who was also among the besieged, simply cabled the paper saying, 'Have just read obituary in *The Times*. Kindly adjust pay to suit.'

I was born at Peking, on the day the Japanese blew up the Russian flagship *Petropavolsk* at Port Arthur, and spent the first few weeks of life at Wei-hai-wei, which until a couple of years before had been the headquarters of the British-officered Chinese regiment which my father had seen as a primitive instrument of the

Sino-Indian plan. People used to stare northwards across the sea at night and claim they could see the flashes of great naval battles in the Port Arthur direction. My Chinese amah, who had seen the looting of Peking by the foreign troops, expected the Japanese or the Russians to land at any minute and massacre everyone. She was glad to take me to England, but there the boys shouted and threw stones at her in the street because she wore blue trousers, and she longed to return.

My father became Minister to Korea while it was still nominally independent, and then Consul-General as the Japanese progressively took over control. He thought the whole British agreement with the Japanese on the Korean issue disastrous. He was offered another ministerial post. Quite suddenly he announced he was weary of the whole business and retired, saying that at forty-nine it was high time to start leading an entirely new sort of life.

We rented four or five different houses in four years. Each of them was discovered, after a few months, to have some intolerable defect. Secretly, as he admitted to me later, my father had come to the conclusion that it would really be more satisfactory to buy a house in the hills west of Peking, but he wanted to give England every chance. According to my mother, the house in Hertfordshire lasted longer than the others only because it had this shed or barn which was so suitable for housing the War Game.

I had played Germans and English with the tin soldiers for a couple of years when I thought I, too, would like to learn to play the War Game. I was disappointed. Neither my father nor my uncles would teach it to me. They had given up playing it themselves. They said that to learn it now would be not only pointless but actually misleading because very soon now there would be a new war which would make all strategy, tactics and rules of the War Game obsolete.

2   Holes in the Fence

VIRTUS LAUDATA CRESCIT, or 'virtue grows with praise', was found, at the last moment, to be the motto of the school I was to go to, and if arrangements had been less far advanced I believe my father would have changed his mind and sent me somewhere else. It was symbolic, he felt, of a state of mind – a lax state. All very well to take the view that a pat on the back could occasionally make goodness better; but very improper, he opined, for a school, of all places, to turn this notion into an official motto. To do so was virtually to flaunt a conviction that people cannot be expected to be any good *unless* they are patted on the back for it.

It was one of those small pointers that suddenly indicated to him the extent of the gulf existing between his own ideas and those of the age in which his children were to grow up. Useless to point out that the motto was not modern – had, it was understood, been the family motto of the school's founder, in the mid sixteenth century. What, might one ask, was known of *his* character and achievements? But it was too late to back out now. We had already taken a house in Berkhamsted so that, at any rate to begin with, I could attend the 'Preparatory' section of the school as a day boy rather than a boarder.

By the time I went to it, Berkhamsted School had five hundred boys and was poised somewhere between Stalky and Co. and the welfare state. The Rugby Tradition, the standards of the barrack-room, and intimations of modernism and 'progressive' education overlapped or struggled confusedly for supremacy.

It was also taken for granted that any boys left alone and unoccupied for more than a few minutes were going to get up to vicious mischief, with the result that efforts were made to fill every interstice of every day with public and communal activities – many of them conducted, like the drill of the Italian bersaglieri, at the double. Paradoxically, Sunday was the moral danger zone, because to work would have been to break the Fourth Commandment and to play games would have been shocking to local opinion. Even two chapel services could not be stretched right across the gap, and there were a couple of hours on Sunday afternoons when we had to be allowed to go for walks, in couples or groups.

On Mondays, Wednesdays and Saturdays in the summer we played compulsory cricket from two in the afternoon until dusk, and on the other days from noon until lunch-time, and again in the evenings from five o'clock – when school ended – until the light mercifully failed. The playing-fields were at the top of a steep hill about half a mile long, and to get from one end to the other of it on time one usually had to do it at a brisk jogtrot. During all the years I was there I made a total of only seven runs.

In winter and spring there was nothing between us and the perils of leisure except football, running and the school Cadet Corps. With most of us the Corps was unpopular, but I liked it. I had been brought up in expectation of a war, and there was a war going on during a good deal of the time I was at school. The thing seemed to make sense. It was a game with a visible point to it. It seemed realistic. You would be out one day on a field exercise, firing blank ammunition under command of a prefect who was also your platoon commander, and a few weeks or months later you would hear how he had been killed in genuine battle in France. I, too, became a cadet officer in the end, and used to enjoy explaining, in elaborately military terms, to elderly and diffident officers of the Brigade of Guards who came to inspect us, what we imagined we were up to.

All the other games seemed to me terribly like hard and, on the whole, uncongenial toil. But the teaching was so stimulating that what was described as 'work' often seemed an entrancing game.

Regimentation of the kind we were subjected to is supposed, I believe, to destroy individuality, and conduce to the development of a conformist attitude. I have no notion whether this is a general truth or not. I can only say that, as a direct result of all this supervision and ordering about, one of the most valuable lessons my school taught me was how to break other people's rules. And at sixteen I read and profoundly appreciated Bernard Shaw's invaluable advice to 'get what you like, or you'll grow to like what you get'.

Relief from our routine was provided by the accident of our headmaster being a chess addict. When the craving for chess came on him, he had to play; in the fire of this passion rules, regulations and routine were reduced to ashes. As I was supposed to be the best chess player in the school, I was often invited to play with him, and at such times I would sit securely, and for hours on end, at one side of a table by the fire in his study, listening contentedly to the imperious, but temporarily innocuous, jangle of bells summoning people to get on with something or other, and the shouts of prefects driving others along cold corridors without.

Charles Henry Greene, this headmaster, gave the impression of conducting the affairs of the school and viewing life in general with the same smouldering, sometimes explosive intensity which he brought to the chessboard. He was a man of powerful and vivid reactions. Certain events, sometimes major, sometimes quite trivial, seemed to strike his mind with the heat and force of a branding-iron, and for a long time would remain in the forefront of consciousness, to be referred to, commented, brooded upon aloud in a singularly sonorous voice, and with occasionally florid eloquence.

His history lessons to the sixth form were not so much history lessons as comments on a state of affairs in which history had taken a distinct turn for the worse. For the most part he treated history simply as a series of signposts to the probabilities and possibilities of the present. Most of them pointed to ruin. For Charles Greene was, in the widest as well as the party-political sense of the word, a Liberal, and in the crack-up of Liberalism he saw the mark of doom.

When he looked at the Treaty of Versailles, his slightly bulbous grey eyes rolled, shone and started from his head, and his yellow moustache bristled. It reminded him of every disaster in the history of treaty-making since the errors committed by Pericles. As he spoke of it he sank back in his chair, pulling the mortar-board farther and farther down on his forehead as though to shield his eyes from the sight of so much folly and horror. 'When I gaze,' he said, 'upon the activities of Mr Lloyd George, when I consider the political consequence of Mr Clemenceau, my mind, abdicating its intellectual function, shrinks, half-paralysed, from the very attempt to contemplate the abyss which opens, inevitably but unregarded, before us.'

Reading the news from Moscow and from the various fronts of the war of intervention, he would sink into an almost luxurious awareness of impending doom. The spirit of Bolshevism, he said, was permeating everywhere, and the most ordinary events and *contretemps* of everyday life confirmed his view.

Bored at the fact that they were mobilized months after the ending of the war, the soldiers camped outside the town became drunker and drunker, and once rioted, breaking into the school itself and threatening to throw the headmaster into the canal. It was Bolshevism.

Prefects neglected their duties; a French master turned pacifist and started teaching his pupils that the whole war had been a monstrous mixture of crime and blunder in which people had been slaughtered for nothing; and a conspiracy was uncovered among the older boys to wear dark-blue serge suits to chapel on Sundays instead of the short black coats which were required by regulation.

All these were manifest indications of the bolshevistic way things were tending.

And then death-watch beetles were found at work in the timbers of the high roof of the Elizabethan Hall. It was horrifying, but in its awful way satisfactory – a climatic symbol of decay and violent collapse. 'Once again I have reports of slackness and indiscipline, everywhere I detect a falling off in keenness. The pernicious and destructive doctrines of Marx and Lenin are tapping away at the foundations and at the roof beams of civilization like the death-watch beetle which even as I speak is carrying out up there, invisible to us but none the less menacing for that, its work of voracious disintegration.' Since he said all these things with a vivid sincerity, and these extravagances were the product of genuine and agonized beliefs, the effect was not at all grotesque, but as vividly impressive as a revivalist meeting.

He worried sometimes about my political future. He wanted me to have a political career so that I could take a hand at halting the general decline, and possibly reverse the trend. I held strong Conservative views, and he, though a Liberal, thought that on the whole that was probably a good thing – I should enter the Conservative Party and so stimulate its moral sense and moderate its crassness. At lunch in the schoolhouse, when no one could leave the table until the headmaster had stood up and said the Latin grace, our arguments on the origins of the Boer War, or the policy of Palmerston, used sometimes to be prolonged for as much as a quarter of an hour after the last crumbs of the suet and treacle pudding had been eaten. The discussion was conducted amid a rising shuffle of impatient feet and the rebellious tinkling of spoons on empty plates. Sometimes he would use his initiative of the grace to cut short an argument which displeased him or to which perhaps he did not see an immediate rebuttal.

'Well, well, Cockburn,' he would say, getting slowly to his feet, 'I don't see how civilization's going to be saved Benedictus Benedicat.'

Disruptive tendencies were at work even in the circle of his own family. As was the custom of many old-fashioned people at the period, the Greenes used at breakfast innocently to describe to one another anything interesting, bizarre or colourful they had had in the way of dreams during the previous night. Mr and Mrs Greene were unaware that their third son, Graham, had at about this time discovered Freud – an early step, I suppose, along the road he was to take as a novelist. He would leave the bacon cooling on his plate as he listened with the fascination of a secret detective. When necessary he would lure them on to provide more and more details which to them were amusing or meaningless but to him of thrilling and usually scandalous significance.

'It's amazing,' he said to me once, 'what those dreams disclose. It's startling – simply startling,' and at the thought of it gave a low whistle.

Since my father viewed the British Public School system with increasing uncertainty and distrust, I probably should have remained in the semi-detached position of a day boy to the last if the war had not ended when it did. During it my father had returned to government service in some job so hush-hush that neither then nor subsequently did I find out what, exactly, he was up to. When it was over he retired again, intending at last to pursue the new life which he had envisaged on his first retirement in 1908. But it soon turned out that he had miscalculated the rise in the cost of living – or, rather, its permanent character – and was now in a state of acute financial embarrassment.

A friend told him there was a good job going as chief of some inter-allied financial mission to look after the finances of Hungary. Perhaps he would like that? My father asked whether the circumstances of his knowing almost nothing about Hungary and absolutely nothing about finance would be a disadvantage. His friend said that was not the point. The point was that they had a man doing this job who knew all about Hungary and a lot about finance, but he had been seen picking his teeth with a tram ticket in the lounge of the Hungaria Hotel and was regarded as socially impossible. My father said that if such were the situation he would be prepared to take over the job.

Fortunately, it turned out that the work did not, after all, consist in running the finances of Hungary, merely of helping to sort out the financial claims upon Hungary of British, French, Italian and other Allied nationals. He bought a Hungarian grammar and a small book on money, arranged for me to become a boarder at the school, and got into the Orient Express.

The Budapest in which he arrived was like a battlefield where everyone has come to a bad end, where all the heroes are dead and all the great causes are betrayed. 'Freedom from fear' was one of 'the Four Freedoms' very noticeably lacking there. It was a city where everyone was frightened – frightened of being arrested, frightened of being murdered, frightened of just being ruined.

It seemed to my father, surveying Central Europe in the early 1920s, that human nature had deteriorated considerably. And he thought that this deterioration was unnecessary, self-inflicted, self-willed. He startled people sometimes by saying in moments of indiscretion that in his opinion everyone was taking the Great War and its consequences a great deal too seriously. Since he rarely bothered to explain exactly what he meant by this, he gave offence. In the eyes of quite a number of younger men he was a walking embodiment of that type of cynical old man who was supposedly 'responsible' for the war and for the consequent misfortune of the younger generation.

What he really felt was that, after all, he had, so to speak, lived with this war for years before it happened; for years before it happened he had said that it was coming, that it would be terrible, that in his view we should survive.

Since he had never supposed that the war would do anything but incalculable harm to the fabric of civilization, he simply could not understand the frustration and bitterness of the young men who said, 'You told us this was a war for civilization, and now look.' To him the results appeared to be just what anyone in his senses would have expected, and he therefore was suspicious of people who seemed to be taking the war and its results as an excuse for every kind of intellectual, moral and political extravagance.

Because he had never taken seriously any of the high-toned propaganda slogans of the war period, he never came near understanding the rage of those who had believed in them and now felt themselves betrayed. During the war itself he had never for a moment imagined that the battles were being waged in the interests of democracy or civilization, or even of freedom; he found quite adequate inspiration in the conviction that we were fighting to prevent the German Empire from doing us down.

One year, on the way from school to Budapest, I sat, at Oxford, for a scholarship examination. At that time the colleges were grouped for scholarship examination purposes, so that a candidate could compete for a scholarship at five or six colleges at the same time. You could, so far as I remember, state in advance that you would accept a scholarship at only one chosen college of the group, or you could indicate that you were prepared to enter any college of that group which would pay you to do so. Friends of the family, many of them military men who had never been near Oxford, said emphatically that there were only three or four colleges which it was really possible to go up to. They named them. Other friends of the family who had been at Balliol said there was only one possible college.

I had to disregard them. I cared very little what college I went to provided that I went to it almost immediately and thus got away from school. I was sitting on the terrace of the Hotel Gellért drinking iced beer when a telegram was brought to me. It said, 'Are you member Church of England?' After a momentary mystification I realized that I must have won a scholarship to Keble College and that membership of the college must be confined to Church of England members, or at least that only Church of England members were eligible to hold scholarships there.

I was downcast. It seemed to me extraordinarily improbable that I was any such thing. Bitterly annoyed that one's movements should be hampered by what seemed to me an irrelevant obstacle, I took the telegram to my father and said despondently that it seemed that my first raid on the scholarship front had failed. He immediately asked me whether at any time I had secretly but formally been converted into any other faith? Had I, for example, been received into the Roman Catholic or Mohammedan Church? Since most of my ideas at that time appeared to him strange and even perverse, he would not have been surprised to hear that I had secretly become a Buddhist. When I told him 'No', he said that in that case everything was in order. It seemed that once one has been baptized a member of the Church of England, one automatically retains membership for the rest of one's life unless one is formally received into some other faith. Profoundly relieved, I telegraphed to Keble saying, 'Yes.'

3   Oxford Accent

DESPITE everything, despite even the casualty lists of the war years, it would have been just possible at Oxford to imagine that the First World War had not taken place – or at least that it had been merely a big, ugly, necessary episode, in the sense envisaged by my father. Above all it was a fact that for most of us the Bolshevik Revolution remained a nearly irrelevant event. People who regarded it with horror, and those who looked upon it with at least a tepid enthusiasm, were unconsciously at one in viewing it with a more or less comfortable detachment, rather in the mood of people going to see a novel play or a technically revolutionary film.

My own philosophy tutor was a man who appeared to be of the view that philosophy was something like alcohol – amusing and possibly stimulating if taken in moderation, but no use as a sustaining food. Of any philosophical idea less than two hundred years old he would say, 'I think you'll find that it's pretty well been exploded.' Once, straight back from Budapest with a volume of philosophy which had just appeared there, and which he could not possibly have read, I hurried to him saying that I thought this was something really worthy of all our attention. He kept the book for a few hours and on returning it to me remarked, 'I rather gather that the man is likely pretty soon to be exploded.' Oxford was a place where everyone was complacently awaiting the moment when any new idea would be 'exploded', whereas in Budapest it was only the old and the traditional which people expected at any moment to blow up.

One day I was speaking on this subject to a shrewd but eccentric aunt – wildly and harshly, for I just then felt myself overcome by a strong nostalgia for Central Europe – when she said suddenly:

'It's all a question, you know, of the light.'

'The light?'

'Yes,' she said. 'It's a matter of the way in which the nerves of any given person's eyes react to different qualities of light. All the rest – politics, people and so on – are relatively unimportant. It is one's reaction to a particular quality of light which makes one happy or unhappy in a place.'

I had told her that the valley of the Danube was the first area in which I had ever felt immediately and completely at home, not after months or even days of living there, but immediately – within an hour. And this was true at the time, although since then I have twice experienced this same sense of being immediately at home in an entirely strange place – once in New York and once in Oklahoma City.

My aunt said there was nothing unusual in my feeling about the Danube valley, it was simply that the quality of the light in that particular area happened to be the one which I found simultaneously most stimulating and soothing to the nerves. In the same way, the light quality of the Thames valley was evidently unsuited to me.

I believe now that there really is something in this theory, although at the time it appeared to me bizarre. My aunt seemed to be treating as mere secondary trivialities the factors in the situation which I regarded as most important. After discoursing for a short time on this theory of light, she remarked casually, 'And of course having money is so important too. I don't suppose you have enough.'

I said that nobody had. She said, 'I should very much like to give or at least lend you some. It is a pity that the cats take all the spare money I have.'

I said that naturally I entirely understood, and I did, although it did seem rather a pity that there was not enough for all of us. For by this time my debts were relatively enormous – enormous, that is, in relation to any prospect there seemed to be of ever meeting them. They seemed to rise uncontrollably like flood water, without any reference to my efforts to increase my income. For a while I edited the Oxford University weekly paper the *Isis*, I wrote a weekly column during term time for one of the Oxford City papers, and occasionally I sold articles or a short story elsewhere. None of it seemed to make any difference, and the situation was the more harassing because, having for more than two years done almost no work of any kind which could be considered useful for the purposes of my final examinations, I now found myself compelled to get up at 6.30 to start reading, to read intensively most of the day and to dose myself with caffeine tablets so as to keep awake and working until two or three in the morning. I had never been able to attend lectures because they, like public speeches, drove me to a frenzy of boredom and impatience. I never could understand why the lecturers could not spend the time writing down what they had to say and distributing it in convenient pamphlet form. Gibbon took the same view. But, although not having attended lectures was supposed to be disastrous, and was naturally regarded with great disfavour by one's tutor, I did not myself find it much of a handicap, particularly as most of the lectures which I had missed a year or so before had by now dropped into print somewhere. All the same, the amount of reading to be done was prodigious and the repeated irruption of duns distracting.

A few days before the end of my last term, I went – hesitantly – to say good-bye to my tutor. Hesitantly, because he was a man who shunned humans even when they were absolutely calm. Excited or emotional ones affected him like asphyxia. I tried to remain absolutely calm.

Naturally he was always glad to see the last of anyone, but he dreaded the potentially emotional business of an actual 'good-bye'. Wearing a russet-coloured suit, he lay as though camouflaged on a russet-coloured sofa. I saw him groping for some seemly valediction. He looked despairingly at the ceiling and then along the bookshelves all round the room, all full of works by philosophers who either had been, or were just about to be, exploded. 'Hitherto,' he said, 'your life has been neatly criss-crossed by school terms and school holidays, university terms and vacations. Now you are going down from Oxford and you have – well one may say that you have a straight run to the grave.'

Driven by extreme distaste for committing myself at this stage to any particular career, a thought which gave me a kind of claustrophobia as though one were entering a tunnel, I sought almost frantically for possible means of evading such a commitment, and at length discovered the existence of a Travelling Fellowship offered by Queen's College to anyone who had secured first- or second-class honours in the final examinations. Apparently there was a rich man called Laming who had come to the conclusion that British representatives abroad, diplomatic and otherwise, were below par, and he had endowed this Fellowship so that people intending to enter the Foreign Service, or to function more or less permanently abroad in some other capacity, should be enabled, after coming down from Oxford, to reside for two years in any country or countries of their choice on an annual income of £250. And although in most countries of modern Europe this sum would hardly keep a person in cigarettes, at that time there were a number of places where a student without financial obligations to anyone but himself could live in comfort and freedom on that amount.

In preparation for the Fellowship examination I went, for the study of French, to the cheapest section of France I could hear of – a gaunt village in the Cévennes. By a bizarre concatenation of events I even became, briefly, a French Government official – *Receveur d'Enregistrements*, the only Englishman I believe, ever to hold that position. With a strong Meridional accent, I left for Vienna. But passing through Venice I had rashly sold most of my clothes to raise cash. In the summer suit, adequate for the Cévennes, I trembled in Viennese snowstorms and had still no money for fuel. I moved for a couple of weeks to Luxembourg which was cheap, comparatively warm and bilingual. Back in London, I was lent a flat in Bloomsbury but it, too, was cold. When I tired of reading in bed, I took a penny ticket on the underground and went with my books to sit on a little bench on the platform of the Warren Street tube station.

I forget how many people competed for the Travelling Fellowship that year – I think a couple of hundred, or perhaps more. They looked to me horribly intelligent and some of them I gathered had spent a good part of the past month at expensive coaching establishments in Tours or Hanover. More alarming, however, was the fact that so many of them seemed so well dressed, so well groomed. The reason this was alarming was connected with the purposes of the Fellowship as defined by its Founder. It was quite understood that the sort of person he wanted to benefit by his Foundation ought to be not only an efficient scholar, not only have, if possible, the 'right' sort of accent, but also be the type to make a good impression at, for example, a diplomatic luncheon party. In order to examine the qualifications of candidates from this point of view, each in turn had a brief but vitally important personal interview with the Provost and dons of Queen's College.

An attempt was made to give this interview something of the character of an informal social occasion. One was expected to sit at ease in a comfortable chair and was offered sherry.

When I sit at ease I like to cross the calf of one leg over the knee of the other, but unfortunately in the course of my wanderings my shoe leather had worn through utterly, and where the soles of my shoes should have been only my socks were visible. Indeed, having had to walk some distance from my rooms in the college to the place where the interview took place, I could not be sure that my exhausted socks had not given way too, leaving the bare flesh showing. In any case, either socks or flesh would create an abominable impression, so that throughout the conversation I had to sit rigidly in an entirely unnatural position trying to remember, while chatting in an easy manner, to keep my feet flat on the carpet. Also I am in a habit of gesticulating a good deal when I talk; but since the cuffs of my shirt were almost spectacularly frayed and had to be kept out of sight, this habit too had to be abandoned for the duration of the interview, and I sat hunched like some semi-petrified gargoyle, my hands gripping my wrists so as neither to display the frayed cuffs nor even to suggest to the minds of the examiners that the cuffs could not be shown.

Candidates had been required to fill up a form showing where they had been during the period between the end of the last summer term at Oxford and the date of the examination. Simply to keep the record straight I had put down that I had spent a couple of weeks in Luxembourg. After some more or less light-hearted conversation and casual questioning, the Provost suddenly remarked that he observed I had spent some time in the Grand Duchy of Luxembourg. I said I had been there for a bare fortnight.

'And what,' he asked 'did you gather of conditions there?'

I got off a rather sapient piece about the operations of the International Steel Cartel, which had its headquarters there, together with some observations upon the possible effects of a recent Luxembourg decision to hitch the Luxembourg currency to the belga rather than to the franc. Meaty stuff, I secretly opined, after only a fortnight in the country. The Provost tapped the table impatiently, and his expression was that of a man who does not relish having his time wasted by chit-chat about trivialities.

'Yes, yes, yes,' he said, 'very interesting, no doubt, but what I would really like to know is what you gathered about the varying systems of land tenure in the north and south parts of the Grand Duchy?'

All this was harassing enough, but still more disconcerting was the fact that my Oxford creditors had chosen this moment to make an attack in force. Whether this was an unhappy accident, or whether they had somehow learned that I was sitting for this Fellowship examination and considered it a suitable moment to turn on the heat, I have no idea. For whatever reason, they became

28

suddenly implacable and menacing. (In fairness I should say that there were some noble exceptions.) Several of them threatened legal action, and it was grimly evident that although a man with bare feet and frayed cuffs might possibly still clutch at the Fellowship, one who had just been served with several writs could not.

I interviewed the fiercest of the creditors and begged them to hold their hand until after the results of the examination had been announced. They refused. Maddened by their short-sighted folly, which threatened not only my career but the prospect of their ever getting paid at all, I decided that only a bold policy could save the situation. The result of the examination was scheduled to be announced a couple of weeks or so after the written part, which lasted several days, was concluded. I gave them all post-dated cheques for sums adequate to satisfy them temporarily, dated for the day the results were due to be announced. Personally I had no doubt that I should win one of the Fellowships, and of course in that case the bank would be quite happy to advance the money. But I could see that the creditors probably would not be entirely satisfied with this security, and I did not mention to them the fact that the cheques would be payable only as and when I was successful in the Fellowship examination.

Although as the written examination proceeded I became more and more confident, I was undoubtedly aware of a sense of tension and excitement which probably was not shared by candidates in more comfortable circumstances. The examination ended and a week or so passed, and then something happened which made me feel that fate was deliberately hitting out at me.

My father had told me long ago that if one wished to be lucky one should always believe in luck – that people who cursed their luck suffered for it. I did my best to carry out this policy now, but it was difficult because what had happened was that one of the examining dons had caught a cold, or contracted some other minor ailment, and the announcement was made in a notice to the candidates that declaration of the results would be postponed by a week beyond the scheduled date.

It was only after a half-hour of despair that a possible solution occurred to me. I wrote to one of the principal examining dons – a charming man who had already showed me great kindness – saying that I had just heard that a relative of mine, who had helped me greatly throughout my academic life and took a passionate interest in my career, was dangerously ill. In fact it was doubtful whether this relative could survive for more than a few days. Surely, it would be tragic if, on account of this accidental change of schedule, my relative should pass away without knowing whether I had succeeded or not – particularly tragic if I had succeeded and this news came too late to cheer the last hours.

The good-hearted don wrote to me immediately – I had of course taken the precaution of going to London before sending him my letter so that his reply, if any, would be in writing – saying that he could not in any way officially anticipate the result, but that, speaking as an individual, and purely on the basis of his own personal estimate, he would say that I would not be deceiving my relative if I indicated that I had obtained the Fellowship. With this letter I dashed back to Oxford, interviewed the bank manager, who fortunately was aware of the position of the don in question on the examining board, and asked him whether on the strength of this he would meet the cheques which were now due to be presented within a matter of three or four days. He agreed.

Naturally I had to sign documents which in fact meant that in the course of the next couple of years something like half the whole of the Fellowship payments would have to be handed over to the bank.

The prospect did not bother me. It seemed to me that these were rivers that could be crossed when we came to them.

Also those early years in Budapest during the inflation time, when the value of money in your pocket could be halved between breakfast and lunch, and halved again before dinner, had made it hard for me to focus at all steadily on any financial problems, or to treat such problems otherwise than as entirely fluid and impalpable.

And when it was indeed oficially confirmed that I had gained the Fellowship, all this optimism seemed fully justified.

Months before, I had told my tutor that I vaguely planned to start my 'run to the grave' by connecting myself with *The Times* newspaper. My tutor thought it a fate considerably worse than death. Did I realize I would probably have to speak to comparative strangers, and write about events as though they were important? But being very properly uninterested in my future he made no other attempt to dissuade me.

At the outset, before I had heard of the existence of the Travelling Fellowship, a job with *The Times* had been a mainly negative ambition, formed to avoid the Foreign Office which had been so long and so highly recommended that I could think of it only in the words of the songster as 'a wonderful opportunity for somebody – somebody else'.

To the advocates of a Foreign Office career the notion of 'going in for journalism' was pitiably degrading. 'And mark you,' as a friend of my father told me sternly, 'split what hairs you will, mince words as you may, in the last analysis *The Times* is nothing more or less than *sheer journalism.*'

It seemed certain that journalists had the choice of being absolutely servile (as reported by another very old friend of the family who had the latest information from Germany under Bismarck), or corrupt (the conviction of another who had personally known Caillaux), or intolerably vulgar (the view of a fourth who had always said Lord Northcliffe should have been hanged).

I discovered very soon that these hesitations and *hauteurs* were paralleled at Printing House Square. Applications for employment poured in, sometimes producing a kind of *folie des grandeurs.*

Brilliant and sound I grant you. But brilliant and sound enough for The Times? *This one mentions his triple First, his double Blue and his uncle the Bishop. Estimable, but the dear good chap does only speak four languages. Is one justified in giving him a trial when some nearly perfect aspirant may already be on his way from Winchester to Balliol? Is, indeed, anyone, anywhere, truly worthy of* The Times?

This was the awfully solemn thought which at that time sometimes oppressed Printing House Square, and if held long enough, could have led to a total depopulation of *The Times* offices everywhere. For even correspondents of the London *Times* sometimes perish or lose all sense of values and seek other employment. I had myself already met one who had resigned – for a reason which, though uncommon, seemed sufficient. He had formed the opinion that his appointment as a part-time correspondent had been a Parthian act of malicious sabotage by a retiring foreign editor with a grudge against the paper. 'My having the job,' he said with candour, 'was intended simply to discredit *TheTimes* in the eyes of the world.' His resignation was a touching gesture of loyalty to the paper's best interests.

In these circumstances I had been warned, back in the previous summer, that to fill up one of the regular application forms for a job with *The Times* would be worse than useless. To begin with it would reveal the fact that one was actually in need of a job, a state of affairs which could be regarded as ignoble. However, before entering the Fellowship examination, it had been necessary to state in an application form what exactly one proposed to do after the two years' period of the Fellowship – in what capacity was one going to take advantage of the benefits received from the Fellowship and fulfil the wishes of the founder.

Most people said that they were aiming for the Diplomatic Service: a few whose fathers or uncles controlled businesses operating abroad indicated they would be ambassadors of commerce. I had been warned, indirectly, that merely to say that one had an idea of being a journalist, a foreign correspondent of some kind, would be absolutely fatal. There were bound to be several among the examiners who would instinctively feel that the fewer British journalists running about the world the better. Also they would take the view that any man of birth and education who deliberately announced his intention of becoming a journalist probably was beyond salvation, even by the exceptional facilities afforded by the Travelling Fellowship. 'But *The Times*,' I said. 'Surely if I say I am going to be a correspondent of *The Times*? Think,' I said, 'of Russell! Think of Dr Morrison! Think of Wickham Steed!'

My adviser agreed that *The Times* would probably pass muster, 'Although,' he said dubiously, 'it *is* journalism, you know.'

Thus, unknown to *The Times*, I was forced to commit myself to becoming at some future date one of its correspondents.

The residential conditions attaching to the Fellowship were elastic – you could spend the whole two years in one town or country, or you could keep moving about. The only absolute condition was that you must be in a town with a university. I wanted to go back to Central Europe, and just after the results were announced I met a man who said he was a good friend of *The Times* correspondent in Berlin and would give me a letter of introduction to him. Up to the last moment I had been wavering somewhat between Berlin and Vienna, but this decided me. I bought, on that wonderfully long Oxford credit, some suits which more than adequately expressed the gaiety and even flamboyance of my mood. To compensate for the distress experienced at the interview, I had four pairs of shoes very expensively made for me and had a lot of silk shirts made for me too. When all these garments had finally been constructed, I took off for Berlin.

When I got there it emerged that the man to whom I had the letter of introduction had been transferred – had not been in Berlin for nearly two years. But by that time I was there, and the smell of Central Europe had a new tang to it.

4   The New Voice

TOADS used to come out of swampy ground in the Tiergarten and sit looking out of the backs of their heads at the packed buses, the racing taxis and the limousines and the huge German touring cars, roaring eastwards and westwards on the Charlottenburger Chaussee, which strikes unswervingly across the green heart of Berlin.

The toads, motionless except for the slow blink of their eyelids, were the only immobile creatures in sight, and gave an impression of cynical watchfulness. Their performance was corny but impressive; by hindsight even more impressive than it seemed at the time.

The sight of those squat, old-looking observers, gazing backward at everything that happened, sharpened the sense of impermanence, of foolish vulnerability in the face of inimical and indifferent forces of destruction, which could always be felt so strongly in Berlin. In Berlin you felt that the deluge was always just around the corner. There is a book or short story (well known but I have forgotten who wrote it), about a city which establishes itself in the sandy desert, defeats the desert, and just when things seem safest is – at first almost imperceptibly – attacked by the desert, defeated by it and finally engulfed. Similarly in Berlin you could without difficulty believe in a day when the toads and perhaps worms and snails would, after so long awaiting their opportunity, note that the human defences had collapsed, and take over.

I have known scores of people who have lived in Berlin most of their lives and always had this sensation about their city. It would be oppressive or stimulating according to one's mood or temperament. What caused it I do not know. It cannot have been, as some people have suggested, the relative newness of Berlin compared to,

33

say, Vienna or Paris, for great areas of Paris and Vienna are no less modern than most of Berlin, and in any case neither Chicago nor Kansas City produces this sensation. Pehaps my aunt was right and it is a trick of the light playing on the nerves of the retina. I think it is a character of Jean Giraudoux's *Siegfried et le Limousin* who remarks that there is more mystery and terror in a single pine tree in the streets of Berlin at midday than in an entire French forest at midnight.

After discovering on the first day I was in Berlin that the man whose presence there had been the whole reason for my coming to this capital was no longer present, I got the name and telephone number of his successor as *The Times* correspondent and the next morning rang him up – at 8.30 a.m. so as to create a good first impression of alertness, not one of those slouching Oxford decadents.

This might have been disastrous, because the correspondent had only just reached bed after one of those tiring journalistic evenings in the Berlin of those days, which used to start about six in the afternoon and rarely ended until six or seven in the morning. However, Mr Norman Ebbutt was a man of warm-hearted goodness and this he displayed immediately, pretending that it was time for him to get up and behaving in general as though I really were an old friend and had come with a letter of introduction to him. He even pretended to believe that I might actually be of use to him in *The Times* office in Unter den Linden. With extraordinary tact he somehow managed to suggest that I might be doing him positively a favour by coming and 'helping'. He must have known that he, of course, would have to spend hours teaching me to do things he could have done himself in a tenth of the time.

It was true that he was alone and grievously overworked, because at that period a mild manpower crisis, starting in remote parts of the world, but developing by a kind of chain reaction, was afflicting the foreign organization of the paper. Two correspondents had acted vexatiously and had to be transferred to other posts.

In those days it was nearly impossible to be sacked by *The Times*. You just got a less important and less interesting job at about the same pay. This civilized policy worked excellently and removed the root cause of many journalistic crises. This cause is fear of the sack. It is fear more potent and menacing in journalism – at least in foreign correspondents' journalism – than in most professions, because in so many cases the foreign correspondent has through no particular will of his own been suddenly whisked on to a standard of living obligatorily high on account of the paper's prestige, and has often inadvertently convinced some girl that this is the standard of living to which she may confidently become accustomed, and then found himself involved in a fearful rat-race of competition, pursued – at least in his nightmares – by other young men who want to live on that standard too and will put him off it unless he quickly and repeatedly does something that will impress the London office. As the London office frequently does not know what is really impressive about the events in the country to which its correspondent is accredited, and is thinking only about what it imagines will impress Birmingham or Newcastle tomorrow morning, the correspondent is tempted into vicious journalistic ways.

One of the two unfortunates of *The Times* who had to be transferred had developed 'views' on something or other – and in *The Times* language 'viewy' was a dreadfully damaging epithet. Another had embarrassed the British Legation in a capital city in Latin America, where he was a part-time correspondent. He had turned up with a girl to whom everyone was quite prepared to believe him married. But he was painfully high-principled, and he publicly disabused them of this idea. For valid reasons he was not, and could not be, legally married to her. He wanted to make that perfectly clear. On the other hand he must insist that she be invited with him to all official functions as though she were indeed his wife. Otherwise he would feel obliged to boycott such functions and make scenes.

The Legation in the foreign capital wrote to the Foreign Office, and the Foreign Office wrote to *The Times* asking them to reason with their man. Could he not, *pro forma*, and to avoid affront to stuffy foreign diplomats, courtiers and ecclesiastics, pretend he was married to the girl? Or at least cease to deny it? Or else leave her at home?

The Times wrote to the part-time correspondent, so reasoning. Much later one of the foreign editorial staff who had been in charge of the delicate negotiations told me the outcome. 'He simply wrote that she was his wife in the eyes of God. Surely,' he said, sighing, 'he couldn't have expected *The Times* to see eye to eye with God, could he?'

Norman Ebbutt was intelligent and courageous, and he needed to be, for he was a man of goodwill. He even believed that one day he would go to the British Embassy in the Wilhelmstrasse and find out what the policy of the British Foreign Office was, and perhaps that would turn out to be intelligent and courageous too.

Politically he was, I suppose, what could be described as a left-wing Liberal, which meant, at any rate in his case, that he hoped for the best in everyone. He used to take me to drink beer with Herr Stresemann, who was Foreign Minister, and in whom at that time Liberals believed. Personally I found that Stresemann was entertaining provided that you did not believe in him. He was one of those Germans who had, at a fairly early date, discovered that the way to get away with being a good German was to pretend to be a good European. He had a wonderful act in which he pretended to be not only fat, which he was, but good-hearted and a little muzzy with beer into the bargain. In reality he was as quick and sharp as a buzz-saw, and if being a sharp, fast-moving buzz-saw was not enough, he would hit you from behind with a hammer. We used to sit in the late spring in the garden of the Foreign Office drinking beer and playing a kind of diplomatic chess game which would have been risible if it had not been serious.

I think it was Stresemann, sitting under a fruit tree, talking about European unity, who first sowed in my mind the doubt as to whether my warm-hearted enthusiasm on behalf of the victims of the World War, my romantic belief in the nationalist movements of Central Europe (nationalist even when they were disguised as the resurgence of Central European democracy), and my conviction that the Treaty of Versailles had been a disastrous diplomatic crime, really covered all the facts.

I do not mean to imply that I cleverly saw what the old boy was really up to. I simply had an impression; an impression, that is to say, that if this was the kind old boy I had been feeling sorry for and enthusiastic about all this time, I probably had been making a mistake.

These encounters with Stresemann produced, in fact, a jolting dissatisfaction with a whole body of 'liberal' political ideas which, in the sixth form at Berkhamsted, at Oxford, and in Budapest had seemed to me axiomatic. This sort of liberalism was still, basically, nationalist. The nation states were still the determining factors. The questions it posed concerned their proper relationships and policies. It could be said to be a strictly vertical view of the situation, hardly taking into account the horizontal divisions – that is to say, the social, class divisions existing within those states and prolonging themselves beyond their boundaries.

And soon I came, in Berlin, into contact with an attitude to life and politics which immeasurably increased the dissatisfaction engendered by Stresemann and the friends of Stresemann. The contact was not gradual but sudden. It occurred at a party – the first of many – given (in this case at the Kaiserhof Hotel) by a Viennese baroness comfortably equipped with advanced political views and a banker for a husband. She also had wide philanthropic interests, and her parties were given to promote these causes.

I have forgotten which of these causes this party in the Kaiserhof Hotel was in aid of, but in any case the people I met – the Viennese bankers, the diplomats suspected of undue brilliance by their Foreign Offices, the industrialists suspected of improper relations with socialist politicians, and the socialist politicians suspected of improper relations with industrialists, the painters, film directors, publishers, writers, dancers and musicians – would have been present whatever the object of the Baroness's party, because they were all members of a kind of perambulating salon which functioned sometimes in Berlin, sometimes in a huge chalet, formerly an hotel, on the shores of a lake in the Austrian Alps where she went for the summer.

Naturally I cannot remember now just what was said or done at the party in the Kaiserhof Hotel and what was really said and done much later in Vienna that spring or in the summer by the lake. But I do remember that after a few hours of conversation at the Kaiserhof I had that sensation you get when you look with an inexperienced eye into a microscope, seeing nothing on the slide below but a confusing blur, and then someone adjusts the instrument to an effective focus.

Ever since I returned to Central Europe, the slide which earlier had been so clear had become increasingly blurred, and now it seemed that I had only been waiting for someone to make the adjustment. The Viennese essayist Polgár wrote that the Café Central in Vienna 'is not a coffee house like other coffee houses, but rather a way of looking at life'. And that could truthfully have been said about the people who at various times and places frequented the Baroness's travelling salon. Their opinions, of course, were diverse and usually passionately conflicting. Yet they had more in common with one another than any of them had with, let us say, the Oxford Liberals, or Norman Ebbutt and the corps of foreign correspondents in Berlin.

Although people who disliked the Baroness referred to her circle of friends as a 'set', a 'circus' or even a 'menagerie', all these epithets, kindly or hostile, were wide of the mark, because in reality the salon was a fluid affair and – which was more important – was very far from unique. You could have found replicas of the same people all over Central Europe, and even in Paris. And it was precisely this fact of their not being unique, nothing special, which gave them their significance.

Probably I had met them – them or people like them, I mean – often before, but inside some cocoon of sentimental Hungarian nationalism or Oxford Liberalism, had been impervious to the contact. This, in other words, was a noise which had been going on all the time but to which I had never been attuned. And this was true although neither at the Kaiserhof nor afterwards was there as much political conversation in the ordinary sense of the word as one could hear at any gathering of Anglo-American journalists in Berlin. But in politics, in the wider sense, these people were drenched, steeped, dyed.

They were for the most part Austrians, Hungarians, Poles or Russians, and some were Bulgarians or Rumanians. Most of them, too, were between the ages of twenty-five and forty-five. That is to say, all of them had been inescapably involved in the social up-heavals and conflicts of the years after 1916 and had thus been involved at an age when they were still young enough to adjust themselves to those conditions. Also, being people of energy and intelligence, they were able to accept the facts of life as they knew it and, where others saw chaos or defeat, to see a pattern; a pattern, moreover, which people of energy and intelligence could take hold of, to perfect or change.

What all of them, despite their curious differences of view, shared and could not help sharing, however much it might irk them, was – to put it with a bluntness which would have offended many of them by its lack of subtlety – a recognition of communism as the central dominating fact of our generation and indeed of our century. A platitude of course. To people nowadays such a recog-nition may seem a somewhat limited achievement, but I am speaking of the year 1927.

I dare say that before then I had often nodded 'yes' to this platitude myself, but it had not in any way affected my attitude to life – to, for example, the Treaty of Versailles, or the policies of either Herr Stresemann or the London *Times*. But these people had been impregnated by their experiences. They could no more ignore the facts of revolution and class conflict than they could the facts of astronomy. And the views of those who deplore these facts were as deeply coloured, and as pervasively informed by them, as were the beliefs and attitudes of those who continued to look upon them with enthusiasm.

When some direct references to current politics did occur, it was immediately borne in upon me that whereas I had been aware almost exclusively of the, so to speak, vertical divisions between peoples and policies, to my new acquaintances the horizontal divisions were more absorbing and in the end more important.

People who believe that the earth is round do not keep asserting that it is so, yet their attitude to everything is profoundly affected by that assumption. And the assumptions of these people were apparent even when the talk was farthest from politics. There were often moments in our early acquaintance when, after I had made some statement which seemed to me simple and even self-evident, I would be asked to repeat it as if it had been some astounding paradox, and I presently found that the reason for this was that people could not believe that I had really said what I had said, because to them so many of my assertions sounded like assertions that the earth is flat.

'Perhaps,' I said to Madam T., the Viennese draughtswoman and painter 'they think I am merely idiotic.'

'No, no,' she said, 'they expect anything of an Englishman.'

I began to be irked by my own ignorance of the events and particularly of the writings which had so profoundly affected these people's lives. Reluctantly, because I felt sure it would be tedious and utterly wrong-headed and mistaken, I bought in Vienna on my way to the chalet in the Austrian Alps a volume – nicely printed now and freely displayed in the bookshop – containing all those pamphlets and manifestos of Lenin and Zinoviev which eleven years before had had to be smuggled dangerously across Europe, and were now collected under the general title *Against the Stream*.

'The Stream' was of course the current majority socialist opinion in most of the belligerent countries in favour of the prosecution of the war. In the intervals of canoeing or boating on the icy, brilliantly blue waters of the Grundlsee, climbing to high places to see the shining or shadowy panorama of the Alps, chattering lazily under the fruit trees with fellow guests, or walking over the grassy hills by moonlight to drink freshly distilled plum brandy in the kitchens of upland farms, I set myself to examine in a rather desultory fashion those hysterical polemics, packed tight as shell-cases with high explosive. I found them shocking, repugnant, alien. They pricked and tickled like a hair shirt. They seemed to generate an intolerable heat. They existed in a world of notions with which I had no contact, and, exasperatingly, they dared totally and contemptuously to disregard most of the assumptions to which I had been brought up and educated, or else to treat them brusquely as dangerous delusions peddled by charlatans bent on deceiving the people.

I was bewildered, too, and shaken by a mysterious and violent quality of style, as though some intellectual masseur had got one's brain down on a slab and were twisting and pummelling it. 'As to that,' said the poet Ezra Pound, 'in the style of Lenin the space between word and action is less than in that of any other writer I know.'

Accompanied by the composer George Antheil, Pound had turned up in Vienna, and having read a fiction story of mine which he liked in the New York *Dial*, sent me – the first and only written communication I had from him – a note written apparently on lavatory paper in blue chalk saying, 'Hail. Dial story great. Can we meet? What chance you coming this city jolly month June?'

By his own writings I had been more profoundly affected – 'changed' one could almost say – than by anything else I had read during the previous few years, and I hurried to Vienna to meet him. I could afford only a couple of days there, but we spent several hours of them together. At that time Pound had the idea of establishing himself in Vienna and thereby, as he said with his characteristic mixture of arrogance and irony, turning the place into the cultural centre of Europe.

I returned to Berlin to find that *The Times* which, a few weeks before, had repeated its insistence that I was not to be allowed to write anything – they were afraid, Ebbutt gathered, that I was trying to chisel myself into a position where I would suddenly demand a job or a quantity of back pay – had suddenly reversed itself. Despite their injunctions I had written an article about the Hugenberg Trust, the vast newspaper, advertising and cinema combine controlled by the extreme nationalist, Alfred Hugenberg (later a patron of Hitler), and particularly about the use of the German films of extreme nationalist propaganda. *The Times* published it, and now had written to suggest that the best thing for me to do was to leave Berlin immediately, return to England and start going through the hoops which, by what *The Times* liked to consider an unbreakable law, had to be negotiated before one could hope to become a foreign correspondent.

Theoretically, candidates deemed worthy of trial were sent first to serve an apprenticeship on some newspaper in Liverpool, Newcastle or Nottingham. If they survived that, they did a spell in the home room of *The Times* occupied with domestic reporting, and were then – assuming that worthiness was maintained – transferred to the Foreign Room. After that all was uncertainty. Some people, who had entered the Foreign Room in the belief that they would be out of it again in a year or so and on the way to *The Times* bureau in Vienna or Buenos Aires, remained there for years and years, and in the end often lost any inclination to be anywhere else.

The prospect of abandoning for Nottingham or Newcastle the Berlin which I was just beginning to discover presented itself as both distasteful and ridiculous. In particular, the violent voice I had heard for the first time by the Grundlsee kept exasperatingly ringing in my head. It was a low insistent drumming, and annoyed and disconcerted me, but it had the effect of an assurance that there existed unknown territories and horizons, which, if I were now to involve myself in regular 'gainful employment', would never be visited or viewed by me. Just then my father died, and England seemed more distastefully, more drearily alien to me than ever.

I wrote rejecting *The Times*'s offer. I thought that probably this meant I should never be a correspondent of *The Times* at all, but Ebbutt, on information received from London, said that on the contrary the people at Printing House Square had been shocked but rather pleased – for years nobody had actually refused a job on *The Times*; they thought this showed originality. It was agreed that I might occasionally write short items of news for the paper under the strict supervision of the regular correspondent, which was, in fact, what I had been doing for weeks past.

Then, towards the end of a blazing afternoon, tornados of rain rushed suddenly down on Berlin, and there were reports of a cloudburst on the borders of southern Saxony. The reports in the evening papers had that curious smell about them which suggests immediately that somebody somewhere is trying to conceal something. Ebbutt was away on a couple of weeks' leave and his place was being taken by a Mr Barker. He and I both had this curious impression that something rum, and possibly sensational, had taken place in the mountains down there beyond Dresden.

I went there at my own expense – an alarming speculation. I got there at dawn, observed with satisfaction that there were no other journalists about, and found that, in one of the strangest small-scale catastrophes of the decade, the cloudburst had poured unheard-of quantities of water into mild little mountain streams, which tore down trees formerly far above their beds, jammed the broken trees against the bridges until they formed high timber dams, and, pushed higher than ever by the dams, rose and rushed along the streets of sleeping villages on the valley sides, peeling off the fronts of houses like wet cardboard, and killing more than a hundred people in a few minutes. Half a mile of that little valley smelled of death. There were corpses in the mud and in one house the table in an upper back room had been laid for breakfast. In several other houses canaries were singing or moping in their cages.

No other newspaper in London had had a man on the spot, and their stories were scrappy compared to the column *The Times* had next day. After that *The Times* wrote again, suggesting that perhaps I might be permitted to cut out the period of apprenticeship in the English provinces and go straight into the Foreign Room in London. And, when I refused this offer too, they presently wrote a third time proposing that I should cut out the Foreign Room, too, and simply stay where I was as assistant correspondent in Berlin. This blithe disregard of the hoops which I had always understood it was necessary to pass through quite worried me. It seemed to me almost as though the Church of England had told someone that he could be ordained without bothering to get confirmed first. Finally I asked a visiting High Priest from Printing House Square about it. His reply was an exhilarating example of what perhaps may be called *The Times* spirit.

'That,' he said – referring to the traditional hoops – 'is our rule. Unwritten, but I hope you take it no less seriously for that.'

'Not at all,' I said hastily. 'I just wondered...'

'And a very sound rule it is,' said the High Priest, sternly. 'Very sound indeed. Remember that.'

I never, as a matter of fact, heard of the rule again.

However, with every day that passed my claustrophobic distaste for immuring myself in a regular job increased, and again I refused. My resolve was strengthened, no doubt, by the fact that I had recently sold a few articles and short stories to German and American newspapers.

Even Ebbutt, always optimistic on my behalf, thought that this third refusal might have put an end to my beautiful friendship with *The Times*. However, nobody seemed to mind my continuing to occupy the centre room at the Berlin office, working there as I chose without pay except for special articles, and without any definite obligations.

A little later in the summer, rioting broke out in Vienna on a scale which caused many quite serious observers to believe that the second wave of East European revolution was beginning; the chief correspondent – either Ebbutt or Barker, I forget which at the moment – had to rush off at a moment's notice, and nobody seemed to find it odd that I should be left in sole charge of the office in Unter den Linden.

Quite a number of my friends and acquaintances from the party at the Kaiserhof had dashed to Vienna to see the revolution if that was what it was really going to be, or to observe at close quarters this extraordinary explosion in the midst of a relatively calm European summer. When they returned, their circle had been enlarged to include, temporarily, a lively section of the United States in the shape of Mr Sinclair Lewis.

German friends begged me to take them to a party to meet this great Voice of America. Their earnest intention was to spend an hour or so happily cross-questioning Mr Lewis on such matters as Americanism, Babbitry, and the Philosophy of Main Street. Lewis, however, was tired and turned up rather drunk. From beneath his jacket hung the ends of two towels clearly marked with the name of his hotel. He had them knotted round his waist to keep his trousers up. Some German at once thought this significant of something or other – the American revolt against convention, perhaps. But when he mentioned it to Lewis, the novelist looked at the knotted towels with an air of surprise as if he had only just noticed them and merely said he supposed his belt must have got broken or lost.

The German guests wished to start a discussion of trends in modern world literature. Lewis, for his part, was anxious to give a rendering of a song he had just heard or just composed, a parody of 'I didn't raise my boy to be a soldier'.

'I didn't raise my boy,' he chanted loudly, 'to be a bourgeois, I raised him to be the Third International's pride and joy. But the son of a bitch has gone and gotten rich, my boy! my boy! my boy!'

I undertook a forlorn and stumbling attempt at explaining the joke – starting with the origins and political character of the original song. It was hopeless from the start.

In the spring I was waiting anxiously for the last instalment of my Fellowship payment to arrive, and at length wrote urgently and rather irritably to Queen's College to inquire about it. The reply was disconcerting. It pointed out that the instalments had all along been paid in advance, and I had had the last one a month ago. There was nothing more to come at all. In these circumstances I wrote to *The Times* saying that although I had previously rejected their offers, I had now finished the period of my Fellowship, and would like to work as a *Times* correspondent provided, however, that I could do so in New York.

The reason for this was that by now I had widely extended the studies I had begun beside the Grundlsee, had read *Das Kapital* and the *18th Brumaire* and *Civil War in France* and other works of Marx; read Lenin's *State and Revolution*, and *Imperialism*, and *Materialism* and *Empirical Criticism*, and been particularly impressed by Bukharin's *Historical Materialism*. Yet at the same time highly informed books continued to appear in quantity, proving that what was happening in the United States in that year of boom, 1929, was making the sheerest nonsense of Marx, Lenin, Bukharin and everyone else of their way of thinking. The United States hung over my thoughts like an enormous question mark. I felt that I should never be able to make up my mind about anything unless I went there and saw for myself.

Mr Geoffrey Dawson, then editor of *The Times*, did not have the reputation of a particularly warm-hearted or sympathetic man, but his response to my letter was a gesture which indicated a quick sensibility to my situation, and a realization that maximum speed might be of very considerable importance to me, as indeed it was. He did not write, he simply telegraphed. 'Have no fear for tomorrow. Return at once. Job waiting.'

5 Printing House Square

NOTHING sets a person up more than having something turn out just the way it's supposed to be, like falling into a Swiss snowdrift and seeing a big dog come up with a little cask of brandy round its neck.

The first time I travelled on the Orient Express I was accosted by a woman who was later arrested and turned out to be a quite well-known international spy. When I talked with Al Capone there was a sub-machine gun poking through the transom of the door behind him. Ernest Hemingway spoke out of the corner of his mouth. In an Irish castle a sow ran right across the baronial hall. The first Minister of Government I met told me a most horrible lie almost immediately.

These things were delightful, and so was the first view of *The Times* office in London. In the Foreign Editorial Room a sub-editor was translating a passage of Plato's *Phaedo* into Chinese, for a bet. Another sub-editor had declared it could not be done without losing a certain nuance of the original. He was dictating the Greek passage aloud from memory.

That very first evening I saw the chief sub-editor hand a man a slip of Reuter's Agency 'tape' with two lines on it saying that the Duke of Gloucester on his world tour had arrived at Kuala Lumpur and held a reception. It would run to about half an inch of space, and on some newspapers I dare say might have been got ready for the printer in a matter of minutes. I was glad to see nothing of that kind happen here.

The sub-editor, a red-bearded man with blazing blue eyes, who looked like a cross between John the Baptist and Captain Kettle, had at the age of twenty or thereabouts written the definitive grammar of an obscure Polynesian language and gone on to be – a curious position for an Englishman – a professor of Chinese meta-physics in the University of Tokyo. He took the slip of paper into the library and then to the Athenaeum, where he sometimes used to go for a cold snack during *The Times* dinner hour.

His work on it was completed only just in time for the ten o'clock edition. It had been a tricky job. 'There are,' he explained, 'eleven correct ways of spelling Kuala Lumpur, and it is difficult to decide which should receive the, as it were, *imprimatur* of *The Times*.'

All foreign correspondents believe sub-editors to be malevolent troglodytes, happiest when casually massacring the most significant lines of an informed, well-balanced dispatch. Sub-editors believe foreign correspondents to be flibbertigibbets, uselessly squandering enormous expense accounts, lazy and verbose, and saved from making fools of themselves in print only by the vigilance of the staff in the Foreign Room.

Sharing, myself, the correspondents' views of people working at the London headquarters, I was naturally nervous. However, *The Times* people proved genial and made kindly efforts to put me at ease. One told me that, although the London climate was lethal, one could prolong life by getting up very early three times a week and travelling to Southend for a brisk twenty minutes' walk on the sea-front.

'And of course,' he said, rather mysteriously, 'being in the train so much gives one more time for thinking and reading.'

(He was, I need hardly say, a Fellow of All Souls.)

I said I hoped to be leaving shortly for New York. He was sincerely sorry for me – such an awfully long way from healthy Southend.

This conversation took place at tea, a rather serious function performed round a large oval table in a room on the ground floor of Printing House Square. We reached the office at about four in the afternoon and went straight down to tea and a half-hour's conversation before going up to the Foreign Room, a big, well-lighted place overlooking Queen Victoria Street, furnished principally by a long narrow table, extending from the inner wall almost to the windows. Junior members of the Foreign staff like myself sat at the part of the table nearest to the chief Foreign sub-editor. The seniors at the far end barricaded themselves with volumes of the *Encyclopaedia Britannica* or other large books and thus were able, as one of them remarked to me, to 'get on with our work without being disturbed'.

I did not at first see why this type of protection should be necessary, but later learned that several of them were engaged in writing historical works of their own, or authoritative treatises for various learned reviews, on the subject in which they were particularly expert. Mr Scott Moncrieff, the translator of Proust, worked there at one period, and I was told that the business of *The Times* was often held up for as much as a half-hour at a time while everyone present joined expertly in a discussion of the precise English word or phrase which would best convey the meaning and flavour of a passage in *A la Recherche du Temps Perdu*.

For further entertainment in the long evenings, someone had invented a game – a competition with a small prize for the winner – to see who could write the dullest headline. It had to be a genuine headline, that is to say one which was actually printed in the next morning's newspaper. I won it only once with a headline which announced: 'Small Earthquake in Chile. Not Many Dead.'

From five until about eight o'clock work continued without a break, and then people went to eat at their clubs or *The Times's* dining-room or the canteen. Unless you were on late duty you finished work at about eleven o'clock.

At first I was fascinated by the work, but after a few weeks I became bored and rather nervous because I was still afraid that someone would notice that I had not gone through any of the proper hoops, and pack me off to Newcastle instead of New York. Sometimes it seemed to me that I caught one or other of the High Priests looking at me somewhat askance, as though, perhaps, I were not, after all, worthy of *The Times*. My alarm was increased by the discovery that everyone already knew the story of something which had happened in Berlin one day when Ebbutt was on holiday and his place had been taken by a man called Pugge or something similar. Extensive unrest and street fighting were going on in Berlin at the time – I think it arose out of a demonstration on May Day. It was a confused situation and many people opposed to the unemployed demonstrators also thought the Prussian police were acting trigger-happy. Pugge, the newcomer, had no doubt that it was a straight fight of law and order versus the licentious mob. Any hesitant angels caught loitering were apt to get a sharp pushing around when Pugge rushed on to the scene.

Irked somewhat by his attitude I wrote, one afternoon when he was out watching the shooting, the dispatch which I conceived Pugge would have written – From Our Own Correspondent in Jerusalem – had he been covering events there approximately two thousand years ago. It was a level-headed estimate studded with well-tried *Times* phrases. 'Small disposition here,' cabled this correspondent, 'attach undue importance protests raised certain quarters result recent arrest and trial leading revolutionary agitator followed by what is known locally as "the Calvary incident".' The dispatch was obviously based on an off-the-record interview with Pontius Pilate. It took the view that, so far from acting harshly, the government had behaved with what in some quarters was criticized as 'undue clemency'. It pointed out that firm government action had definitely eliminated this small band of extremists, whose doctrines might otherwise have represented a serious threat for the future.

I put it on Pugge's desk. Glancing rapidly through it after a tiring day and seeing familiar *Times* clichés – small disposition to attach undue importance, government acting with firmness, band of extremists – all bowing and scraping at him from every paragraph, Pugge did not bother to read it properly, and passed it, together with his own dispatch, to the telephonist.

By a piece of ill-luck it chanced that *The Times* had recently reorganized its European telephone system, with the result that the Berlin office was used as a relay centre for dispatches from a number of smaller capitals which formerly had communicated direct with London.

The telephonist was already vexed by the extra work involved. Now he came rushing back from the switchboard waving my dispatch in a mauve fury.

'What's all this?' he shouted. 'Are we taking flaming Jerusalem now?'

Mr Pugge was abominably shocked. I had always hoped to hear someone use the phrase 'in the worst possible taste'. Pugge did. He did his best to bring home to me the appalling character of my action.

'Do you appreciate,' he said, 'that what you have done is to attempt to play a joke on *The Times*?'

This he obviously felt was the most blasphemous aspect of an altogether blasphemous bit of work. And in my present state of anxiety it seemed to me that there were several people around Printing House Square who would probably share this view. I began to wonder whether the job that had been waiting for me was really the New York job or something quite different and, from my point of view, unsuitable.

It was difficult to find out, because Mr Geoffrey Dawson had perfected a technique for not telling people anything much, and yet appearing all the time both approachable and communicative. His room had two doors. When you had been announced, and had entered, you found him standing in front of his desk, poised always on the same mark on the carpet, both hands slightly outstretched and his whole attitude that of one who has been unable to prevent himself bounding from his chair and rushing forward to meet you. Already touched and impressed, you were further overwhelmed by the warmth of his greeting and the voluble geniality of his conversation as he put his hand on your shoulder or took your arm.

There you were, pacing the floor of the sanctum of the editor-in-chief of *The Times*, and he concentrating on you while his secretary, you could imagine, told anxious cabinet ministers and bishops over the telephone that the editor was in conference. The effect was practically hypnotic, and in this state of partial hypnosis you were scarcely aware that with one arm across your shoulders the editor was with the other hand opening the door at the far end of his office and pushing you gently into the corridor, bidding you a warm farewell after an interview which had lasted approximately eighty seconds.

Nothing had been promised, nothing decided; but for several hours you certainly felt that you had accomplished something or other.

As things stood I need not have bothered about my position because, without my knowing it, Sir Campbell Stuart, at that time one of the most energetic directors of *The Times*, and the man who had played a major role in preventing the paper being acquired by Lord Rothermere after the death of Lord Northcliffe, had been kindly watching over my interests, for he was a Canadian and a friend of my Uncle Frank. I had told my uncle that I wanted to go nowhere but New York – though I had concealed from him the full reason for so wishing. My Uncle Frank, who looked upon Europe as little more than a fascinating museum in which it was good for people on holiday to pass a certain amount of time each year, was enthusiastic about my decision, and he enlisted the help of Sir Campbell Stuart to ensure that I was not disappointed.

Sir Campbell Stuart lived with his mother in his suite at the top of the Hyde Park Hotel, and when I finally went to call on him there, he lay almost flat on his back in an armchair, and with his extremely long and angular legs extended to the fire, smiled at the ceiling in a whimsical manner as he explained to me the real reason for the delay in my appointment and the apparent inability of the editor to make up his mind.

'They are afraid,' he said, 'of Louis Hinrichs.'

This character, of whom I had never previously heard, immediately assumed formidable proportions in my eyes. To be a man of whom *The Times* was statedly afraid was sufficiently imposing. Who and what was Louis Hinrichs? And why was *The Times* afraid of him?

Well, it appeared that Louis Hinrichs was the New York correspondent of *The Times* and had formerly been the Wall Street correspondent of *The Times* and the *Daily Mail* when the two papers were in the same ownership. *The Times*, said Sir Campbell Stuart, was afraid of him because he knew about finance, Wall Street, stocks and shares, things like that. Sir Campbell spoke of *The Times* with a mixture of respect and affectionate derision, as though of a distinguished but elderly uncle having venerable abilities and a good many more or less ludicrous quirks of character. Or, as I sometimes suspected, he felt himself rather in the position of the able butler when the entire family of aristocrats is marooned on a desert island and the butler, despite his comparatively lowly colonial origins, is the only one who knows how to deal with reality and pull them through.

Smiling at the ceiling, Sir Campbell Stuart explained to me that *The Times* had a certain awe of anybody who in fact understood finance. 'They think, in fact,' he began to giggle at the idea, 'that Hinrichs is a holy terror.'

The Times, in fact, liked its correspondents to be familiar with history, archaeology, the classics and the higher reaches of diplomatic society in whichever capital they happened to be established, but it was bothered by people who knew too much about money and economics and even tended to regard these subjects as of greater importance than the personal relationship existing between a cabinet minister, member of political party A, with a politician, member of political party B. The idea that they had a correspondent who really understood Wall Street and positively regarded Wall Street and its problems as essential in the affairs of the world, was to *The Times* awe-inspiring. Hinrichs, in fact, was to them a Man from Mars. And in consequence one had to act pretty gingerly in deciding whom to send him as his office mate and assistant correspondent. Therefore everyone had to mark time until Hinrichs, in the late spring, arrived in London and could be confronted with the candidate for this office – that is to say myself.

Since I was determined to go to New York in any case, and the question of whether I went there with a comfortable amount of money and prestige as *The Times* correspondent or had to struggle off again under my own inadequate steam, depended upon this Louis Hinrichs, I was naturally in a nervous state of mind when I went to call upon him at the Waldorf Hotel at teatime one after-noon. I can still recall more or less clearly the brutal figure I had expected to meet, and during the first ten minutes of conversation with Louis Hinrichs I was tormented by the fear that some appalling mistake had been made and that I was talking to the wrong man. He peered at me over a cup of China tea with a mixture of hope and despair. By an extraordinarily courteous piece of acrobatics he managed to reverse our true positions.

'I do hope,' he said, 'that after this meeting you will not re-consider your wish to come to work in New York.'

As we drove down Fleet Street he said, 'You know, I wish I did not have to go to *The Times*. I wish one could simply telephone them to say that everything is all right and that I hope to see you in New York soon. *The Times* frankly terrifies me.'

Recalling vividly that he terrified *The Times*, I could think of nothing to say. He added, just as the taxi swung into Queen Victoria Street, 'You know, sometimes I feel that I really ought to write a letter to *The Times* explaining to them that I am not at all the sort of man they imagine I am.'

In Printing House Square he interviewed Mr Dawson, who was as usual delighted to find that 'everything was all right' and therefore required no supervision or attention on his part. We then went together to see Mr Ralph Deakin, entitled Foreign and Imperial news editor. Mr Deakin was believed to be the originator of the statement that nothing was news until it had appeared in the columns of *The Times*, and at that period he gave – from his shining shoes to the beautifully brushed bowler hat on the rack behind him – an impression of mental and physical discretion and complacency which could have been offensive had it not been, in its childish way, touching. Certainly nobody could have guessed from his manner that he was the sort of man who would saddle himself with an employee of whom he so clearly disapproved.

Deakin had never made any secret of the fact that he was dubious as to whether I was the 'right type' for *The Times*. He was obviously a little surprised that Hinrichs should accept me. He would have expected him to stand out for someone a little more svelte, or else a little more businesslike in appearance. Resignedly he turned from the immediate topic of my impending journey to New York to discuss the fate of one of my predecessors, a former assistant to

Hinrichs, who had been brutally murdered by the hangers-on of some Chinese war-lord under the walls of Peking. Hinrichs expressed his sorrow.

'Nevertheless,' said Deakin, 'he had his reward.'

Hinrichs and I, simultaneously startled by this observation on the death of that distinguished young man, exchanged rapid glances, each of us wondering what comment one could possibly make on such a statement. Also it occurred to each of us at the time that this could only imply the existence of some bitter feud between Deakin and the victim of the banditti, and each of us was horrified to realize that Deakin apparently was prepared to continue this feud beyond the grave. There was a moment of danger during which either of us might have made some extraordinarily ill-placed remark had not Deakin added with a note of extreme satisfaction in his voice, 'Yes, he had his reward. I mean a column-and-a-half obituary in *The Times*.'

'You see,' said Hinrichs as we left the building, 'what I mean about *The Times*.'

6   Grand Slam

IN New York, you could talk about prohibition, or Hemingway, or air conditioning, or music, or horses, but in the end you had to talk about the stock market, and that was where the conversation became serious. Unless you understood this, and it took me quite a while to understand, you caused that shadow to fall. There was a 'mystique' about the market. You could argue about the merits of this stock or that, you could analyse earnings, you could consider rationally the effects which the weather in, say, Missouri was liable to have upon the stocks of companies producing agricultural machinery. But what you could not with impunity do was suggest, not by words only but by so much as an intonation, that there was any doubt about the fact that the market as a whole was going on up and up, that every 'recession' there might be in the near future would be 'temporary', 'technical', 'an adjustment', after which the new era of American life would resume its swift, inevitable progress towards a hardly imaginable stratosphere of prosperity. To hint that you regarded such an assumption as in any way questionable was – whether you were talking to the Italian who kept the nearest speak-easy or to your hostess at dinner in the East Sixties – to put yourself in the unpleasant position of making some vulgarly ironic reference to the Holy Father in the house of devout Roman Catholics. There was an element of sacrilege about it, but it was worse than that. For in this 'mystique' of the market there was an element of sympathetic magic too. Deep in people's consciousness there was an instinct, like that of a primitive African, that to speak ill of the market was in itself unlucky, a proceeding capable of bringing upon not only the speaker but all associated with him the wrath of the Market God.

Most people are capable of carrying more or less incompatible ideas in their head at the same time, and the same man who had convinced himself, by a study of innumerable market reports and statements by economists, that the level of stocks was fully justified by the underlying economic situation, and that a rise was predictable in the light of factors which could be analysed and calculated, also often believed in his heart that the whole thing was a kind of marvellous subjective trick; a séance where the table moved, and the spirits spoke, by virtue of the combined will power and capacity to believe of all present – a beneficial atmosphere which could be dissipated or seriously affected for the worse by the presence of an unbeliever. Perhaps that was only another way of stating the simple fact that if enough people started to disbelieve in the future of common stocks, common stocks would cease to have a future, but that was not the way in which most people put it to themselves. If they had, the existence of just one unbeliever would not have alarmed and wounded them so gravely.

In cold blood, and by hindsight, these attitudes can sound childish, and furthermore can support that tediously erroneous Anglo-European view of the Americans as people who are unduly – in the vulgar sense of the word – 'materialistic'. If the attitude of the Americans to the stock-market boom in the summer of '29 proved anything, it proved the opposite – for it showed that they believed in miracles. Myself I find this an endearing quality. The idea that two and two can never make anything but four is in itself depressing and limiting, and turns out, in the higher mathematical regions, to be probably untrue. This belief in miracles is simply an expression of the notion that if you try hard enough you can make wonderful things happen. The chief trouble with the Americans of 1929 was that they had their money on the wrong miracle.

The situation was no doubt absurd, and after the ball was over there were plenty of people to point out just how 'crazy' the country had been at that period. But to see it as merely absurd is to miss the pathos of what was happening there and, in the welter of greedy gamblers, to lose sight of what was tragic and even noble in this grotesque scene. For it was a scene which could have been enacted on that scale only in America, and this was so because it was a brief re-enactment of what was essentially an old American dream. They had dreamed that if you could get away from the principalities and powers of old Europe you could found a free and noble society. And when the eastern seaboard became an area oppressed by new principalities and powers, they dreamed that in the Middle West and the Far West the miracle could still happen. From the harsh necessities of millions of emigrants in the mid nineteenth century was distilled a new and heady component of that dream-liquor, a faith that there was still room on earth for the kingdom of heaven. And the people to be pitied were perhaps not those who had that faith, however naïve, but those who had lost it. Even the most superficial student of our day is familiar with the fact that the American Civil War was an affair of inextricably confused motives, of gigantic political swindles, of meanness masquerading as patriotism, and avarice disguised as love of liberty. Yet it would be a pity to forget that there really was more to be said about John Brown than that his body was mouldering in the grave, and that the sentiments expressed later in the Battle Hymn of the Republic are not invalidated by the fact of political intrigues, however sordid. The eyes of the corrupt army contractors and later of the carpet-baggers had not 'seen the coming of the glory of the Lord', but the eyes of a lot of other people had seen something like that, and the fact that the glory of the Lord did not in the end turn up did not make the hope of it ridiculous. What it did do was to add something to the sometimes overpowering American sense of frustration.

The big bull market, as Frederick Lewis Allen wrote later in *Only Yesterday*, was a compensation for innumerable disappointments and disillusionments of the past. And it was this which gave the atmosphere of the summer of 1929 its peculiar quality. There were moments when you said to yourself that this was just a casino. And then you had to admit that at the same time it reminded you of a revivalist meeting and even of the starting of some kind of crusade. It seemed like the pleasantest kind of crusade – one in which the whole world was going to get happy by getting richer and richer. It would start of course with people who were gambling in American stocks getting rich, and then the rest of the Americans would become prosperous too, and pretty soon the whole world. America felt kindly towards the world that summer – when it had a moment to think of it at all. In any case, there was no need to think of it much, because America was going to solve all the world's problems automatically.

The atmosphere of the great boom was savagely exciting, but there were times when a person with my kind of European background felt alarmingly lonely. He would have liked to believe, as these people believed, in the eternal upswing of the big bull market, or else to meet just one person with whom he might discuss some general doubts without being regarded as an imbecile or a person of deliberately evil intent – some kind of anarchist, perhaps.

I did not at all wish to be regarded as any such thing, and I kept my doubts pretty carefully under wraps, especially as they did not, after all, arise from any expert assessment by me of the immediate factors in the situation, but simply from the 'academic' theories of the Marxist and Leninist writers whom I had studied in the apartment on the Kurfuerstendamm and my studio in Paris.

From Louis Hinrichs I was particularly anxious to conceal my schizophrenic frame of mind, to hide from him the fact that as I read the market reports, the innumerable expert predictions of the financial writers, or listened to the talk of brokers and financial editors, I was only a little more than half-persuaded that those Marxist philosophers were wrong. I thought it would be a confession that would shock and perhaps alarm Hinrichs. I did not at that time know him very well. In any case, my comprehensive ignorance of the factual details of the present situation, as distinct from some general theory of economic movements, made it easy to avoid generalizations. I had too many questions to ask. Naturally Hinrich's knowledge of the stock market and of the 'over-all picture' of American business conditions was encyclopaedic, and in addition to that he had a fascinating sort of physical intimacy with the financial district of Manhattan. Most days we used to walk about there, going from office to office to see people who, he thought, might be useful to me later on. I had arrived with a preconceived notion of Wall Street, and that whole area, as a roaring, pulsating jungle, but under Hinrich's gentle guidance one had, surprisingly, rather the impression of going on a conducted tour of a village; a largish village and one full of oddities and unexpected situations or characters, but still a place where you could soon learn to find your way about, and one which you could hope, after not too long, actually to comprehend. This impression was curiously deepened by the physical qualities of the financial district itself. As one approached this hub of one of the world's largest cities one subconsciously expected a crescendo of mechanized noise. But the fact was that here traffic congestion had reached its logical paradoxical conclusion.

There was a time, I suppose, when everyone tried to drive along Wall, Pine or Cedar Street in a motor-car, but what had happened by now was that since there was not conceivably room for all the mechanical wheeled traffic which wanted to use those streets, mechanical traffic had virtually abandoned them, and the crowds padded about their business on foot.

56

The result was that when you turned out of Lower Broadway into one of these side streets you were conscious of a kind of hush, and the noise of tens of thousands of people moving about on their feet without engines reminded you of Venice.

This powerful, towering village, the activities of whose inhabitants could tilt whole nations, was familiar to Hinrichs in all its aspects. He knew who was who now and who had been who when, and as you toured it with him you thought that here as much history had been packed into a couple of decades as had occupied a century elsewhere. We had just passed, one day, the bomb-scarred offices of the House of Morgan, its windows now heavily protected in case anyone should want to throw a bomb again – that earlier bomb had been in itself the violent expression of an earlier American dream – when Hinrichs stopped in a disconcerting manner he had when he wanted to make an important point, and spreading his fingers in the fluttering motion which expressed uneasiness and a certain bewilderment, he said,

'All the same, Claud, I don't believe it.'

In New York at that moment there was only one 'it' of which you could say that. I was as astonished as a member of some underground movement in an occupied country who discovers that the local Captain of Police is of the same opinion as himself.

Strangely, for it was quite unnecessary, yet significantly – for it was an indication of the hypnotic effect of the climate we had been living in – we both of us, I noticed, as we walked along, lowered our voices. In the sixty-six-storeyed shadow of the Manhattan Bank Building Hinrichs began to explain to me what he felt about the bull market, and why he believed not only that it would not continue, but that it was a possibly monstrous delusion which could do serious harm to 'my dear America'.

We had many such conversations and from these emerged, paradoxically, the fact that, although we had reached a somewhat similar conclusion, we had reached it from premises which were diametrically opposite. Apart from the fact that I had acquired my doubts on a purely theoretical basis, whereas Hinrich's were the result of expert practical knowledge, mine had their roots in revolutionary soil, whereas his grew from the most orthodox conservatism. He knew the form book and he went by it. He could see nothing in the history of American development to suggest that, on behalf of the American Joshua of 1929, the Lord God was going to suspend the laws of economics.

Excited by the extraordinary disclosure of Hinrichs's scepticism,

I drew exaggerated conclusions.

'Then you mean,' I said, 'that you believe that the capitalist system won't work?'

But this was not what he meant at all. He meant simply that the capitalist system – a phrase he somewhat disliked, I think, because it implied the existence of other, equally valid systems – would proceed as usual by a series of jerks frequently interrupted by catastrophes. To 'defend', so to speak, the catastrophes seemed to him unnecessary, for he considered them as inevitable as sunrise. There was not, in his view, a 'system' to blame; if one had to blame anything, then it was just life. The capitalist system was life, and therefore attempts to substitute any other type of 'system' were both nonsensical and dangerous. You could not step out of life.

He was a warm-hearted man, generous and sympathetic towards all individual miseries, but he saw no cure for the general miseries of the human race – such as want and war – and thus, at least in conversation, took the view that people who proffered such cures were mentally defective or else quacks.

Our theoretical discussions in *The Times* office were frequently broken in upon by one who might be said to have been the embodiment of the Spirit of the Boom – namely, Mr Frederick Bullock, correspondent of the *Daily Mail*. In Northcliffe's day the *Daily Mail* and *The Times* correspondents in New York had naturally shared offices, and after the papers separated no one had thought it worth while to change the layout of the office. Thus we had, on the floor above the *New York Sun*, three fair-sized rooms of which the centre one was occupied by our joint secretary, and those on either side of it by *The Times* and the *Daily Mail* respectively. It is hard to imagine how more comparatively incompatible elements could have been jammed into so small a space.

The communicating doors were usually left open, and behind Hinrichs's most delicately learned exposition of some point in the past policy of the Federal Reserve System could be heard the rising bellow of Freddie Bullock's Rabelaisian laughter, or the cheerful bark of his bullish orders being shouted into the telephone to his broker.

He was a short, enormously muscular man of sixty or so, and when you first saw him you saw a huge cigar, a pair of tufted eyebrows and hairy muzzle, combined in a face which seemed designed for durability rather than elegance. You were just deciding that what you had to deal with here was a somewhat roughly constructed cannonball, when the cannonball would come to sudden rest, the cigar smoke would cease to swirl, and you were being examined hopefully by shrewd, alertly sparkling eyes, which brimmed with amusement, eagerness and goodwill. Their expression said that if you were a member of the human race you would certainly get from Mr Frederick Bullock the benefit of any doubt your conduct might occasion. He had the candour and exuberance of a twelve-year-old schoolboy, and the theatrical instincts of a first-class clown. He smelt rather than understood Hinrichs's scepticism about the market, and as a result regarded Hinrichs with a kind of derisive compassion. He would come steaming into our office behind his cigar, launch a general discussion on the state of financial affairs, listen impatiently for a few moments while Hinrichs attempted in the most meticulous fashion to explain his point of view, and then with something between a bark and a guffaw go steaming out again, pause for a moment to tell, or attempt to tell, an indecent joke to the handsomely blonde and strictly respectable secretary, and dash into his own office where the telephone was ringing. We would hear him shouting and laughing into it, and a few minutes later he would come rushing back again, sometimes executing a burlesque dance step as he did so, and – thrusting his half-smoked cigar under Hinrichs's nose by way of emphasis – shout out the news which his broker had just given him, to the effect that some stock in which he was interested had already risen four points that morning. In his estimation this was momentarily conclusive proof that the sceptics were a lot of nervous old women who, pusillanimously, or as a result of academic inhibitions, were letting slip the opportunity to make a million dollars.

A million dollars or thereabouts was in fact the sum which Freddie Bullock had made on paper by gambling on the stock market during the past couple of years. He used to tell with glee, and at the same time a touch of melancholy, the story of his most recent visit to Europe where, in Paris, he had had breakfast with the then Lord Rothermere. For a time, under Lord Northcliffe, Freddie Bullock had been, so far as I recall, a director of the *Daily Mail*, and had been on intimate terms with Lord Rothermere. He had looked forward to seeing him in Europe after a separation which had lasted several years. Lord Rothermere asked him to breakfast at his hotel in Paris. There were a lot of people there, and as Bullock came into the room Lord Rothermere bounded through the crowd and gripped him by the hand, shouting, 'How much did you make? How much?' By this Bullock was somewhat vexed and disappointed – he had expected at least an inquiry after his health, or an expression of gladness at seeing him again. He shrugged.

'In your terms, nothing worth writing home about,' he said. Lord Rothermere became almost violent in his impatience. 'I'm asking you,' he shouted, 'how much did you make?'

'But I tell you,' said Bullock, 'in your terms it's the merest bagatelle, nothing.'

'I'm not asking you for that kind of answer,' said Rothermere. 'I want the figures.'

Bullock paused to make sure that he had the full attention of the roomful of editors, financiers and politicians. 'I tell you,' he said airily, 'it's nothing – peanuts. In fact I can say that during the past three months I have not made more on the market than about six times the annual salary of a first-class man on the *Daily Mail*.'

He was a real Anglo-American. You could say that he was Americanized, yet you had to admit that he was as English as an Orange Pippin. In this Englishness of his he profoundly believed, and was proud of it. As an Englishman (he came, I think, from the West Country) he took the view that, unlike Americans, who are prone to hysteria, English people sternly control their feelings, never display emotion. In a roomful of American friends gambling like himself on the market, he would bound about shouting with excitement and begging everybody to keep perfectly calm. At dinner one day at his home – a costly penthouse apartment just off Washington Square – the talk turned on the sufferings of Great Britain following the First World War. Everyone present, except myself and Bullock, was American. Bullock gave them a patriotic little lecture on how to face adversity. 'Don't think, you fellows,' he said, 'that because we English ride our feelings on a tight rein we don't feel these things deeply. It simply,' he said, his voice trembling, 'means that even when we are thinking most deeply of all our country has been through, we never show it.' His voice trembled more and more, and the glass of wine shook in his hand. 'We never,' he sobbed, 'show a trace of emotion.' He drank deeply and two large tears rolled from his eyes.

Together with journalism, stock-exchange gambling and women, medicine shared his keen interest. He believed that almost any time now medical science would come up with some gadget which would enable people of nearly sixty to live at top speed without the slightest ill-effect upon their health and in a general way prolong life more or less indefinitely. He was thus the victim of countless expensive quacks.

His attitude to modern medicine resembled in some respects my father's attitude in the old days to the motor-car. For years, when he was younger and poorer, Bullock had pooh-poohed new-fangled medical notions, as being certainly decadent and probably fatal. He spoke of 'nature's remedies', and implied that what was good enough for his father's body was good enough for his. When, however, he did start to take an interest in it his position reversed itself: his objection now was not that its pretensions and achievements were too great but that they were not great enough. Just as my father had thought that if you were going to have a motor-car at all it ought to be capable of taking you from here to there in virtually no time, so Bullock felt that if you were going to pay to have the wonders of science let loose on you, you ought to get something spectacular in the way of health and vigour for your money.

Though nobody formulated it quite like that, this was a notion quite common in the subconscious minds of people in New York at that time. Quacks of every description from half-trained psychiatrists to golden-tongued doctors with multi-purpose hobby-horses throve upon it. One of them, franker than most, told me that, in his opinion, this obsession with health, this nervous preoccupation with the possibilities of disease on the one hand, or of prolonging life on the other, was simply an inevitable symptom of the gambling fever and the gambling boom itself. How horrible to think that Anaconda Copper might go to 150 and you would be too ill to care; how dreadful to die and miss the universal Utopia which was just coming up.

When Bullock was not chiding or commiserating with Louis Hinrichs for his stiff-jointed inability to grasp the opportunities offered by the stock market, he was upbraiding him on medical grounds, pleading with him not to pass up, too, the opportunities offered by modern medical science.

Significantly his feelings on this score were if possible more passionate than those he had about the stock market, and it was evident that here, too, lurked a belief in sympathetic magic – he manifested an obscure fear lest Hinrichs's lack of faith, not to mention his open derision, might be actually weakening the power of the doctors.

7 Storm

THE morning of Thursday, October 24th, was like the morning of a battle which people are beginning for the first time to realize may be lost. Until soon after the opening of the market on the previous day, nobody had thought of such a thing. It was assumed, as it had been assumed on each previous occasion when a break in the market had occurred, that this was a temporary setback, a 'readjustment' – the bulls were losing a skirmish or two but they were not going to lose the battle.

But by the close of Wednesday's market the *New York Times* averages for fifty leading industrial stocks had lost over eighteen points, and long after the close Freddie Bullock, in the intervals of trying to reach his brokers on the jammed telephone lines, kept coming into our office talking, arguing and listening for the first time to Hinrichs with a kind of nervous awe. Bullock came across from his apartment to have breakfast with me that Thursday in the café of the Hotel Lafayette. He needed company, and I dare say, too, he needed the peculiar atmosphere of the Hotel Lafayette which took you a little bit out of this world. It was owned by Raymond Orteig, who had put up the original prize of twenty-five thousand dollars for the non-stop flight between New York and Paris ultimately won by Colonel Charles Lindbergh. The Lafayette was no mere curiosity, a French hotel in New York. It was, on the contrary, a first-class hotel and one which was simultaneously as French and as American as the French district of New Orleans. The food was the best in New York, and if you were a resident and took your meals in your own apartment you could get the benefit of one of the best cellars in New York too – the management of the Lafayette taking the view that prohibition did not apply to resident guests.

We had breakfast at a marble-topped table in the café at the end of which there was a ticker machine. Bullock kept jumping up and walking over to it by force of simply nervous habit, because at that hour the ticker could tell us nothing that we did not know already. Yet that morning there was a stream of men trotting up to the ticker and standing for a few minutes gazing at it in an unusual silence.

It takes nothing less than a major air raid to produce any visible change in the social 'atmosphere' of London, but New York lives more externally, and on the subway to the City Hall Square the change was as evident as a notable change in the weather. At the *Sun* office there was just that nip in the emotional air which you get on the day after a big air raid, when people have grasped that the bombers really did get through last night and may do so again today. It was a situation in which nobody says much but everyone knows what everyone else is thinking and knows that everyone else is a little frightened too.

As the electric clocks ticked off the minutes until the opening of the market, the tension was nearly intolerable. I do not mean that any of us had much idea of what was really going to happen except perhaps Louis Hinrichs. None of us, I am sure, thought, 'This is a turning-point one way or another in the history of the twentieth century.' None of us was sapient enough to reflect, 'Upon what happens today hangs the fate of nations. A way of life is going to survive or is going down the drain. After today, either everything will be as it was, or else nothing will ever be quite the same again.'

There were some very smart people hanging over the ticker at the opening of the market that morning in the *Sun* office, but none of them was quite smart enough to know that, as they saw in those first few astounding minutes shares of Kennecott and General Motors thrown on the market in blocks of five, ten and fifteen thousand, they were looking at the beginning of a road which was going to lead to the British collapse of 1931, to the collapse of Austria, to the collapse of Germany, and at the end of it there was going to be a situation with Adolf Hitler in the middle of it, a situation in which no amount of get-togethers on a log at Rapidan was going to do much good, a situation in fact which was going to look very much like the fulfilment of the most lurid predictions of Marx and Lenin.

I kept being reminded of the old story about the enthusiastic American who took his phlegmatic British friend to see Niagara.

'Isn't that amazing?' said the American, 'Look at that vast mass of water dashing over that enormous cliff!'

'But what,' said the Englishman, 'is to stop it?'

There was nothing much to do that morning except just to watch Niagara. It seemed pointless to go through the usual routine of telephoning to 'contacts' and informants and asking for their comments on the situation. There was no sensible comment that anyone could make, and furthermore you had the feeling that there was no question you could ask which would not strike the man at the other end as some kind of affront. Even so I scarcely began to guess how bad the situation really was until Hinrichs, in a low voice, said to me: 'Remember when we're writing this story the word "panic" is not to be used.'

At length we left the crazy-looking ticker and started to walk through the bright streets towards Wall Street, walking in silence because, in the light of the enormity of the event, anything that one could say seemed intolerably trivial. Thousands of other people were streaming towards Wall Street and they were walking in silence too.

In the Street itself there was an enormous murmuring crowd, and the people pressed close around us were talking, when one listened to them, almost in whispers. Every now and then you could hear quite distinctly a hysterical laugh. As time passed, the crowd grew thicker and noisier, and then there was an eddy in the middle of it and a man in shirtsleeves was pushing his way across the street in the direction of the Morgan offices. Hinrichs nudged me sharply. This was an easily recognizable denizen of the Village, namely Charles E. Mitchell, Chairman of the National City Bank, the leader of the bull market and the champion of the 'expansionists' against the 'restrictive' efforts of the Federal Reserve Board. He pushed his way into the offices of the house of Morgan and a little later we learned what he had gone for. He and the other leading bankers of Wall Street had been summoned there to establish a multi-million-dollar pool in an attempt to steady the market.

Silver-haired Mr Thomas W. Lamont, J. P. Morgan's second-in-command, received us with a manner so reassuring that, upon me and many others, it had the same effect as Hinrichs's warning against the use of the word 'panic'. It was like the manner of the man who comes on the stage of a burning theatre and urges everyone to keep perfectly cool, stating there is no cause for alarm. He made soft, soothing gesticulations with his pince-nez as softly, gently, almost stammeringly, he deprecated anything in the nature of sensationalism. His first sentence has been aptly described as one of the most remarkable under-statements of all time.

'There has been a little distress selling on the Stock Exchange,' he said, 'and we have held a meeting of the heads of several financial institutions to discuss the situation. We have found that there are no Houses in difficulty and the reports from brokers indicate that margins are being maintained satisfactorily.'

The pince-nez gently waved away ill-informed rumours of the disaster, moving to and fro in the dim light from the high window heavily covered with anti-bomb steel netting. Nothing fundamental, he said, had changed. There was nothing basically wrong with the country's economy. What had occurred was due simply to 'a technical condition of the market'.

Since becoming a journalist I had often heard the advice to 'believe nothing until it has been officially denied'. But, despite this, even the ominous blandness of Mr Lamont did not shake me into full awareness of what was going on. The shake came a little later at lunch with the Edgar Speyers.

'Edwardian' was the adjective which inevitably occurred to you in the presence of Edgar Speyer, and equally inevitably he recalled to me the Rothschilds as I had seen them in my boyhood days at Tring. He was an American now, had been an American for years, and he and his brother were not only millionaires but had made themselves powerful figures in the cut and thrust of Wall Street, but the aroma of Edwardianism still hung about him like the scent of a good cigar. This was natural enough since it was in Edwardian England that this originally German Jew had risen to wealth and prominence. He had been Sir Edgar Speyer then, and a Privy Councillor. Then he was caught in the storm of indignation against Germans in high places in England which at the beginning of the First World War swept even Prince Louis of Battenberg out of the Admiralty. He could afford to recall what for many people might have been a disaster with an amiable shrug. His enforced good-bye to all that had by no means been disastrous for him. He just got on a boat and went to Boston and made a couple of million dollars. Later he advanced triumphantly on New York and, at the time I knew him, lived in one of the lovely rose-coloured houses on the north side of Washington Square. It housed, not in any special gallery but as part of its furnishings, a small but luminously beautiful art collection composed chiefly of Chinese paintings and porcelain. The atmosphere was one of elegant calm in which the rich odour emanating from pots and pots of money was naturally, but not disagreeably, perceptible. It was at that time one of the few houses

I visited in New York where you did not have to talk about the stock market or any other form of business, and the food and wine were so good that nobody thought it odd if at lunch or dinner you were perfectly silent for minutes on end. There were a middle-aged English butler and a youthful English footman, but, except for their age, one might have supposed that they had been trained in Edwardian England and come over with Speyer on the boat to Boston in 1914. Their only departure from an older tradition was that they both of them left the room as soon as each course had been served by the footman under the butler's supervision.

Leonora Speyer was a writer. She had, as I recall, recently published a volume of poems, and on this October 24th of 1929 the Speyers and their four guests were talking about modern American poetry. I was eating pompano and listening to somebody telling something about some poet I had not yet heard of, when I perceived to my astonishment that some kind of disturbance was going on at the other side of the dining-room door, which faced me as I sat at the table. Something had certainly bumped against the door. I heard a very faint thump, and I saw the door shiver slightly. The idea of anything, as it were, untoward occurring in the Speyer household was nearly inconceivable. I concluded that they must be the owners of some large dog which I had never seen, and that this dog had escaped and was probably at this moment being hauled off to its proper place by the footman. And just then as I was about to give full attention again to the conversation, something else happened.

The handle of the door turned very very slowly, the door shuddered again and moved an inch or so inwards. Then it closed again, and again the handle very very slowly turned in the direction opposite to its direction before. There was no longer any doubt about it. Either somebody in an ecstasy of indecision was trying to make up his mind to come into the room, or else, as seemed more likely, two people were struggling over the handle of the door, one of them trying to open it and the other to keep it closed.

In any other house there might have been a dozen explanations for this – children loose in the passage, for instance. Perhaps children playing with a big dog. But in the Speyer household things were so ordered that a disturbance of this kind was as startling as it would have been to find the dining-room too hot or too cold, or to have a draught blowing down one's neck. Fascinated by the mysterious struggle behind the door, I found myself gazing at the man who was talking intelligently about this poet with an expression, as I could see from the surprised look he gave me, of absolutely idiotic vacancy. I was so placed that I was the only one at the table who, when the door opened, could see right down the corridor outside, and what I saw, when the two manservants came in to put a saddle of lamb in front of Speyer, was that at the end of the corridor either four or five maidservants of various ages were grouped together in what seemed to be an excited attitude and one of them – unless I was under some kind of hallucination – had actually shaken her fist at the footman as he came through the door.

Within a few minutes the butler and footman had again withdrawn, but we had swallowed no more than a mouthful or two of lamb when the noise in the passage became so loud that nobody in the dining-room could even pretend to ignore it. A woman shouted, 'Go on – or else! –' and then the door was burst open and the butler, very red in the face, nearly bounced into the room as though he had been pushed violently from behind at the last moment.

He closed the door and as collectedly as possible marched across the room to Speyer and in low apologetic tones begged him to come outside for a moment. Listening with an air of astonishment, Speyer, after a few seconds' amazed hesitation, left the room with him. Almost immediately Speyer came back again looking a little dismayed. He begged us to excuse him. The staff, he explained, had of course their own ticker-tape in the kitchen premises and of course they were all heavily engaged on the stock market. And now the ticker was recording incredible things. In point of fact the ticker was by that time running just over an hour and a half late, owing to the enormous volume of trading, so that the prices which the Speyer staff were reading with horror at a quarter to two were the prices at which stocks had changed hands at the very worst moment of the morning before the bankers had met and the formation of the bankers' pool had been announced.

The staff saw their savings going down in chaos; since they were certainly operating on margin, they might at this moment already have been wiped out. Among the stock in which all of them had speculated was that of Montgomery Ward, and that had dropped from an opening price of eighty-three to around fifty before noon. And all this was going on before their eyes while their employer, reputedly one of the shrewdest financiers in New York, was calmly sitting upstairs eating pompano and saddle of lamb. They absolutely insisted that he go at once with them to the kitchen, study the situation, make telephone calls if necessary, and advise them what to do for the best.

Speyer left the rest of his lunch uneaten, and his wife and her guests finished the meal under conditions of confusion and make-shift which probably had never been seen in the Speyer household before. I left as soon as I decently could and did not see Mr Speyer to say good-bye. He was still in the kitchen. I hurried to the office to write my story, beginning at last to be aware of what the great crash meant.

8   While the Roof Fell In

THE next week was just the same and every day people said that everything was going to get better, and every day it got worse. Things reached a point where it became almost impossible to face one's friends or acquaintances in New York because everything that had happened or was happening seemed to make them out to be fools, and just because at one time or another one had questioned their judgement in the grand old times of ten days ago, one seemed to be swaggering with superior knowledge. Superior knowledge which of course one did not possess.

I was thus both happy and tremulous when I suddenly received the news that *The Times* correspondent in Washington, Mr Wilmott Lewis, had been summoned to London to attend some international conference or other, and the plan was that I should immediately go to Washington and take over his job. I was elated because I was glad to get away from the gloomy atmosphere of New York at this period, and to get also to the political centre of affairs. On the other hand, I was nearly unnerved by the thought that I was suddenly, at so brief a notice, and with such minimal knowledge and journalistic experience, to take over what by this time had become the major political bureau of the London *Times*. I left for Washington on the night of December 31st, 1929.

Sliding into Union Station, Washington, in the darkness of New Year's Eve, I reflected momentarily that the last member of my family to visit the American capital was Admiral Sir George Cockburn, who had burned the White House and the Capitol, and much else of Washington besides, in 1814. Not, I had always thought, a very nice kind of man. For example, when he was in command near Annapolis before the assault on the city, he considered the food and drink available in the camp not up to the mark. He had also heard that there was an excellent restaurant on Pennsylvania Avenue in the enemy capital. Sensibly enough, he made arrangements to visit this restaurant every evening in disguise. However, no memory of these pleasant little soirées prevented him later from cantering up and down Pennsylvania Avenue on his horse urging the soldiery to further acts of rape and arson. The proprietress of the restaurant is said to have been very much wounded by his behaviour.

As I left Union Station there was a considerable glare in the sky. The dome of the Capitol had just burst into flames.

Startled, I drove to the house of Wilmott Lewis where I was to stay. It was our first meeting. He was entranced by the occurrence at the Capitol. Holding both my hands in his he beamed upon me and, 'Now,' he said, 'one sees at once that you have been born under the right star. You have luck – and that is the most important thing in life.

'Even with your outstanding abilities – which I may say I have for some time been noting from afar with admiration – it might have taken you weeks to make your mark, to become any kind of a lion in the Washington Zoo. Now, as a result of this happy concatenation of events – call it luck, call it destiny, call it what you will – you will be at least a lion cub no later than tomorrow morning.'

Before he had even finished speaking he had lifted the receiver of the telephone in the hall and communicated the story of my well-timed arrival, decorated with some remarkable grace notes of his own, to all the columnists in Washington, and to two in New York. In the brief intervals between the calls he gave me a little lecture on the values of publicity in facilitating one's serious work, and smoothing the path towards one's real objectives.

'Do any of the people you have been talking to,' I asked, 'know what actually caused this fire tonight?'

'They suppose,' he said, 'that it was a painter. The inside of the dome is being redecorated. One of the painters, no doubt drunk, since it is New Year's Eve, probably dropped a cigar among the paint and varnish and so on. However, it is what one may call the "Cockburn angle" that really makes the story.'

Still talking, he led me into the drawing-room, where an exhilarating symphony of noise and almost overpowering volume of sound proved after a time to be composed of the Philharmonic Orchestra playing something rowdy on an enormous radiogram, about thirty of the best-informed people in Washington rattling the tall windows with their gossip, and the yells and incantations of two senators, a congressman, several journalists, and the then Mrs Lewis, daughter of the owner of the Associated Press, who were on their knees shooting craps in the middle of the carpet.

'Curiously enough,' said Lewis, towards five in the morning when the party was beginning to break up, 'I feel a little tired. I must be getting old.'

He was then in his early fifties. For all these hours he had 'conducted' that party of star performers as a conductor conducts a band. Reeling to bed when the last guests had gone, I passed the open door of his study and saw him in his shirtsleeves, his dinner-jacket draped over the back of his chair, thoughtfully beginning to tap out two or three pages of notes recording impressions, potentially significant pieces of information, dropped into his attentive ear in the course of the evening.

'There are a million pieces in the jigsaw,' he said. 'At any moment you may unexpectedly find that you have just picked up the one you need.'

I had met a lot of colourful and impressive personalities that evening, but before I finally got to bed I could not feel that any of them was quite as impressive as my host. Nothing in the years that I knew him altered that opinion.

Strangers thought he must be a famous actor or Envoy Extraordinary of some very civilized state. In the grey dawn of an all-night poker session he seemed, rather, the phantom of the original Mississippi Gambler, so sardonic, debonair and quick on the draw. Or smiling thoughtfully in the inner circle round the President at a White House reception, he suggested an angularly handsome Mephisto, wondering whether or not to wave a conjuring hand and transform the company into swans and bullfrogs.

High-placed Americans insisted he was the secret chief of the British Intelligence Service in the United States, and, years before he became officially 'Sir' Wilmott Lewis, American colleagues recognized the panache of his personality by referring to Wilmott Harsant Lewis as the Knight of New Hampshire Avenue, where his big house was situated. When he was knighted they asked him whether they should address him in some new way.

'You will continue,' he said, 'to address me as "You old s.o.b.", but from now on you have to smile as you say that.'

Up-to-the-minute as a portable voice recorder, he yet had about him a flavour which evoked Europe of the late nineties. In his teens he had been at the universities of both Heidelberg and Paris, and one of a group of *avant garde* poets and critics who met at the

Closerie des Lilas. He admitted occasional nostalgia for the continent he had scarcely seen in twenty-five years.

'Nevertheless,' he said, in his habitual style of faultlessly elaborate parenthesis, 'Washington – which Viviani, when he led the
French delegation to the Disarmament Conference, was tactless
enough to describe as *"un Versailles nègre",* thus (for you figure to
yourself the reactions of Southern senators to whom his ill-timed if
apt remark was, I need hardly tell you, instantly communicated)
stabbing himself in the back, a performance singularly otiose in a
city where so many stand only too eagerly ready to do it for you –
Washington has many amenities and compensations, not least
among them the fact that it is the last world capital still resisting
Americanization.'

Among the amenities he enjoyed were the rare, perhaps unique,
local prestige and international influence his ability had achieved
for him during his first years in the capital. He had come to be
regarded generally as more important than most Ambassadors
most of the time and always much more fun. It was a situation he
appreciated without illusions.

'The advantage,' he remarked to me once, as we sat eating
enormous oysters in a tiny yacht on the Potomac, 'of having spent a
good deal of one's early life on – not to put too fine a point on it –
the bum, is that one learns never to take even a square meal
entirely for granted.'

As a very young man he had been for a time an actor, down and
nearly out. He had sat up at night in an Eastbourne lodging-house
writing fresh material for the bankrupt troupe, himself among
them, to act next day. It was presumably during this period that he
had acquired a kind of barnstorming fruitiness and floridity of tone
and gesture which sometimes disconcerted the stolid.

'As you gaze, Mr President,' I once heard him say to President
Hoover, 'into the future, as you peer down the grey vista of the
years, do you not apprehend, sir, that the problems of the United
States are problems not only of growth, but' – the voice sank to a
vibrant whisper – 'of decay?'

The President seemed bemused alike by the question itself and
by the sudden extension of arm and hand which accompanied it,
the index finger pointing menacingly down the grey vista. The
incident must have disturbed him, for later he made a speech in
which he said the problems of the United States were those of
growth only – not of decay.

Lewis would describe as poignantly as though it had happened yesterday the occasion when after starving for nearly four days in London he had found a shilling or so in the lining of his jacket and rushed out to buy a tin of beef or something of the kind. When he got it back to his room and had hacked it open, with the saliva running down his chin, he found that the beef was hopelessly maggot-ridden.

'It is a good thing,' he said, 'to remember, that, however nicely we may be doing, to millions and millions of people all over the world, privations and disappointments of that kind are happening all the time.'

He told me when I came to know him well that he thought probably the most 'formative' influence in his early life had been the occasion when as a very junior reporter he had been assigned by the *Daily News* to write a preliminary 'feature' story about the Diamond Jubilee Review to be held at Aldershot by Queen Victoria in 1897.

'I went to Aldershot and viewed the sand-dunes, the broad driveway where the Royal cortège and the whole pomp and panoply of Empire, the Kings and Queens and Princes, were to be assembled, where troops from twenty races and from every continent were to pass in view. As my mind's eye envisaged the superb spectacle, my physical eye detected an unexpected movement among the sand-hills on the other side of the reviewing place. Mildly curious, I moved in that direction. I soon saw that the movement was caused by human figures.

'Approaching still nearer, I perceived these to be the figures of women in rags and horribly decayed. At that time, you know, there was in the British Army no proper system of education and instruction on the subject of venereal disease – it was thought that to introduce such a system officially might be offensive to the "respectable" public, and perhaps to the Queen herself. These women, then, were former prostitutes of Aldershot, so diseased as now to be unable to pursue the practice of their profession and living in the most miserable shacks and shanties among the sand-dunes. One must admit, of course, that they were excellently placed to enjoy the prospect of the great Diamond Jubilee Review.'

An abruptly switch-backing course took young Mr Lewis from London to the Far East, where he was alternately on top of the world and reduced to helping to manage a tough bar at the Shanghai race-course. Soon after that his astounding energy shoved him to a point where he was internationally recognized as one of the most ingenious and brilliant war correspondents in the Russo-Japanese War.

He edited a newspaper in Manila, worked as a sports writer in San Francisco, was 'hard pressed' again in New York, emerged penultimately in Paris at the moment of the Versailles Conference. Deeply impressed, Mr Wickham Steed, then editor of *The Times,* introduced him to Lord Northcliffe. The meeting was in a sense a failure. Apparently Lewis, as was his habit, illustrated his conversation with rather frequent quotations from the French minor poets. Lord Northcliffe complained that the man was a damned foreigner. He compromised by agreeing that he be hired, provided he was sent somewhere far off. They thought first of Tokyo, finally agreed on Washington.

By the time I met him his prestige was alarming, and his dispatches were misleadingly described as models of what such things should be – misleading because anyone trying to imitate these superbly individual works of art would have come a nasty cropper. Sometimes he spent three or four days or even a week preparing and polishing a dispatch on some aspect of American affairs which would be filed to London at a moment when an event, foreseen by Lewis, occurred to form the 'news peg' upon which the rest of the carefully prepared message was to be hung. More often he wrote his dispatches or articles very fast, but this was only because he was, so to speak, permanently 'in rehearsal'. He was always rehearsing, mentally or in conversation, the formulations or comments which would be appropriate to this or that development of the situation, so that when the development actually occurred, the polished phrases and considered judgements poured from the typewriter at a pace which, but for the unending 'rehearsals', would have been incredible.

I was to have only forty-eight hours with him in Washington before he left for London. Considering my ignorance of this vast and complex stage, the experience would have been very alarming had not Wilmott Lewis, by a kind of courteous hypnosis, succeeded in creating for myself and almost everyone else the illusion that I was a person of such enormous experience and ability that – with a hint or two, probably unnecessary, from him – I could effortlessly take charge of the situation.

Just before leaving, he suddenly presented me with the first of two pieces of journalistic advice which were the best I had ever had.

'I think it well,' he said, 'to remember that, when writing for the newspapers, we are writing for an elderly lady in Hastings who has two cats of which she is passionately fond. Unless our stuff can successfully compete for her interest with those cats, it is no good.'

Months later, when he was back in Washington, I once submitted to him a two-column article for *The Times* on which I had worked hard and of which I was extremely proud. Lewis read it with close attention. As he nodded appreciatively my pride and pleasure increased. He read it for the second time. Then, holding it between his finger and thumb, he said, 'Old boy, this piece is not only informed but erudite. Its material is solid and accurately observed; its style polished – and, in my estimation, witty. In fact it is everything which one imagines to oneself an article in *The Times* should be. Yet I'm afraid – my instinct tells me – that,' he opened his finger and thumb and the pages dropped into the wastepaper basket, 'the cats will have it.'

Despite the intensive forty-eight-hour course in Washington affairs which I had gone through under his guidance, I was uneasy. Left to myself, I thought, I should write something terribly mistaken, causing panic in London and upsetting the Empire. Sensing my emotion, Lewis pushed head and shoulders out of his departing taxi and gave me the second piece of admirable advice.

'Whatever happens,' he shouted, 'don't be nervous. Remember, old boy' – the taxi was moving faster now and he had to shout through the driving sleet – 'whatever happens, you are right and London is wrong.'

He had been away many weeks, was in fact just returning, before I grasped the full extent of his own faith in this statement. He had invited me to stay in his house and also use it as my office. He had omitted even to mention that there was in fact a *Times* office in Washington. I found it by accident one day when I was wandering through a downtown office building looking for something else. It was locked. I obtained a pass-key. The door moved with difficulty. When I did get inside, I found the door had been jammed by a cascade of cablegrams and letters pushed daily for weeks and weeks through the letter slip.

Most of the cables were from *The Times*, some of them sent since I had taken over, most of them of earlier date. They said 'Urgently require 700 words on. . .' and 'Please cable most urgently full coverage of. . .' 'Must have tomorrow latest. . .'

Appalled, I met Lewis on his return with the dreadful news; I supposed it to be due to some ghastly mistake by the Cable Company. He looked at the cables distastefully.

'Ah yes,' he said, 'perhaps I should have told you about that office. London, you know, *does* these things. I've always found it best to maintain a certain distance. Better to decide for oneself what to send and when to send it.'

Relieved by his explanation of the business of *The Times* office in Washington, I asked him why he had refused the Foreign editorship of *The Times*, which I knew had been offered him during his most recent visit to London.

'I am too scabrous an individual,' he said, 'to survive for long the rarefied air of Printing House Square. I did, however, offer to become their *London* correspondent – reporting, you know, on the motives and personalities of political activity in England with the same interest and detachment that one seeks to display here. Would it not, I suggested, be an excellent idea for *The Times* to be as informative, and when necessary as candid, about people and events in Westminster, Whitehall and the City as it is about goings on in Washington or Paris? They didn't,' he said, looking happily out at Washington, his expression more Machiavellian than usual, 'seem awfully keen on the idea. I wonder why not?'

The roar of the Press Club dining-room engulfed me. Lewis, listening to a fierce political discussion, seemed a little tired. He said he kept remembering the dream a French poet friend of his had once had, in which he saw the whole world covered by an inundation. Only the tops of the highest spires and steeples peeped above the flood, and the only survivors were some parrots which perched on these and, taught by man, kept screeching out 'Justice, Progress, Freedom!'

Somebody said, 'Bill, you're a nasty old cynic.'

Wilmott Lewis looked at him shortly. 'Cynic? Not at all, old boy. If humanity leaves such memories to the birds, it will have been a considerable achievement, something of which we may all be proud.'

During the first two and a half years of that decade, when I was in Washington, sometimes for months at a time, sometimes only for a few weeks or even hours, things to take pride in seemed to be what we were rather short of. First we had a crisis which no one would admit officially existed, so that – somewhat like the prostitutes at Aldershot who became diseased because the army did not dare officially to admit the existence of syphilis – unemployed men in Chicago had to fight one another for first grab at the garbage can put out at the back doors of the great hotels because a full and proper system of unemployment relief would have been 'socialistic', and above all would have been an admission of the existence of a crisis of scarcely believable proportions.

Later the crisis was admitted all right, and what we had then was something very like chaos. It was one of those situations in which deterioration and collapse are so rapid that even quite sensible policies always seem to be put into operation too late. There were flashes of hope and optimism which as they flickered out only emphasized the surrounding gloom. It seems odd, almost ludicrous, perhaps, by hindsight, that the so-called Hoover moratorium – the suspension of payment on all international government debts – should have appeared to enormous numbers of people as equivalent to an announcement that salvation after all is just around the corner, that God, after some agonizing stumbles, is once again marching on. Yet it was so. The atmosphere of those sweat-soaked summer days when the moratorium was announced throbbed anew with the electric impulses of American evangelism, of that enthusiasm for the crusade which in America can be touched off so easily because the American heart feels so deeply the need of it.

Austria was going to be saved from financial collapse and Germany from communist revolution and Hitler. All Europe was to be saved from financial collapse, or from the preventive war which it was then commonly supposed in Washington the French were about to undertake. For a few days Washington felt itself the headquarters of salvation. The New World was going into action to put the Old World on its feet. America was going once again to assume its natural leadership as the champion of peace, unity and common sense – its policies could be seen by all to be far-sighted, generous and altruistic. And since Heaven must surely be on the side of the good, and the good need to eat, Heaven would certainly see to it that the idealism of the good paid off pretty damn quickly, rewarding America by ending its depression, restoring its prosperity and getting things back to normal before the hire-purchase men finally came to repossess the car.

I saw President Hoover several times at that period, and if ever a man was transfigured with pleasure and a sense both of rightness and righteousness, it was he. Secretaries used to run in and out of his office with the latest quotations from stock markets all over the world – Berlin, New York, Chicago, London, New Orleans, Tokyo and Sydney. For long years Mr Hoover had accepted the view that the way things look on the ticker is as important as the way things really are, or, rather, is the same as the way they really are. Now everything was going up. The depression was over. If it was not over, why was everything going up? I noted at the time that 'it was just the sort of public mood that the President liked best: *carte blanche* and no maddening interruptions from the blundering crowd. He is the Great Executive again, the Great Engineer of modern society, and he has pulled the right lever at last.'

The shock was naturally all the more severe when it became evident that the declaration of American policy had solved almost nothing, and the optimism and enthusiasm petered out in a long and violent wrangle over the exact terms of the moratorium between Washington and Paris. When 'agreement in principle' was finally reached, M. Paul Claudel invited a number of American officials and others to the French Embassy to celebrate the event. Worn out with quarrelling and heat, the guests looked forward to the ceremony with gloom. There would be rhetoric and platitudes, speeches dripping with false optimism like the leading articles in the newspapers.

In the drawing-room at the Embassy M. Claudel greeted them.

'Gentlemen,' he said simply, 'in the little moment that remains to us between the crisis and the catastrophe, we may as well take a glass of champagne.'

9   Mr Capone, Philosopher

In Chicago the Director of the Illinois Central Bank, to whom I had been putting solemn questions on the subject of car loadings, commodity prices and the like, said moodily, 'Hell, boy, the capitalist system's on the skids anyway, let's go and get a drink.' I was glad of this attitude on his part because I had not really come to Chicago to discuss commodity prices in the Middle West, but to report the background to a murder. A couple of days before, we in New York had read the news of the killing in broad daylight of Jake Lingle, then crime reporter of the *Chicago Tribune* and – as emerged later – an important liaison officer between the Capone gang and the police department. It was one of the most spectacular and, for many reasons, looked like being one of the most revealing Chicago killings of the period when Al Capone was at approximately the height of his power. From a friend in New York who knew Chicago I learned enough of the background of the crime to make me very eager to go to Chicago myself. Hinrichs, who thought it would be a splendid story, was nevertheless hesitant. He explained to me that whenever *The Times* published a crime story from the United States somebody from the American Embassy or the English-Speaking Union or some other agency for promoting Anglo-American relations would ring up or would attack the editor at dinner, saying how much he had always previously admired *The Times*'s treatment of American affairs, and could there not be at least one British newspaper which did not represent the United States as a land dominated by gunmen and hoodlums? Hinrichs thought we had better cable London asking whether they wished me to go to Chicago.

As an assignment to report a murder the reply from *The Times* was probably a classic. 'By all means,' it said, 'Cockburn Chicago-wards. Welcome stories ex-Chicago not unduly emphasizing crime.'

By the time I was in the air over Cleveland the difficulty of carrying out this directive successfully had notably increased. Ex-Ambassador Charlie Gates Dawes had impetuously been 'drafted' or had drafted himself to act as 'strong man' of the situation, to put himself, it was stated, at the head of 'the better element' and to 'clean up' Chicago. Before I touched down at Chicago airport he had arrested nearly six hundred people and a number of others had been wounded in indiscriminate gun-play. I drove to the Criminal Courts Building and sought the advice of the dean of Chicago crime reporters, the original, I believe, of one of the central characters in Ben Hecht's play *The Front Page*. I showed him my cable. His deep laughter shook the desk. What, he asked, did I want to do? I said I supposed the first thing to do was to interview Mr Capone. He suggested that I listen in on an extension while he telephoned Mr Capone at the Lexington Hotel where he then had his offices. Presently I heard Capone's voice on the wire asking what went on. The crime reporter explained that there was a Limey from the London *Times* who wanted to talk with him. They fixed up an appointment for the following afternoon and just before he rang off the crime reporter said, 'Listen, Al, there's just one thing. You know this bird's assignment says he's to cover all this "not unduly emphasizing crime".' Bewilderment exploded at the other end of the line. 'Not what?' Capone said. 'You heard me,' said the crime reporter. 'Not unduly emphasizing crime.'

The Lexington Hotel had once, I think, been a rather grand family hotel, but now its large and gloomy lobby was deserted except for a couple of bulging Sicilians and a reception clerk who looked at one across the counter with the expression of a speakeasy proprietor looking through the grille at a potential detective. He checked on my appointment with some superior upstairs, and as I stepped into the elevator I felt my hips and sides being gently frisked by the tapping hands of one of the lounging Sicilians. There were a couple of ante-rooms to be passed before you got to Capone's office and in the first of them I had to wait for a quarter of an hour or so, drinking whisky poured by a man who used his left hand for the bottle and kept the other in his pocket.

Except that there was a sub-machine-gun, operated by a man called MacGurn – whom I later got to know and somewhat esteem – poking through the transom of a door behind the big desk, Capone's own room was nearly indistinguishable from that of, say, a 'newly arrived' Texan oil millionaire. Apart from the jowly young murderer on the far side of the desk, what took the eye were a number of large, flattish, solid silver bowls upon the desk, each filled with roses. They were nice to look at, and they had another purpose too, for Capone when agitated stood up and dipped the tips of his fingers in the water in which floated the roses.

I had been a little embarrassed as to how the interview was to be launched. Naturally the nub of all such interviews is somehow to get around to the question 'What makes you tick?' but in the case of this millionaire killer the approach to this central question seemed mined with dangerous impediments. However, on the way down to the Lexington Hotel I had had the good fortune to see, in I think the *Chicago Daily News*, some statistics offered by an insurance company which dealt with the average expectation of life of gang-sters in Chicago. I forget exactly what the average expectation was, and also the exact age of Capone at that time – I think he was in his early thirties. The point was, however, that in any case he was four years older than the upper limit considered by the insurance com-pany to be the proper average expectation of life for a Chicago gangster. This seemed to offer a more or less neutral and academic line of approach, and after the ordinary greetings I asked Capone whether he had read this piece of statistics in the paper. He said that he had. I asked him whether he considered the estimate reasonably accurate. He said that he thought that the insurance companies and the newspaper boys probably knew their stuff. 'In that case,' I asked him, 'how does it feel to be, say, four years over the age?'

He took the question quite seriously and spoke of the matter with neither more nor less excitement or agitation than a man would who, let us say, had been asked whether he, as the rear machine-gunner of a bomber, was aware of the average incidence of casualties in that occupation. He apparently assumed that sooner or later he would be shot despite the elaborate precautions which he regularly took. The idea that – as afterwards turned out to be the case – he would be arrested by the Federal authorities for income-tax evasion had not, I think, at that time so much as crossed his mind. And, after all, he said with a little bit of corn-and-ham somewhere at the back of his throat, supposing he had not gone into this racket? What would he have been doing? He would, he said, 'have been selling newspapers barefoot on the street in Brooklyn'.

He stood up as he spoke, cooling his finger-tips in the rose bowl in front of him. He sat down again, brooding and sighing. Despite the ham-and-corn, what he said was quite probably true and I said so, sympathetically. A little bit too sympathetically, as immediately emerged, for as I spoke I saw him looking at me suspiciously, not to say censoriously. My remarks about the harsh way the world treats barefoot boys in Brooklyn were interrupted by an urgent angry waggle of his podgy hand.

'Listen,' he said, 'don't get the idea I'm one of these goddam radicals. Don't get the idea I'm knocking the American system. The American system . . .' As though an invisible chairman had called upon him for a few words, he broke into an oration upon the theme. He praised freedom, enterprise and the pioneers. He spoke of 'our heritage'. He referred with contemptuous disgust to socialism and anarchism. 'My rackets,' he repeated several times, 'are run on strictly American lines and they're going to stay that way.' This turned out to be a reference to the fact that he had recently been elected the President of the Unione Siciliano, a slightly mysterious, partially criminal society which certainly had its roots in the Mafia. Its power and importance varied sharply from year to year. Sometimes there did seem to be evidence that it was a secret society of real power, and at other times it seemed more in the nature of a mutual benefit association not essentially much more menacing than, say, the Elks. Capone's complaint just now was that the Unione was what he called 'lousy with black-hand stuff'. 'Can you imagine,' he said, 'people going in for what they call these blood feuds – some guy's grandfather was killed by some other guy's grandfather, and this guy thinks that's good enough reason to kill the other.' It was, he said, entirely unbusinesslike. His vision of the American system began to excite him profoundly and now he was on his feet again, leaning across the desk like the chairman of a board meeting, his fingers plunged in the rose bowls.

'This American system of ours,' he shouted, 'call it Americanism, call it capitalism, call it what you like, gives to each and every one of us a great opportunity if we only seize it with both hands and make the most of it.' He held out his hand towards me, the fingers dripping a little, and stared at me sternly for a few seconds before reseating himself.

A month later in New York I was telling this story to Mr John Walter, minority owner of *The Times*. He asked me why I had not written the Capone interview for the paper. I explained that when I had come to put the notes together I saw that most of what Capone had said was in essence identical with what was being said in the leading articles of *The Times* itself, and I doubted whether the paper would be pleased to find itself seeing eye to eye with the most notorious gangster in Chicago. Mr Walter, after a moment's wry reflection, admitted that probably my idea had been correct.

Even so, when I did start writing my thesis from Chicago – not unduly emphasizing crime – I became aware, really for the first time, that about fifty per cent of what seemed to me to be the truth about the situation in Chicago would certainly be unpalatable and perhaps in parts unintelligible to *The Times*. I struggled with the article, produced a couple of readable pieces, and *The Times* wired me quite a large and much-needed bonus on the strength of it.

As for Capone, one could say of course that he was politically a buffoon, and the fact that his views coincided with those of the leader writers on the paper was a clownish and insignificant accident. But I knew then, and I felt more deeply still in the time that followed, that the incident had only expressed in terms of farce a genuine situation and a genuine problem. *The Times* of the early 1930s was of course a great deal farther to the right than it is today. It is hard to recall so many years later the tenacity with which people hung on to notions and principles which their successors might still consider theoretically desirable but have come to recognize as untenable for any practical purpose. I remember the disconcerting feeling that myself and nearly every serious person that I met in the United States were growing up under the tremendous pressure of the great crisis much faster than the people in Printing House Square. It is true that in many respects *The Times* was a good deal more open-minded, or at least more prepared to consider possible novelties in the situation, than many of the other London newspapers. I can recall very few occasions indeed when it would have been possible to have accused *The Times* of deliberate distortion, suppression or invention of 'favourable' news by means of pressure upon the correspondent.

The Times seldom did anything like that, and to tell the truth I should not have been shocked or startled if it had. It seemed to me that a newspaper is always a weapon in somebody's hands, and I never could see why it should be shocking that the weapon should be used in what its owner conceived to be his best interest. The hired journalist, I thought, ought to realize that he is partly in the entertainment business and partly in the advertising business – advertising either goods, or a government. He just has to make up his mind whom he wants to entertain, and what he wants to advertise. The humbug and hypocrisy of the press begin only when newspapers pretend to be 'impartial' or 'servants of the public'.

And this only becomes dangerous as well as laughable when the public is fool enough to believe it.

Such 'pressure' and 'guidance' as *The Times* did attempt to exercise were usually of a subtle and more amusing sort and caused me neither trouble nor vexation. The pressure of events in the United States – where the prophecies of the Marxist classics were being fulfilled with the punctuality of minute guns – was of a different kind.

The American 'way of life' of the past decade was changing before one's eyes, and the exhilarating sense of change, of history on the march, of new possibilities opening, was all-pervading. There was nowhere you could go in the United States and feel that things were as they had been or as they would be again.

I was privileged to view what I suppose might be called 'the dawn of social consciousness' in the mind of a Middle Western millionaire who had the reputation of being what was then called an 'economic royalist', a political troglodyte, a foe to progress. He was known to his friends as 'Mr Pop', on account of the way in which he made his first pile of money. At that time – at the time, I mean, when Mr Pop was a fairly young man – big developments were taking place in the popcorn-vending industry. There was a continuous effort by inventors and manufacturers to modernize and streamline the machines in which popcorn was visibly popped and sold to the onlookers. As he went about the streets and occasionally stood watching corn being popped in one of these machines, Mr Pop was aware of a sense of disappointment. Ruminating, he at last got his finger on the cause of it – these machines were not like the machines used to be when he was a boy. There were not so many wheels, not so many lathes, not so much to watch. Being evidently a man of humble mind, Mr Pop decided that, if he felt this disappointment, millions of other people must be feeling it too. Acting on this assumption, he went around buying up the patents on the old types of machine – the patents could of course now be had for a song, since the machines, totally unfunctional, were supposed to be obsolete. Mr Pop manufactured these machines by the thousand and put them on the streets, and pretty soon the news came in from the street vendors that the public was flocking to them, happy indeed to watch all those nostalgically whirring wheels and writhing lathes and to buy their corn from the vintage models rather than from the modern types. With the packet of money he made out of that Mr Pop went on and made a lot more, and now he had a big house in southern Indiana with a stream and a road bridge, with towers, which was a model of something he had seen on his travels about the world, I think in southern Germany.

As a result of some muddle in the instructions given to the architect, the house had, as a matter of fact, got built the wrong way round, with its back to the stream. This was unfortunate, but Mr Pop reasoned that it was no ground for piling one misfortune on another, and losing his bridge. In consequence, when one approached the house, one did so by a mile or so of perfectly flat driveway which suddenly humped itself up between the towers of the bridge, and from the top of the bridge you looked down and saw the green grass growing beneath you. Inside, the house was full of 'finds' of archaeological and artistic interest made by Mr Pop on his world travels. Beside each of them was fixed an elaborate bronze plaque describing the nature of the object, its age, and so on. One of them was a tile from the Summer Palace at Peking, which was described on the plaque as being three thousand years old. Rather oddly, when I visited Mr Pop, he explained emphatically to myself and the other guests that there was no doubt whatever that this tile was a fake – manufactured probably strictly for the tourist trade.

The guests on this occasion were for the most part politicians – there was a Republican senator from Washington and a couple of Republican congressmen, the Republican governor of Indiana or his deputy – I forget which – and two or three members of the Indiana legislature. At dinner the talk naturally enough was all of the crisis, of unemployment, of threatened hunger marches, of the bread lines, and of the need for the organization and extension of relief measures. It was the kind of talk which Mr Pop hitherto had supposed was only to be heard among anarchists, socialists, and the long-haired agitators of one kind and another. Coming from leaders and fellow-members of the Republican Party it hit Mr Pop like a blow on the head. After dinner he was sitting with me a little apart from the others, and he presently began to move about uneasily and peer at me with the air of a man preparing to propound a question of supreme importance. At last, peering into his glass, he said: 'Mr Cockburn, may I ask you something?'

I bowed.

'Would you,' said Mr Pop, 'see anything wrong in being the fourth richest man in Indiana?'

I made some incoherent reply.

'Well that,' said Mr Pop, 'is what I am. I am the fourth richest man in Indiana.'

85

I had sympathized with Capone in his human and social pre-
dicament, although I had not found him a particularly likeable
man. And I sympathized now with Mr Pop, whom I had grown to
like, at the moment of his confrontation with the possibility that
there might be some snag, something historically or morally not
absolutely nice, about being the fourth richest man in Indiana in
the year 1931. I sympathized with *The Times*, too, but it did not
make the situation any easier or solve any problem.

In the sense *The Times* entered into the matter only incidentally
– in the sense, I mean, that we were all engaged in the newspaper
business. Had *The Times* been a firm of automobile exporters, and
I their salesman, the problem would not have arisen in the same
form. An automobile salesman can go about – mentally speaking –
in disguise, and I believe many of them do. He can believe passionately that the earth is flat without causing a drop in sales. He can
even secretly hold, and secretly propagate, some unpopular political or religious opinion without going to pieces and without – if he is
careful – being caught at it. For the journalist things are more
difficult.

Essentially, the late Lord Northcliffe was right when he said to
some intellectual who thought himself so very smart that he could
'write popular' and get away with it. 'You can never successfully
seek to put upon the table of Demos what you would not put on
your own table.'

Evidently there are plenty of people in journalism who have
neither got what they liked nor quite grown to like what they get.
They write pieces they do not much enjoy writing, for papers they
totally despise, and the sad process ends by ruining their style and
disintegrating their personality, two developments which in a writer
cannot be separate, since his personality and style must progress or
deteriorate together, like a married couple in a country where
death is the only permissible divorce. It is a fate which through
incompetence or economic necessity may overtake anyone, but
one does not wish to start out by accepting it as one's own.

Although by the beginning of 1932 I was secretly bootlegging
quite a number of pieces of news and articles to various extreme left
American newspapers and news services, I was conscious that my
style – in the narrow and in the wider sense of the word – was
deteriorating.

I decided to make a change. The relief of having taken this
decision was such that I probably should have dithered about for
months without actually doing anything had not my elbow been

jogged by an external event.

What had happened was that Wilmott Lewis, whose doctor had at last succeeded in causing him some mild anxiety about the state of his heart muscle, was beginning to entertain the idea of a partial retirement. He had suggested to *The Times*, and *The Times*, he told me, had agreed *en principe*, that I should be transferred from New York to Washington and there take over the ordinary or day-to-day and week-by-week operation of the Washington bureau. He would retreat to a beautiful winter residence he had his eye on in Georgetown, and in the summer he would live on the Blue Ridge Mountains. He would be 'available for consultation', and occasionally, perhaps once a month, write an article for the paper. He would also read all the books he had never had time to read, and write, he surmised, at least one of the books he had never had time to write. It was a wonderful prospect and his eyes shone with enthusiasm as he first unfolded it to me. Particularly characteristic of Wilmott Lewis and particularly moving was the fact that a great part of his pleasure in this plan was that, as he saw it, the scheme would be as splendid a thing for me as it would be for him. His excitement and his solicitude for my career were so touching that for a moment I felt that it might even be humanly better to abandon my own plans and fall in with his. However, short of that, there was not a moment to be lost in disillusioning him.

He sat for a few seconds in an aghast silence, watching the house in Georgetown, the summer place on the Blue Ridge and all the books fade into thin air. I asked desperately whether somebody else could not take over the role proposed by himself and *The Times* for me. He said it was quite impossible, and I knew that this was in fact the case. Within a minute of two he had entirely recovered himself and with his native and extraordinary delicacy was consoling me as though it were I whose plans had been upset and not himself. He guessed, of course, that I felt a certain sense of guilt *vis-à-vis* himself, as though I had betrayed the years during which he had taught me so much of what I knew about the United States.

'My dear boy,' he said 'any small debt you may have owed me has been long ago repaid over and over again. And if you insist on regarding yourself as my pupil, reflect how far more agreeable it must be for me to have produced one who now moves freely under his own steam rather than being stuck, my dear boy,' he made the last words sound like death, 'in the mud.'

After an equally melancholy explanation to Hinrichs, who tried to take the sadness out of our parting by remarking that for several months he had expected that something of the kind must happen, I wrote to *The Times* announcing my decision. To my vexation they treated my big gesture simply as a sign of a slight over-strain, and wrote back suggesting that I take a couple of months' paid holiday in Mexico. I had to write again in more vigorous terms, explaining, by way of putting an end to any discussion, that my motives were largely political. I was horribly disconcerted to find that *The Times* did not take this very seriously either. Mr Dawson wrote me a letter in which he said that it was foolish in his opinion to give up working for *The Times* simply on account of one's political views. *The Times*, he said, was a vehicle which could be used by people of the most varied opinions. 'For myself,' he concluded, 'I have always regarded *The Times* as something of an organ of the left.' There followed in brackets a classic qualification. 'Though never,' wrote Mr Dawson, 'I hope of the extreme left.'

I had to abandon my naïve belief that however difficult anything else may be, the one thing that is easy, and makes everyone happy, is that you resign. Resigning was proving a lot more difficult than I had expected. A short while after the exchange of letters Mr Dawson, Mr Deakin, the Foreign and Imperial news editor, and one or two of the High Priests who had been to Ottawa for a conference, came down to New York and took it in turns to explain to me the folly of my attitude. One view was that the thing to do was settle the whole business quickly on a cash basis, and there was talk of something in the way of a bonus, plus an early rise in salary. I was humiliated to find that my important decision had been interpreted in these quarters as an act of vulgar blackmail. Others, probably reflecting that they had to do with a wild-eyed intellectual, thought that a more spiritual approach would be the right ticket. They spoke of the good which a first-rate correspondent of *The Times* could do to mankind. When these and other suggestions, which had been made separately, had all failed, we gathered one morning in *The Times* office in New York and were joined by Wilmott Lewis, who admitted to me privately that he had not been able to resist coming up for the final scene. Sitting at what until now had been my desk, Mr Dawson swung his tortoiseshell spectacles lugubriously and remarked, looking at me with a puzzled frown, 'It does seem rather bad luck that you of all people should "go red on us".' His voice put audible inverted commas around the phrase 'go red on us'. At this point Wilmott Lewis, his sense of the theatre overcoming any discretion he may have had, moved to the centre of the stage, or rather of the office, and with a gesture which in some indefinable way suggested that he was flaunting the black cloak of a magician, gazed down upon Dawson and raised his hand in a familiar gesture.

'You speak, my dear Dawson,' he said, 'of luck. Speak rather of history. Throw your mind forward along the path of history. Envisage, my dear Deakin, with the eye of imagination the not too distant future. The time will come, my dear-fellows, when you will hire as correspondents elderly men who will be Conservatives. But many of them, mark you, may well be suffering from heart attacks when the great story breaks. Or, my dear fellows, you may hire young men who will also be Conservative but, note this! many of them may well be too stupid even to know when the great story is breaking. Or you may hire men who are both young and intelligent, and quite a lot of *them*, my dear fellows,' his voice dropped to a menacing whisper, 'will be Reds.'

Dawson, who had put on his spectacles to watch the performance, now peered up at Lewis over the top of them. He gave a small acid-sounding laugh.

I'm afraid,' he said, 'you have been talking too much to your *ex*-assistant.'

Then I knew that I had resigned at last.

10 That Was The Week

To come to Berlin, as I then did, just after New York, was to be whisked down suddenly from the gallery of a badly lit theatre and pushed against the flaring floodlights to see that what you thought you saw from back there is really going on. The act is coming to its horrible climax, and furthermore the man who is playing the part of the murderer really is a murderer. His knife is not a familiar stage property but a real one and he is going to kill people with it.

Already the Storm Troopers were slashing and smashing up and down the Kurfuerstendamm, and there were beatings and unequal battles in the city streets. The toads beside the Charlottenburger Chaussee looked more menacing than ever. The newspapers and the 'thoughtful observers' and the pro and con men went humbugging along, but no one with any feeling for the situation believed them. I several times met Herr Willi Muenzenberg, who was popularly believed to be the real brains and driving force of the German Communist Party, and once I had the opportunity for a short private conversation with General Schleicher, then Chancellor. Each spoke in terms of reasoned optimism, and each gave the impression that he did not give a damn whether you believed a word he said because he did not believe it himself. (Schleicher was murdered sooner than Muenzenberg, who survived until the early 1940s, when he was mysteriously strangled – possibly on suspicion of being a secret Nazi agent – in the forest of Fontainebleau.) A situation in which even the professional humbugs cannot keep a straight face is always somewhat exhilarating, but, as one always finds in those situations, the naked truth can be a chilly, knobbly kind of companion too. Also, just as in New York and Chicago, it had gradually begun to seem absurd the one should spend one's time going about writing articles for *The Times*, so now in Berlin it rapidly began to seem even more absurd to sit observing events and trends, writing an occasional short story, or turning out articles for leftist American newspapers and news agencies. If one were not going to disintegrate under the pressure of events, the thing to do seemed to be to organize oneself into something coherent and effective.

Once again I might have dithered about for weeks or even months had not something jogged my elbow. This time it was Hitler. He came to power. I was high on the Nazi black list. I fled to Vienna.

There I sat down to consider seriously a notion which had been buzzing in my mind for some time. It had started buzzing when I worked – off the record – with a publicity expert in Washington who was conducting a one-man battle against what was known as the Radio Trust. I had noted at the time, and the note appears in the book which I wrote just before leaving Washington, that 'among the technical devices which as everyone knows are revolutionizing the workings of modern government, the humble mimeograph machine is seldom mentioned. Less spectacular than the other wonders of the age, as for instance the mass-production news-paper, the telephone, the radio and the talking picture, it exercises, in its cheap and incessant activity, an influence scarcely less than theirs, and seems to have reached the peak of its activity in Wash-ington, D.C., at the present period. Washington is in many respects the ideal field for a mimeograph machine to work in. For this little device requires for its most effective functioning the smallest pos-sible geographical area, containing the largest number of persons who are influential, either because of the position they hold, or the money they have, or because like newspapermen they are sitting at the feeding end of a pipe-line with millions of people at the other end of it . . . It is commonly agreed that the Press, the radio and the moving picture are the most powerful forces in existence for mould-ing public opinion. To control any or all of them, or even to get the opportunity to use them as a medium, requires a great deal of money. The people who have enough money to control them are therefore sitting pretty in the democracy, but not nearly so pretty as they would be sitting were it not for the mimeograph machine. Naturally they have mimeographs too, but here for the first time their competitors find themselves on an equal footing. The police force can supply itself from larger sources with tanks and armoured cars and laboratories for the manufacture of tear gas. It is only in the possession of the automatic pistol that the enemy of the police finds himself on a level with his opponents. A mimeograph machine is one of the few remaining weapons which still gives small and comparatively poor organizations a sporting chance in a scrap with large and wealthy ones.'

The general idea which I had had then was revived in my mind later in Berlin by, of all people, General Schleicher, who ran, in his own interests, a weekly mimeographed sheet of information and comment which circulated by mail and was not sold on bookstalls. The total circulation was very small, and of course it did not do General Schleicher very much good in the end, but from my viewpoint the important thing about it was that it exercised an influence out of all proportion to its circulation. That is to say, in terms of influence, one reader of Schleicher's sheet was, on an average, worth about five thousand readers of one of the daily newspapers. (It was, for example, 'must reading' for all foreign newspaper correspondents in Berlin, and for all the embassies and legations.)

This phenomenon had reminded me of another aspect of the situation which I had often discussed with Wilmott Lewis in Washington. The discussion had arisen over the late Hamilton Fyfe's *Life of Northcliffe*, in which he makes this central point:

When Northcliffe started the *Daily Mail* in the nineties, Fyfe suggests, he was not 'playing a hunch' but tapping a mathematical certainty. He argued: The Education Acts of the 1860s have changed the entire character and extent of the literate public. But in the years since the 1860s the newspapers have not changed at all. Therefore there must exist somewhere a new pool of potential readers not taken care of by the existing newspapers. And this pool, if correctly tapped, could provide a new multi-million readership.

There was not much doubt in my mind as to the sort of people who would constitute the 'pool'. Anyone in, for instance, London or New York or Berlin or Vienna who frequented any kind of club or other meeting-place where, say, diplomats, lawyers, bankers and newspapermen gathered together and talked, must have been deeply aware of the strange contrast between the colourful information and significant rumours – for rumours can often be as significant as facts – circulating in the clubs, and the awfully tight-lipped drabness of the newspapers being sold on the club doorstep.

I got most of the English daily newspapers in Vienna and was struck once again by the fact that what informed people were really saying – and equally importantly, the tone of voice they were saying it in – were scarcely reflected at all in the newspapers, and that these people themselves were more or less acutely aware of this lack in the newspapers.

A further conclusion followed. It was that such 'pools' could only be effectively tapped by a paper run 'on a shoestring'.

The moment any kind of big financial commitment came in question – even the investment that would be needed to launch a printed weekly paper – it would begin to be necessary to 'broaden the base', 'extend the appeal', in fact lower the Highest Common Factor. The advertisers alone would see to that.

What all this added up to was that I had better go to London and start a weekly paper of a new type. For the third time, extraneous circumstances precipitated a decision. I discovered with dismay that my remaining money was almost gone. It was evident that, if I waited any longer, I should scarcely have the fare from Vienna to London, let alone enough to support me during the two or three weeks which I felt sure would be needed for the organization of the paper.

It took in point of fact nearly six weeks, the result, I suppose, chiefly of the fact that since out of the past six years I had spent only a little over two months in England, and that had been three and a half years ago. I knew almost nobody, and I had forgotten how important people think it in England to know not only where you are going but where you have come from. Also when the news of where I had come from did get bruited it was not always an advantage – learning of my resignation from *The Times*, people on the right thought that I must be a Red and shied off, and the Reds, since I was not a member of any known left organization, were if possible more suspicious still.

The atmosphere was both depressing and exhilarating. Even the most detached citizen must find it occasionally depressing to find his country so reduced in circumstances that it has to have such a man as the late Ramsay MacDonald for its Prime Minister. It was, however, exhilarating because the smug smog in which the press of that time enveloped the political realities of the moment was even thicker than I had anticipated, and thus offered even better conditions for the conduct of my experiment.

The one or two old friends I had, and the people I presently got to know, were for the most part sympathetic but discouraging. And many of my few acquaintances who expressed a flattering and uplifting interest in the idea turned out to be firm believers in the axiom that one should never put off till tomorrow what one might possibly be able to do the month after next. I was constantly frustrated too by the habit people have got into of considering that nothing important can be done without going through the ritual of 'a conference', or better still, a committee. Several times during the six weeks I had to tuck my idea under my arm and run with it to prevent it being suffocated in this way.

Frustrating and even alarming though all this was, it was at the same time amusing, helped me to extend my 'contacts' and to pick up a smattering of information about the state of affairs in Britain. But after the first three weeks or so I realized clearly enough that until I actually produced my paper 'of a new type' I should never be able to explain to anyone what it was I had in mind – and I realized too that a lot of them would not like it if I did.

Everyone had been well-meaningly discouraging about the money. Some said that even the smallest weekly paper could not possibly cost less than £5,000; others said £10,000. It was agreed that such a sum could probably be raised, but I understood now that to raise it would involve introducing the very frets I was seeking to avoid. There would be advertisers and shareholders and even, it was hinted on several sides, some kind of editorial board, and what we should end up with would be just another weekly newspaper.

In any case I had not left *The Times* for the purpose of saddling myself with another editorial board and some more shareholders and advertisers. After thirty days of patient investigating I had grasped more firmly than ever the truth that what one must do was to ensure that this paper was all of a piece and all under one control. That it should express one viewpoint and one viewpoint only – my own. In other words, size must be sacrificed to coherence and to unity of style. Thus after four weeks of bumbling more or less agreeably about London I came to the conclusion that the thing to do was cut the cackle and start the paper regardless of what anybody might say, warn or advise.

I went out to Berkshire and found an old Oxford friend – Benvenuto Sheard, author of a novel called *Men in Shirtsleeves* – who had for some time been vegetating unwholesomely in that section of the home counties. By this time I personally had only five pounds left, and I had reckoned that we would need at least forty pounds to start the paper. I suggested to him that it would be good for both of us if he lent me forty pounds for the paper, in exchange for which he would have a job on it as a kind of manager.He agreed. On the return journey to London I explained to him all over again my precise purpose.

G. K. Chesterton, I reminded him, had written of editors that they lived in the shadow of three fears – fear of misprints, fear of libel actions and fear of the sack. We would aim, I said, to disregard all considerations of that kind, more particularly the second, because what we had in mind was a revival of the uninhibited eighteenth-century English tradition of the newsletter, It was going to give the customers the sorts of facts – political, diplomatic, financial – which were freely discussed in embassies and clubs but considered to be too adult to be left about for newspaper readers to get at them.

I pointed out to him that by the method we proposed to use – that of the mimeograph machine – we should kill two birds with one stone: we should on the one hand ensure that we were in total control of our own paper, and on the other that people who wanted to bring libel actions could of course do so, but probably would not, because most libel actions are brought for the purpose of getting money, and it would be evident to one and all that we had no money of any kind.

After that things moved at a fairly brisk rate. We found an attic in Victoria Street approached first by a shaky lift and later by a staircase which was rather more of a ladder than a stair. There was room in it for a kitchen table, four chairs and a smaller table on which we installed a duplicating machine bought on the hire-purchase system so that the libel-mongers would have even less to gain than they might have hoped. We found a brilliant and devoted secretary – again a person who had not been involved in the type of calculation which was so common in London, and at once saw the possibilites of the idea.

At that stage we had only two troubles. The first was a row between myself and my partner, who hoped that the sheet would look clean and dignified. I, on the other hand, thought that the important thing was that it should be noticeable. Given the price of paper and duplicating ink, there seemed no possibility that it could be both. In the end we made it noticeable. It was mimeographed in dark brown ink on buff-coloured foolscap. It was not merely noticeable, it was unquestionably the nastiest-looking bit of work that ever dropped on to a breakfast-table.

The other trouble we had was from people who had heard what we were about to do and wanted to help. There was a man from Vancouver who knew about business and insisted he could get a lot of advertising for the paper. I told him we did not want advertising, but it did not diminish his enthusiasm. He quite evidently regarded me as a kind of babe in the wood who must be protected from the wild animals that are loose. In view of this touching solicitude it was impossible to turn him out of the office, and he used to stand there for hours talking and explaining his general plan for making us more money than anybody could have dreamed of. He stayed with us, in fact, throughout the launching of the paper and for three weeks after it had begun to come out, but then he went out of his mind just outside the Army and Navy Stores where he knelt on the pavement one morning, addressing me as his Brother in the Sun. As I drove him to the nursing-home I realized I had been right all along about advertising.

Lawyers volunteered to help too, but I had to point out to them that either they were good lawyers, in which case they would have to keep saying, 'You can't publish that, it's libellous,' or bad lawyers, ignorant of whether things were libellous or not. In either case what use would they be? It was sad having to fight off so many well-intentioned offers of assistance, but I had to keep firmly in mind that what we were running was a pirate craft and we could not burden ourselves with conventional navigators and mates, however skilled and knowledgeable.

I had decided early on that we would not attempt to sell the paper on the bookstalls and news-stands. To begin with I did not want to get involved in a distributive organization which would be beyond one's own personal control. Also under English law, so far as I understood it, the wholesale newsagent can be held responsible for damages awarded in a libel suit against a paper distributed by him. For this reason the wholesale distributors are forced or encouraged to exercise a kind of long-term censorship over the products they handle. (That was why some time later we had the ridiculous situation in which the people who handled the London circulation of *Time* magazine had to spend hours with scissors snipping out of the paper, when it arrived from New York, those stories which might be considered libellous in England; that was how it happened that when the British papers were keeping mum about the abdication crisis of 1936 and *Time* magazine was running constant stories about the King and Mrs Simpson, *Time* reached the British bookstalls full of holes where the most interesting stories ought to have been. Yet even then you could meet people who would declare that there is no press censorship in England.)

It seemed to me that we could turn this circumstance to account and use it to deepen the 'confidential' atmosphere around our paper. For the same reason I preferred, although it cost three times

as much to do so, to mail the paper to subscribers in closed
envelopes.

All these questions of production and circulation, interesting as
they were, took up a good deal of my time. My partner, as I have
said, was a novelist and short-story writer who had a positive horror
of business, and was totally ignorant of it. He scarcely knew where
to buy a stamp. Also it had been part of our bargain that I should
not bother him with anything of that kind – what he wanted to get in
exchange for his forty pounds was, so to speak, a tiny airstrip in
London from which he could take off for social and literary trips
about the town.

The secretary was a young married woman, Crystal Harding,
daughter of a backwoods baronet living somewhere in East Anglia,
and until about this time her idea of a major event in home affairs
had been the exclusion of some friend from the Royal Enclosure at
Ascot. She was pretty, energetic, intelligent and loyal, but she
could not type and most of the people who dashed in and out of the
attic in Victoria Street were as alien to her as though they had
escaped from the zoo.

However, in addition to her other qualities she had a great deal
of common sense, and the business of occasionally explaining to
her what we thought we were up to helped to clarify one's mind. All
the same, it was difficult in the circumstances to spend as much time
as I should have liked on the organization of our new sources. By
this time of course I had a lot of 'contacts' in London – particularly
in the City. But we could hardly have come out when we did had it
not been for the cooperation of a number of foreign correspondents
in London, many of whom I had known in Berlin or Washington.

Zero hour was a Wednesday in the mid-spring of 1933. We had
chosen Wednesday as 'press day', so that *The Week* would reach
people ahead of the existing weekly newspapers. I had had a great
deal of difficulty in getting hold of a mailing list. There was no
money to hire one of the lists which were available, and instead I
had borrowed one which contained names of the subscribers to the
then temporarily defunct weekly paper *Foreign Affairs*.

It was a list of about 1,200 names. Myself, the manager, the
secretary and the man from Vancouver had spent the previous
night addressing foolscap envelopes, and in the very early morning,
in order to make our deadline as late as possible, I wrote the entire
issue covering three sheets of foolscap written on both sides, and
then cut the stencils.

All the things that always happen on such occasions happened.

None of us had ever used a duplicating machine before and stencils cracked like sails in a gale and the place was be-spattered with sticky brown ink. The valuable Pekinese dog belonging to the secretary became disgusted and spitefully chewed up the reserve tubes of ink. The man from Vancouver was already showing signs of the mental unbalance from which he later suffered more spectacularly. Also the manager's highly developed sense of neatness was offended by the way in which we were folding the foolscap sheets and shoving them into the envelopes and he kept taking them out in order to refold them in a neater but rather delaying manner. By early evening we had the whole lot enveloped and mailed and staggered to the Café Royal to drink champagne.

To my companions and fellow-workers I pointed out that the whole thing was absolutely sure-fire. Here we had a list of 1,200 names. Our product, *The Week*, was sensational, brilliant, irresistible. However, let us be cautious and assume that some of the people on that list are ill – too ill to fill in a subscription form – or they are dead. Say 300 of them. Then assume that there are some fools among them – boneheads or embittered maniacs who will not be charmed by *The Week*. Say 100 of them. That leaves a residue of 800 people who by tomorrow evening will be sitting down to send off their twelve-shilling postal orders for the annual subscription.

Unfortunately no one had warned me that the *Foreign Affairs* list was years old. Forty per cent of the people on it were dead, indifferent, or had radically changed their attitude to world affairs. Also there had been a serious miscalculation regarding the mentality of the British public – its readiness to jump for something new or love the highest when the editor saw it.

The number of paying customers secured by that first circularization was seven. Just seven.

The news spread rapidly among friends and acquaintances that my big idea had misfired.

Personally, since I regarded the existence of the 'pool' as a mathematical certainty, I was not discouraged, although I could think of no convincing reason to offer anyone else as an explanation of my continued optimism.

And yet little less than two years later this small monstrosity, *The Week*, was one of the half-dozen British publications most often quoted in the press of the entire world. It included among its subscribers the Foreign Ministers of eleven nations, all the embassies and legations in London, all diplomatic correspondents of the principal newspapers in three continents, the foreign correspondents of all the leading newspapers stationed in London, the leading banking and brokerage houses in London, Paris, Amsterdam and New York, a dozen members of the United States Senate, twenty or thirty members of the House of Representatives, about fifty members of the House of Commons and a hundred or so in the House of Lords, King Edward VIII, the secretaries of most of the leading trades unions, Charlie Chaplin and the Nizam of Hyderabad.

Blum read it and Goebbels read it, and a mysterious war-lord in China read it. Ribbentrop, Hitler's Ambassador in London, on two separate occasions demanded its suppression on the ground that it was the source of all anti-Nazi evil.

Admittedly none of this seemed at all probable at the end of that first week when the total circulation stood at seven. Apart from the moral shock – disclosure of low mental level all round, nation sunk in apathy – this lack of response left hardly any money to circularize anyone else and raised the whole question of how to go on living at all.

I was forced to live meagrely on the twelve-shilling postal orders which occasionally came in, spending much of my time at the Café Royal, then in its last phase as a gathering-place of just the kind of people who ought to be reading and talking about *The Week*.

It made – since a bottle of good wine cost three shillings – a fine, nearly free, place to do business in. People coming in for drinks who had vaguely heard of *The Week* would often pay over their subscription money in cash, though they probably would never have got around to sending in a subscription form and a postal order. The late Professor Joad brought in quite a freshet one night by shouting his congratulations on *The Week* all over the Café Royal and declaring that no man in the place could claim to have any idea upon what was going on unless he were a subscriber to *The Week*.

Even so, things remained extremely difficult for several weeks until one day, with the circulation awfully steady at thirty-six, Ramsay MacDonald intervened.

The World Economic Conference – some joker had housed it among the fossils in the Geological Museum – was a big thing in his life. Figuratively speaking, he had his name in lights all over it. Yet, the Premier excepted, almost everyone from Leadenhall Street to the Afghan Legation knew that the Conference was dying on its feet. But it was thought not very good taste to point in public. 'Useful spadework' was what the newspapers said was going on.

The Week, in a special issue, reported extensively upon what was really being said *sotto voce* by informed observers. It remarked that the only spade at work on the Conference was the grave-digger's. Quoting Charles Dickens, it saw fit to liken the position of the Conference leadership to that of the Dover Mail, which 'was in its usual genial position that the guard suspected the passengers, the passengers suspected one another and the guard, they all suspected everybody else, and the coachman was sure of nothing but the horses; as to which cattle he could with a clear conscience have taken his oath on the two Testaments that they were not fit for the journey'.

On the day this appeared Mr MacDonald came down to the Conference looking, as someone remarked, as though he were on his way to Clarkson's to hire a crown of thorns. He convened a special off-the-record press conference in the crypt. He said he had a private warning to utter. Foreign and diplomatic correspondents from all over the world jostled past mementoes of the Ice Age to hear him. For as a warning-utterer he was really tip-top. In his unique style, suggestive of soup being brewed on a foggy Sunday evening in the West Highlands, he said that what we saw on every hand was plotting and conspiracy, of this, that and the other kind, in the larger sense, and here in his hand was a case in point, tantamount to just that sort of thing.

Everyone pushed and stared, and what he had in his hand was that issue of *The Week*; and he went on to quote from it, and to warn one and all to pay no heed to the false prophets of disaster, activated by motives of this or that or the other thing. This was good strong stuff and stimulating to these people who hitherto had never heard of *The Week*, and, but for this, possibly never would have.

Regrettably I had to miss a good deal of it. I recalled that this was the hour when the manager would be sitting in a barber's shop in Curzon Street where he spent a rather large part of each morning, and that the secretary was away attending some society wedding. The office was deserted. I urgently desired to know what else Mr MacDonald had to say, but equally I urgently needed to dash back to Victoria Street so as to be there in time to answer the telephone which, as could easily be foreseen, would soon be vibrating with voices of the anxious *cognoscenti* of international affairs.

It was ringing all right. 'This is the diplomatic correspondent of *Le Matin*. I want . . . ' 'Here is the diplomatic correspondent of *Frankfurter Zeitung*. I require immediately . . .' By tea-time the circulation was in the seventies, with 'Pertinax' of the *Echo de Paris* and Mme Tabouis of the socialist paper *L'Oeuvre*, then in their heyday as the two most formidable journalistic pundits in Europe, well up there with the leaders.

And then to prove that it wasn't just raining manna, it was pouring it, another big shower of it fell.

While I was still scribbling down the names of the new sub-scribers, I heard afar off a muttering and puffing, and then upon the ladderlike stair leading to our attic I heard the thunder and crack of impetuous feet. In a split trice the place was heaving and bulging with enormously mustachioed men, and women with mauve veils, speaking excitedly of the Prophet Isaiah. What did they want? They wanted subscriptions to *The Week*. Why? Because at a neighbouring hall – Caxton or Central – there was in session a congress of citizens taking the view that the future may readily be foretold by measuring the Pyramids and that the British (even, stretching a point, the Americans) are the lost tribes of Israel. Someone had read aloud to this gathering a passage from an earlier issue of *The Week*, and it absolutely confirmed, apparently, some-thing Isaiah had said. It could be that *The Week* was divinely inspired by the prophet. In any case they wanted forty subscriptions quick.

They were solid people with cash in their hands, and I could hardly refrain from taking time off to telephone the café manager at the Café Royal to tell him that in an hour or two it would be in order to wipe clean my terribly congested slate.

11   Bloody Facts

'IF you go on like this,' said Mr John Wheeler-Bennett, the head of
the Royal Institute of International Affairs at Chatham House,
'you will soon, I should think, be either famous or in gaol.'

'Lots of people,' I said, 'have been both.'

'That,' he said, turning upon me his luminous smile, and beam-
ing as though an awkward question had now been satisfactorily
resolved, 'is so.'

A lot of people who, by constantly talking of *The Week*, complaining of it, denouncing it as a horrible liar, and even praising it, were
helping to make this tiny sheet 'quite famous', were also of the
opinion that something terrible must be going to happen to *The
Week* pretty soon. The Criminal Libel Law and the Official Secrets
Act, one or other of which we apparently infringed about twice a
month, were the instruments which people imagined were going to
send me to gaol. Since, as I have said, I had no lawyer to bother me
about such things, and since nobody but myself could possibly be
involved in whatever unpleasantness might arise, I was saved all the
advance worry which nags at people on other types of paper when
they are handling dynamite, and by being simply ignorant of whether
I was infringing some law or not, saved myself from the temptation
which otherwise I have no doubt would have often been irresistible – to omit or tone down reports of facts and reports of rumours
merely on the ground that to publish them might land one in the
Courts. We were of course repeatedly threatened with libel actions,
but none of them was ever brought and none was ever settled out of
Court. When deciding whether or not to write a story which was
obviously, in the legal sense, libellous, but which I believed to be
true and of some public interest, I used instead of a lawyer a simple

criterion of my own.

In case he brings an action, I asked myself, which of us in the end will look more ridiculous? On the whole, this criterion worked fairly well. When the emissaries of the libelled came to see me with threats and menaces, they were immediately discouraged by the evident poverty of our organization. Their usual technique was then to demand an unqualified apology. This I invariably refused on principle, although always expressing readiness to write another story on the same subject giving any facts they might choose to supply tending to show that the earlier story had been baseless. It was at this point that one could usually detect from their expression that the thought passing through their minds was that which had passed through mine earlier – namely that if their client took the case to Court he would probably make more of a monkey out of himself than he was likely to make out of me.

How often we really infringed the Official Secrets Act, or were suspected by the authorities of espionage or improper relations with public servants for the purpose of extracting state secrets, I have no idea. For the first eighteen months or so, at any rate, we were highly suspect– naturally, and for the same reason I had been suspect in Berlin, namely that we had no easily recognizable fancy dress and the authorities were somewhat in the position of the drunken Dutchman in the musical comedy who gets by accident into the middle of a fancy-dress ball and runs frantically from person to person imploring them, 'Do please tell me once and for each what are you as?'

Obviously the authorities would much rather deal with people who are visibly members of some recognized political organization, and I had a lot of evidence that they were considerably worried by not knowing what I was 'as'.

Long ago Wilmott Lewis had drawn my attention to what he called 'the factual heresy' or 'the illusion of spot news'.

It would be tedious to examine the historical phenomena which has produced in the public mind a belief that the desirable thing to read in a newspaper is 'the inside news', and still more the illusion in the public mind that the newspaper, or rather the reporter, really has 'inside news'.

Wilmott Lewis, who was usually right about such matters, took the view that about ninety per cent of what the public conceives to be 'inside news' or 'spot news' is either something so trivial or obvious that it is not worth writing about, or else is not 'inside news' at all in the sense of being something secret and confidential, but is the kind of information which any highly informed and reasonably intelligent person could piece together from, say, a week's reading of all available newspapers and a week's conversation with all available sources. And even this, he used to insist, is not enough. News, he used to say, is in itself nothing. Presentation is almost everything. The entire question, he would insist, is a question of style.

I have seen people who, as he made these observations, came rapidly to the idiotic conclusion that the creative journalistic process is much simpler than it really is – you could see them beginning to imagine that all the man had to do was to sit about reading and talking and presently, having developed his 'style', present the matter in coruscating prose. This of course is untrue too, and the reason why Lewis, for example, leaned over backwards talking about style, and the reason why it is necessary to do so repeatedly, is that, although in the early days of journalism style was empha- sized to the point where the role of the 'facts' was merely forgotten, nowadays the 'factual heresy' is a dangerous one.

To hear people talking about the facts you would think that they lay about like pieces of gold ore in the Yukon days waiting to be picked up – arduously, it is true, but still definitely and visibly – by strenuous prospectors whose subsequent problem was only to get them to market.

Such a view is evidently and dangerously naïve. There are no such facts. Or if there are, they are meaningless and entirely ineffective; they might, indeed, just as well not be lying about at all until the prospector – the journalist – puts them into relation with other facts: presents them, in other words. Then they become as much a part of a pattern created by him as if he were writing a novel. In that sense all stories are written backwards – they are supposed to begin with the facts and develop from there, but in reality they begin with a journalist's point of view, a conception, and it is the point of view from which the facts are subsequently organized. Journalistically speaking, 'in the beginning is the word'. All this is difficult and even rather unwholesome to explain to the layman, because he gets the impression that you are saying that the truth does not matter and that you are publicly admitting what he long ago suspected, that journalism is a way of 'cooking' the facts. Really cunning journalists, realizing this, and anxious to raise the status of journalism in the esteem of the general public, positively encourage the layman in his mistaken views. They like him to have the picture of these nuggety facts lying about on maybe frozen ground, and a lot of noble and utterly unprejudiced journalists with no idea whatever of what they are looking for scrabbling in the iron-bound earth and presently bringing home the pure gold of Truth.

When I had to start explaining what *The Week* was trying to do, I did myself a good deal of harm by being rather too frank about this matter. To make matters worse, I went about saying that rumours were just as important, just as significant, just as – in the last analysis – 'valid' as facts.

This shocked people horribly, although if you pressed them and asked whether it was not true that ninety per cent of 'information received' by such serious persons as Ambassadors and Chiefs of Police really consists in significant rumours which can be interpreted by the person who knows enough rumours, they were usually bound to admit that this is the case. Contemporaries on the existing weekly newspapers used to complain that *The Week* published rumours which they themselves refused to publish until they were confirmed. One was reminded of the atheistic young man who told the believer that he would never believe anything that he did not understand, to which the believer replied, 'Young man, your beliefs are likely to be small.'

In the same way people who refused to print anything that was not a confirmed fact were likely to print very little of general interest. And I found that attitude arrogant, for, unless one imagines one is God, how on earth can one tell truth from rumour in less than perhaps fifty years? And fifty years is too long to wait if one is in the business of issuing a weekly newspaper.

So far as *The Week*'s news-gathering operations were concerned they were conducted for the most part on a barter basis with a group of what were then the best-informed and most lively-minded correspondents in London.

They included Mr Farson, correspondent of the *Chicago Daily News*; Mr Stefan Litauer, correspondent of the Polish News Agency; Mr Paul Scheffer, correspondent of the *Berliner Tageblatt*, and a varying group of French correspondents.

Two or three times a week we met around noon in Mr Farson's office at Bush House and pooled our information. And on the days we did not meet we pooled information over the telephone. To describe this pool as a 'group' would be to use too formal a word, but – owing, I think, to Mr Farson's guidance – we all of us came to realize that there was something to be said for regular exchanges even when there seemed to be no news at all. The mere fact of each in turn going through a kind of 'total recall' of what had been said by informants – diplomats, financiers and others – during the course of the past forty-eight hours was clarificatory and often produced a piece of the great jigsaw which otherwise could have been overlooked or forgotten. Usually of course there was plenty of news. There was news which – for example – Mr Farson could not handle for his paper but which was exactly suited to *The Week*. Everyone had something to contribute, everyone picked out of the bag what suited his own requirements. Apart from what *The Week* could directly contribute to the pool, it had a special role to play, a special utility. There were innumerable stories which, for example, Mr Farson or Mr Litauer could not venture to send directly to their papers or news agencies but which they could send if they had just appeared in *The Week* and could thus be quoted instead of being sent on the responsibility of the correspondent.

The French were particularly good at playing this game. And, as time went on, this group – every member of which had his own special contacts with news sources in London, his own confidential sources of news in his own country and a lively awareness of the difference between the apparently significant news and the news that really was significant in the light of knowledge of the basic trends – made up a pretty formidable information centre.

And then naturally the whole business 'snowballed'. When it was seen what kind of stories *The Week* uniquely would handle, all sorts of people – for motives sometimes noble and quite often vile – would approach *The Week* to draw its attention to the most extraordinary pieces of more or less confidential information. Sometimes it came from frustrated newspapermen who could not get what they considered vital news into their own papers. More often such confidences were the outcome of obscure financial or diplomatic duels. They would come, for instance, from the Councillor of an embassy who was convinced of the wrong-headed policy of the Foreign Office and the Ambassador, and wished, without exposing himself, to put a spoke in their wheel.

The savage tensions of the 1930s naturally produced a situation favourable to this type of development. Under the frightful over-hanging menace of Hitlerism, there roamed through the capitals of Western Europe people who were half saint and half bandit – the sort of people who would commit a murder for twenty pounds and suicide for a good idea.

For many months one of *The Week*'s principal informants in Berlin was a principal secretary of Herr von Papen. This man, who at times acted as von Papen's *chef de cabinet*, was an energetically devout Catholic and an astute anti-Nazi.

At that time it was still necessary for Hitler to treat von Papen with caution and a kind of respect, so that it was impossible to conceal from the von Papen bureau more than about thirty per cent of what the Nazis were really up to.

It was of course impossible for this secretary to send his information through the mails and I had, in fact, insisted that nothing must be written down at all. I had a messenger – a former sports writer of the Ullstein press – whom nobody suspected of being anything but a damn fool, travel to and from Berlin to talk with this secretary, memorize his information and bring it back to London.

Unfortunately the secretary was less careful than he should have been. He kept a file of *The Week* in order to check up on the way in which we were handling the information which he gave us. One day in June my messenger, who generally had very little interest in politics and was not particularly alert to what was going on, arrived in Berlin and went to see the secretary.

The copies of *The Week* were covered in blood – the man had been shot at close range by the S.S. assassins who had just invaded the house. Our liaison man escaped, by an estimated four minutes, before they returned to the lower floors after a search of the bedrooms to find someone else they might like to kill.

Probably this was one of the reasons – this event and its repercussions – that Herr von Ribbentrop, German Ambassador, thought I and *The Week* were the centre of all anti-Nazi intrigue and propaganda in London.

The fact that he thought so – that he could be such a fool as to think so – helped to give me a measure of the Third Reich which could employ such an Ambassador. One is not much alarmed about people who are reasonably intelligent. What was terrifying about this man was that he was a damn fool – and could only have been employed by a régime of, basically, damn fools, who could blow up half the world out of sheer stupidity.

A satisfactory thing about Ribbentrop was that you did not have to waste time wondering whether there was some latent streak of goodness in him somewhere. He was all of a piece. He had me followed about London by enormous blondes. From the fact that *The Week* often spoke disobligingly of the Foreign Office, too, he of course deduced that it must be secretly run by the Foreign Office. The disobliging remarks were a clever blind, and there was Ambassador Ribbentrop seeing right through it. Vansittart foiled again.

Also, to help mould his ideas, I had arranged to have conveyed to him the information that my real name – now clumsily translated from the German – was Hahnbrandt, and that my father came from Czernowitz. Supposing that this piece of intelligence had been treacherously sold to one of his agents by a friend of mine, Ribbentrop was inclined to think it true. He never really believed any report honestly come by.

The blondes were sometimes female, sometimes male. One of the males had the job of getting a seat beside me on one of those plush-covered benches by the marble-topped tables in the old Café Royal, which at that time I used as an alternative to my office, on account of the superior amenities. Most of the full-time Nordic representatives one encountered were swarthy chaps about five and a half feet high, but this fellow would have made Lohengrin look quite a dago. Often he got so close that you could see the tiny yellow hairs quivering deep inside his ear.

Not wanting anyone's time to get wasted, I arranged for use on these occasions some informative little dialogues with whichever friend happened to be sitting with me.

Me: Say what you will, you cannot deny the Gentiles started the last war. Wormed themselves into key positions everywhere. Asquith, Bethmann-Hollweg, the Hohenzollerns, Poincaré – all Gentiles, old boy.

Friend: But look at the thing broadly – think of their contribution to literature, culture in general. Look at Shakespeare.

Me: Shakespeare I grant you – if he really was a Gentile. But if you want to talk about writers, what about Wells, and Shaw? Typically disruptive, *negative* Gentile mentalities. Mind you, I've many good Gentile friends myself. But taken in the *mass* . . . Besides, I always think there's something queer about their eyes.

Ten minutes of this, and the horrified Wandervogel had had about all he could hold, and was off to the little door on the Duke of York's steps to report on the swelling arrogance of crypto-Jewish conspirators, and add another page or so to my dossier.

12 Pundits and Friends

IT was about this time that Mr Pollitt, Secretary of the Communist Party of Great Britain, whom I had never met, was suddenly announced on the telephone – would I, he asked, take the next train, in twenty minutes or half and hour, and report a mine disaster at Gresford, North Wales? Why? Because he had a feeling that there was a lot more in it than met the eye. But why me in particular? Well, because, it seemed, Mr Pollitt – who was worrying at the time about what he believed to be a lack of 'reader appeal' in the *Daily Worker* – had been reading *The Week* and thought I might do a good job.

I like sudden decisions, and went, and I did a good job.

And a few days after it Mr Pollitt asked me to call on him and said to me, 'How much d'you make?' I told him I had never figured it out – I kept getting new jobs, like being newly appointed first London correspondent of *Time* magazine, and then, as a result of complex journalistic fantasy, first London correspondent of *Fortune* – magazine of American Big Business.

Mr Pollitt said, 'Well, anyway, do you make more than thirty pounds a week?'

I could not deny that I did.

To this Mr Pollitt replied, 'Well, how'd you like to work for about four pounds a week – and half the time you won't get even that? How'd you like to work for the *Daily Worker*?'

This suggestion would probably have been in any case irresistible – and it was the more so because of my experience among the British Labour people and Liberals. I was as certain as I ever have been of anything that I could never possibly appreciate their viewpoint – not, that is to say, to the extent of becoming enthusiastic

109

about it, writing honestly and creatively in favour of it. To put it in slang, the Labour people seemed to me to be about where I had come in in Germany years and years before. And if there were things to disagree with the communists about, what I felt at the time was that they were a lot nearer being a creative force in British politics than any other that I could see.

Also they were a force that was small, poor and adventurous, and the distance between their thoughts and their actions appeared to me to be a lot shorter than it was when you came to the Labour people, the 'progressive intellectuals'.

Decisive in this situation was that I had, for a short time – some months before Mr Pollitt made his offer – worked for a weekly newspaper called the *Clarion*, run by Odhams Press, owners of the *Daily Herald*. I wrote a weekly page of paragraphs on foreign affairs. It was not a bad page, but it had something false and brittle about it, and I knew the reason – the things I really thought were happening could not be expressed directly in that Labour-organized newspaper, and once again I faced the same inhibitions and distortions of expression, of style, as I had faced at *The Times*.

Misled, probably, by sensational literature and the motion pictures, people said one thing was certain, and that was that the *Daily Worker* would be very, very different from the *Times*. Like most statements made without fear of successful contradiction, this one turned out to be full of error. One look at the expression upon the face of the van-driver waiting to rush next day's paper to the stations, and I became aware of something at once rare and familiar. I had seen it on the faces of *Times* drivers, but – until now – nowhere else.

It was an expression which said the edition was going to come off the press long behind schedule, and he was going to risk his neck tearing along the streets to Euston and Paddington, and if he caught the trains at all it was going to be a flaming miracle. And just why was the paper going to be late? Not, you could bet your life, because a big murder story broke at the last minute, or floods menaced thousands, or heiress's secret wedding exclusive, or any of that class of caper, but because the leader-writer – the flaming *leader-writer*, well, I ask you – was still batting out a pronouncement on something or other and they were holding the whole edition for him while he reached for the *mot* flaming *juste*.

A nice state of affairs in the middle of the twentieth century. Who did he think he was? Gladstone?

Within the building, at the entrance to the editorial offices, the sense of familiarity, of *déjà vu*, deepened. This was not entirely due to the fact that at that date the offices of both newspapers looked, in contrast to Fleet Street, like something Dickens had set out to describe, and then left to be continued by someone who was just starting to read up on this new-fangled steel construction you heard about. Functional they were not. They reminded me of Boston. But, more than this, it was an organizational detail which evoked a memory of Printing House Square.

Naturally, all newspapers have guardians whose business it is to prevent eager but irrelevant people bursting in and disturbing the editorial inmates at their tasks. At *The Times*, when I worked there, this protection had been considered particularly important. And I had been told that as for the *Daily Worker* I should find it guarded, they said, like a fortress.

Of course, the character of the most probable intruders differed, up to a point, in each case. *The Times*, I had always been given to understand, was protecting the editorial staff against the onset of people with plans to reorganize the Church of England, people who wanted it to publish a five-column letter demanding state subsidies for otter-hunting, and people who were going to beat up the racing correspondent because of the ruinously misleading thing he foreshadowed about the third race at Newmarket.

At the *Daily Worker* the job of the man on the door was rather to keep out people with plans to reorganize the Communist Party, people who wanted to get a five-column letter published demanding state subsidies for Esperanto, and people who were going to beat up the racing correspondent because of the ruinously misleading thing he foreshadowed about the fourth race at Wolverhampton.

First time I called at *The Times*, I got right to the editor's door without being questioned, and learned that the obvious reason for that must have been that the person who kept people out had had to slip away for a minute to make some tea. At the *Daily Worker*, the arrangements were, in truth, more elaborate. There was a cubby-hole for the guardian to sit in, and a small *guichet* for him to peer out of, and a door which would open only when he was satisfied and pulled a string. On this occasion the door had been wedged open with a piece of wood, the cubby-hole was empty, and as one walked unchallenged up the stairs one caught, at the end of a passage, a glimpse of the guardian's back as he pored over a gas-ring, making some tea.

On the voyage to the interior, other well-remembered sights were witnessed. That man, half-crazed by worry and frustration, shouting about trains leaving and peering over his shoulder towards

111

the leader-writer's room with the mixed rage and awe of one who is trying to get an archdeacon to step on the gas, must obviously be the manager. These chaps, eruditely discussing in a mood of high-minded levity the racial composition of the Saar and that business about the M.C.C., can be none other than the Foreign editor and the diplomatic correspondent. And clearly the tense-looking man scribbling away at the end of the table is the world's greatest expert on something and, though ostensibly sub-editing a small item of late news, is really writing a definitive article for a quarterly or monthly review.

After all this, the sight of the leader-writer himself, a Scotsman, it need hardly be said, or at any rate one of Nature's Scotsmen, came as no surprise at all. One had seen virtually the same man coolly holding up production of *The Times* while his sinewy pen wrestled mightily with Unrighteousness, a spiritual descendant of Covenanters and of the sort of preacher who held that if a full and proper exposition of The Word was going to cause the sermon to go on for five hours, then five hours was what the sermon was going to go on for. Featherpates might babble of parishioners falling exhausted in the aisles, or trains leaving the termini without the paper. That was just too bad about the parishioners and the disappointed readers.

Occasionally, in those early days of the *Daily Worker*, the readers at the far end of the long-distance lines would get together in protest, claiming they would rather have a paper with a political howler in paragraph four of the leader than no paper at all. The explosions shook the building. Campaigns were initiated for more hustle, modernity and snappy popular journalism all round. People sat gazing sadly at the *Daily Express*, with a view to imitating it. Over the problem of how to get snappier there raged discussions comparable to those at *The Times* office when some ruthless modernist, shouting for the Common Touch and plenty of it, came in with that shockingly vulgar suggestion about sticking in a crossword puzzle.

In the midst of one of these periods of controversy, I came down to the office to find a big section of the library space occupied by a broodingly thoughtful Burman, the entire table before him covered with books, brochures and manuscript documents. It looked as though the article he was evidently going to write on the situation in Burma was going to cover the subject pretty comprehensively. Next day he was still there, writing down figures in long columns – statistics of rice production, I supposed. His books and papers now took up so much room that it was hard to move about the library at all. It seemed it must be going to be quite a series of articles. And about all this research there was something impressive and solemn, making one feel that any other article written for the paper was going to look trivial and superficial.

On the third day I took alarm and placed the whole question squarely before the editor.

I yielded, I said, to no one in my appreciation of the gravity and world importance of the situation in Burma. A couple of rousing pieces about it were, I did most profoundly realize, what the paper needed as badly as anything. But, so far as I could judge, our friend aimed at turning out a minimum of twenty such articles, and frankly, and without in any way seeking to minimize the vital urgency of getting the facts in front of the public, was this project entirely in line with decisions recently taken about developing more zing, zip and popular appeal? Would a series of twenty articles on Burma Today be the snappiest thing imaginable? As a circulation-getter, was it just what the *Daily Express* would do?

The editor, who personally would rather have enjoyed reading twenty longish articles subjecting the Burmese situation to an exhaustive analysis, listened with an air of melancholy. Painfully, as though revealing that in the rush for the Common Touch we had decided to go in for some kind of pornography, he explained the position. The Burman was not, in fact, writing an article about Burma. He was not an expert on the country. What he was an expert on was greyhound racing. And what he was doing with all those books and papers was working out greyhound form for the coming season. Thereafter a section of the paper was going to be devoted to greyhound tips and greyhound results.

So, indeed, it came to pass. People who were expecting a piece denouncing the Bank of England and found instead a bit tipping Blazing Killarney Boy for the White City were disgusted, and wrote letters saying this could never have happened in the Old Days and the Tolpuddle Martyrs were rolling in their graves. Others were delighted, for, however shaky he may have been on Burma, as a dog-tipster he was the tops. In the raw financial blizzard which blew continuously through the office for months on end, he was a big comfort to the staff. Perhaps if the Moscow Gold other people wrote about had really existed one would not have bothered so much about what was going to happen at the tracks. Things being as they were, Blazing Killarney Boy was worth a whole lot of imaginary roubles.

The financial blizzard affected me less seriously than others because – although I had had to abandon *Time* and *Fortune* simply because I had no working hours left after dealing with *The Week* and the *Daily Worker* – *The Week* was now climbing steadily, and even making a profit.

It was also exerting a certain – quite undefinable but still perceptible – influence.

About the time when Hitler was marching into the Rhineland, in the spring of 1936, I was somewhat diffidently approached by Mr John Strachey, with a mysterious, if trivial, proposal. He desired me to furnish him with a potted autobiography. It must be done at once. It must be impressive. And I must not ask for what purpose it was wanted.

Mr Strachey was at that time very far indeed from being a member of the government. On the contrary, he wrote for the *Daily Worker*, was generally, though mistakenly, believed to be a communist, and spoke harshly of the leaders of the Labour Party. He was in touch with some of the Churchillian group of the Conservatives who were already alive, like him, to the Nazi menace. Also, as it turned out, he knew a man who knew a man who knew the King.

'But what *is* it wanted for?' I said once, twice and three times, and the third time Mr Strachey agreed to tell all, but not where walls might have ears. We hurried out and walked round and round Primrose Hill. 'It's simply,' said Mr Strachey in a low murmur, 'that the King wants to know who you are.'

Mr Strachey, it seemed, was the friend of an intimate of Lord Louis Mountbatten, reputedly one of the closest and most influential advisers of King Edward VIII. And Lord Louis Mountbatten, said Mr Strachey, was a student of *The Week*.

Lord Louis was an early and, at that time, somewhat lonely anti-Nazi in high places. He was, Mr Strachey murmured to the discreet air of Primrose Hill, using *The Week* to convince King Edward that the real shape of things to come was very different from that foretold by Premier Baldwin and his colleagues. *The Week* had recently given a good deal of rather sensational advance information on Nazi moves which had proved correct. The King, it appeared, was impressed. 'But,' he had complained to Lord Louis with understandable petulance, 'you are asking me to prefer the information of an obscure political scandal-sheet, run by someone I never heard of, to that of all my Ministers.'

This was where the potted autobiography was to come in. It was to show His Majesty that the editor of the obscure scandal-sheet was one of the Right People, with ancestors, and an Oxford accent and a former connection with *The Times*. In the interests of this high-powered and beneficent project, I reached for a halo and rapidly presented Mr Strachey with a glowing testimonial to myself in about four hundred words. Later I received messages saying that things were going well. I gathered that *The Week* had become required reading at Fort Belvedere. I hoped His Majesty would not leave it lying about where an archbishop might see it. I also hoped we might soon see some practical political results.

I waited for months, and what I saw in the end was Mr Strachey, more serious than ever, suggesting that we take another open-air walk – this time, as I recall, in St James's Park.

We were in the middle of the Abdication Crisis. The newspapers were victims of a more than usually painful attack of discretional lock-jaw. They were determined to show responsibility, delicacy, restraint and the Best Possible Taste if it was the last thing they did before total paralysis gripped them. In the suffocating silence the trend was running strongly against the King.

In this situation, Mr Strachey murmured to a passing swan, Lord Louis Mountbatten had conceived the idea that if certain 'inside information' of a particularly sensational character could be suddenly forced into the open, the trend might, just possibly, be reversed in the King's favour. There were facts which it was thought the regular newspapers and weeklies would be most unlikely to print. On the other hand, it had been noted that on several occasions in the past *The Week* had succeeded in securing wide publicity for matters thought 'not fit to print'. Things had, apparently, come to the paradoxical point where the 'obscure scandal-sheet' might be the most effective weapon available to save the King.

Lord Louis, I was informed, was of the opinion that if he could present the King with this concrete possibility, the King might agree to try it. The question therefore was: would I, 'in principle', be prepared to publish certain facts if they reached me from Fort Belvedere? I was warned that they would immediately be denied by the cabinet, that the resulting row would be certainly appalling and possibly catastrophic. His Majesty, I was told, as yet knew nothing of this project.

I was rather far from being a passionate champion of the monarchy, but the atmosphere of pompous discretion was almost unbreathable, and anyway it looked as though whatever happened we should have a lot of fun. Also, one got the impression that Lord Louis Mountbatten was a bonny fighter who ought to be encouraged. I accepted, of course.

Mr Strachey rushed to and fro with mysterious messages. I said that I would publish the story that was to save the King in a special edition of *The Week* – we could turn it off on the duplicator in a couple of hours. The police always showed a keen interest in the contents of *The Week*, and there was just a chance that it might be held up in the mails. I therefore arranged that there should be a score or so of my friends with cars and motor-cycles ready to rush a few hundred copies by hand to a selected list of influential subscribers in London and the home counties.

Late one Thursday afternoon I received word that the material would be in my hands within the next few hours, and should be published immediately. It would be brought by a dispatch rider to *The Week*'s office in the garret in Victoria Street.

I mobilized the necessary typists 'for special duty' and overhauled our rickety second-hand duplicator. The flying squad of distributors was alerted, and its members told to stand by their telephones.

At eight in the evening the main door of the office building was closed, and a sentry had to be posted there to meet the impending messenger and get the documents from him.

The two typists, the boy who turned the handle of the duplicator, the two friends who would stuff the finished product into the envelopes, and myself, sat eating sandwiches in the tiny office which would comfortably accommodate three people.

At eleven o'clock there was a telephone message to say that there had been a 'slight delay', but that the material would reach us before midnight.

By half an hour past midnight I was standing on a chair to lean out of the small, high window of the garret, listening to the profound silence of Victoria Street.

It was nearly one before I heard quite a long way off the loud noise of a big motor-cycle being ridden very fast.

I rushed down five flights of stairs and got to the street door at the same time as the dispatch rider, who had shot past and had to turn. He handed me a small unaddressed envelope, and I knew from the size of it that it was going to be no good. I called him to wait, there might be an answer. He said no, he had been told there was no answer. Inside the envelope was a single sheet of plain paper with this typewritten line.

It read: 'The situation has developed too fast.'

But for a good many months I could devote very little time to it. The Spanish War had broken out.

13 Lost Sierra

HARDLY anybody under the age of about sixty today has much notion of what the Spanish War meant to the people of the period in which it was fought. Yet almost everybody is aware, dimly or otherwise, that it was an event of huge – and to some, mysterious – significance.

Politically and militarily it could truthfully be described as the great divide in the period between the wars. Politically, on the most general level, it suddenly and lethally confirmed theories that had been forgotten or become cobwebbed in complacency. It showed, that is to say, that despite all the hopes and indeed the virtues of Western democracy, a genuine democratic surge which challenges an established order would not be allowed to continue in existence without violent challenge by the old order. People who had supposed that democratic advance in Spain would proceed without that challenge were violently proved wrong.

Thus, throughout the spring of 1936 there had occurred in Spain a convulsive, spontaneous, tumultuous development which, if the word had any meaning, had to be recognized as democratic. In the February elections of that year, the parties of the Popular Front had won 278 seats in the Cortes. The parties of the right, combined in the National Front, had 134 seats. Despite massive intimidation by landowners in a manner traditional in rural Spain, the vote for the Popular Front was 4,176,000. The vote for the National Front was 378,000. The Popular Front included Left Republicans and the Republican Union with 126 seats between them. The socialists had ninety-nine, the Catalan Separatist Left had thirty-six. The communists had seventeen.

Yet when the right organized its armed rebellion against the

Popular Front, this was successfully 'sold' to the British and American publics in particular as being an attempt to save Spain from a red government dominated by the communists. It was the classic pattern of right-wing violent intervention in the supposedly normal course of democratic development, and also the classic formula for justifying this violent intervention to the public opinion of the older-established Western democracies.

Apart from its immediate menace to the interests of the land-owners, bankers and industrialists, the explosion of the February elections represented a subtler threat to the established forces of the right, not only in Spain, not only in the fascist countries, but also in Britain and France.

For in a way exhilarating to many, horrifying to many others, the Spanish outburst was a repetition of those great European explosions of the nineteenth century in which millions of people were motivated and propelled by a good hope that a moment had come when man could remake his world; that he could master his circumstances; that liberty should cease to be an empty word, and work be no longer a dreary one. It was supposed in Spain that, after all, Utopia need not be a sick delusion, or indeed a delusion at all. This, as everybody can see, represented a dangerous example for the working masses of Britain and France who for many decades had become forcibly accustomed to a view of the future which to some looked black, to others grey, and bright to very few. They had succumbed to a kind of fatalistic belief in the consequences and penalties of some unnamed Original Economic Sin. It seemed that they, like the people of Kansas City in the song, had gone about as far as they could go.

The event therefore sent a terrible *frisson* of dismay, not often acknowledged as such, through all the establishments, whether nominally Conservative or nominally Labouristic, in the whole of Europe.

There was another politico-military sense in which the Spanish War marked a fatal divide in the inter-war politics of Europe. The first year of the war represented the high water mark of Soviet Russian involvement in European politics. When the Italians and Germans intervened in Spain (their intervention had in fact occurred before the overt revolt of General Franco), the Russians, after a pause of a couple of months, responded with a massive intervention of their own. This was in fact the most spectacular possible reaffirmation by Moscow of its continued fidelity to the slogan announced by Litvinov a couple of years earlier: 'Peace is indivisible'.

The adherents of the Litvinov policy were seen by many in Moscow as the War Party. At no time did the Litvinov doctrine win complete acceptance in high quarters in Moscow. It had to be defended and demonstrated with the utmost vigour.

In the Spanish War it was thus demonstrated and defended. At all times it could be pointed out by its opponents in Moscow that the Soviet Union was thereby running unnecessary and inadmissible risks in order, in effect, to pull the West's chestnuts out of the fire. When France and Britain not merely remained passive but in fact, by their 'non-intervention' policy, aided and abetted Franco and his backers in Rome and Berlin, it became evident that these risks were becoming insupportable. It was clear enough that if a government victory in Spain were to loom as a real possibility, the likelihood was that the British and French would align themselves even more shamelessly with the Germans and Italians. It would not be one step from this to a united attack by the West, spearheaded by the Germans, upon the Soviet Union itself.

Since several books would clearly be necessary to tussle with all these factors and generalizations, it is better perhaps for the moment at least to remember some pictures of the war as it happened.

Although I had a good idea from Spanish friends in London, including the new Spanish Foreign Minister, Alvarez del Vayo, who was in Britain for an international conference, that 'something' was about to explode on the right in Spain, I had gone there that July of 1936 on holiday, unaware that this was going to be very far from a holiday.

The man everyone went to see, if they could, was General Mangada – the only army general who had not joined General Franco's revolt and instead had remained loyal to the Republic. He was, I believe, a Cuban, or half a Cuban, and he looked strangely like some sort of cross between Gandhi and Gandhi's goat.

The other man who drove out with me to see him at his head-quarters in the Sierra was a young man described as a 'Mexican', who, in reality, was one of the first of the Russian technical advisers to Spain.

General Mangada, after we had drunk a glass or two of sherry with him, asked if we would care to visit the front. We walked for a mile or so across lovely, deserted country – partly a sort of parkland, partly mountain foothills, with outcrops of rock baking in the sun.

We passed small detachments of troops sitting in what shade they could get, and then – after another mile or so during which we had seen nobody – we saw, perhaps six or seven hundred yards away, a line of riflemen in open order, moving about on the low ground ahead of us.

'Those, I suppose,' said the 'Mexican', 'are your advance patrols?'

'Not at all,' said General Mangada, surprised, 'those must be the advance patrols of the enemy.'

It was an ugly moment. There we stood in no-man's-land, and there seemed a high possibility that within ten minutes Spain's only loyal General was going to be captured by the enemy, I was going to be shot as a red agent, and the 'Mexican' – unless his gullet was wide enough to swallow a lot of documents very fast – was going to be Exhibit Number One in a nasty international incident.

Awfully slowly, as it seemed to me, the General – who had the air of a man walking around his estate in Somerset on a Sunday afternoon – turned from his dreamy contemplation of the enemy patrols and we strolled back to his headquarters.

The 'Mexican' – a conscientious young man – said that perhaps he might be privileged to meet the General's Staff. General Mangada shook his head in his gentle manner. 'No Staff,' he said. 'In war Staff means betrayal.'

The 'Mexican' said, 'Well, I am afraid we do not have a great deal to offer, but we have made some remarkable progress recently in mapping, and it occurred to me that our experience in that department might possibly be of some assistance to . . .'

Mangada interrupted him. 'No,' he said, 'no maps.' He put his chocolate-coloured hand on his left breast and tapped it gently. 'In war,' he said, 'the heart must be the map.'

In the vast requisitioned convent in northern Madrid where was being organized at nearly breakneck speed the Fifth Regiment, which was to become the model and nucleus of the New Army of the Republic, I talked one night with the Commandant and organizer-in-chief. At that time I knew this husky, bull-necked man, who combined almost super-human driving power with an unbreakable gaiety, simply as Carlos, and all I knew of his past was that he had once been a steel-worker in Chicago. Later, he turned out to be an Italian called Videla, who was supposed to have organized the assassination, in Mexico, of Leon Trotsky.

He spoke of the problems of the New Army, and while he was talking one of them blew up right outside the room. From the former chapel of the convent we heard first the sound of shooting – volley after volley – and within minutes the barrack square was a scene of the wildest riot and turmoil. We rushed out, Carlos carrying a pistol in each hand – and he needed them because what we ran into outside was a mob of armed militiamen milling about in the moonlight, looking for the Commandant and threatening to lynch him. By an extraordinary effort of domination and the help of the pistols, Carlos held them at bay long enough to get them sufficiently calmed down so that they allowed the man who seemed to be their leader, or one of them, to start to explain what it was all about.

The men were recruits – very poor peasants from somewhere in the south, who had, of their own free will, marched half across Spain to join the New Army and fight for the Republic. They had reached Madrid and the convent late in the evening, and had been hastily bedded down for the night on the floor of the chapel. They had fallen into exhausted sleep, but a couple of hours later, when the moon rose, two or three of them had awakened, and what they saw was the moon shining upon the statues and images of saints which it had not occurred to anyone to remove. The men's reaction was one partly of terror, partly of rage – terror because these images could ill-wish them, could be far more dangerous warriors than the Franco troops they expected to meet on the battlefield, and rage because they believed they had been lured into a trap; whoever was responsible for exposing them to these deadly powers must be an agent of the enemy.

The first men to wake up grabbed their old rifles or sporting guns and started firing at the images and statues, yelling to the others to wake up and help them fight their way out of this trap. Everyone started firing at the saints, and then rushed out to find the Commandant and kill him, too.

'You see,' Carlos said when things had quietened down under a powerful jet of oratory and exhortation from himself, 'our problems are not quite simple.'

They changed, but they got no simpler. When I, some weeks later, joined this same Fifth Army as a private and went to the Sierra Front with a company of barely trained peasants, the first time we went into action – our commander, a former captain in the Foreign Legion, soon deserted to the enemy, and in his capacity as military saboteur had ordered us to charge straight up a bare hillside against a fort full of Moorish machine-gunners – a lot of the men charged holding their rifles high above their heads with one hand and giving the clenched fist salute with the other.

It emerged that they had taken the highly stylized and symbolic posters designed by the Madrid intellectuals, showing a Soldier of the Republic in this posture, as illustrations of correct military practice.

When they saw me dodging along, bent half-double and taking whatever cover there was, they thought the posture unworthy, despicable. A lot of them were killed or wounded before they got converted to the idea that, as instructional diagrams, there was something wrong with those posters.

For people who, like myself, have a claustrophobic distaste for organization and discipline, this makeshift, ramshackle quality of the Spanish War, which could be terrifying because it kept reminding one of the odds against our sort of forces being victorious over the trained troops of the other side, was also a factor compensating the periods of terror and the periods of tedium which are, alternately, so large a part of any war.

Also the nature of my job kept me moving fairly briskly between Madrid, London, Paris, Geneva and Gibraltar – where I went to do a mixed job of propaganda and espionage, and escaped being assassinated only because a pro-Republican waiter in the hotel where I stayed warned me just in time to get out of town. I was afraid at the time I might be taking unnecessary precautions, but years later I met one of the organizers of the attempt who assured me the waiter's warning and my own fears had been perfectly well grounded.

I had been only a few weeks at the front, and had been promoted corporal after two of our sergeants followed the Foreign Legion captain across the lines to the enemy, when I was summoned abruptly to London to take a hand in the campaign to influence the policies of the Labour Party and Trades Union Congress against non-intervention. Despite my protests, I was billed as the star speaker at an enormous meeting in Shoreditch Town Hall – a grave mistake, because I am one of the worst public speakers who ever bored and exasperated an audience. I always had the feeling that no member of the audience at any of these meetings would ever read my written reports with much confidence again.

I was thankful when I was summoned to the Communist Party headquarters by Mr Pollitt and ordered to write a book about the Spanish War instead. 'We need it,' said Mr Pollitt, 'in a hurry.' 'How much of a hurry?' 'Before the end of the week,' said Mr Pollitt, and I was locked into a bed-sitting-room in a nursing-home run by a friend of mine, and told not to come out until the book was done. A nurse was in attendance to give me shots in the arm in case I fell asleep or dropped dead from exhaustion.

When I returned to Spain, this time as the *Daily Worker*'s corres-pondent, the atmosphere was a great deal more harsh, the aspect of the whole war more grim than it had seemed in the summer, but – although Franco was literally at the gates of Madrid – hardly anyone, I believe, even imagined that we could be defeated.

The food had become scarce and abominable, and the shells from the batteries outside the city kept falling in the Gran Via and around the Telefonica building, where the correspondents had to transmit their messages. At breakfast one day in his room at the Florida Hotel, which more or less overlooked the nearest part of the front, Mr Ernest Hemingway was very comfortable about the shelling. He had a big map laid out on the table, and he explained to an audience of generals, politicians and correspondents that, for some ballistic reason, the shells could not hit the Florida. He could talk in a very military way and make it all sound very convincing. Everyone present was convinced and happy. Then a shell whooshed through the room above Mr Hemingway's head – the first actually to hit the Florida – and the ceiling fell down on the breakfast-table. To any lesser man than Mr Hemingway the occurrence would have been humiliating. While we were getting the plaster out of our hair, Mr Hemingway looked slowly round at us, one after the other. 'How do you like it now gentlemen?' he said, and by some astonishing trick of manner conveyed the impression that this episode had actually, in an obscure way, confirmed instead of upsetting his theory – that his theory had been right when he expounded it and this only demonstrated that the time had come to have a new one.

Everyone was very happy to have Mr Hemingway there, partly because he was obviously a fine man to have around when there was war and trouble, and partly because to have so famous an author there, writing on behalf of the Republic, made people feel less alone in the world – in a sense, which was no fault of Mr Hemingway, it helped to foster the illusion that sooner or later the 'world conscience' would be aroused, 'the common people' in Britain and France would force their governments to end non-intervention, and the war would be won.

The Russians, who lived in the Palace Hotel at the other end of the Gran Via, seemed to be the only people who could do without this illusion and still not become defeatist. Although they wrote as big words as anyone for publication, they could get along without them in private conversation. They had an attitude which could be called cynical or just tough. They were refreshing because there were so many people about at the time – particularly the Visiting

Firemen, VIPs of one kind or another from the United States and Britain – who seemed to have an irresistible need to use phrases as though they were facts, and if anyone punctured their phrases they became distressed and frightened about the future.

I spent a great deal of my time in the company of Mikhail Koltzov, who then was Foreign editor of *Pravda* and, more importantly still, was at that period – he disappeared later in Russia, presumably shot – the confidant and mouthpiece and direct agent of Stalin himself. He was a stocky little Jew – from Odessa, I think – with a huge head and one of the most expressive faces of any man I ever met. What his face principally expressed was a kind of enthusiastically gleeful amusement – and a lively hope that you and everyone else would, however depressing their circumstances, do their best to make things more amusing still.

He had a savagely satirical tongue – and an attitude of entire ruthlessness towards people he thought either incompetent or even just pompous.

As the Spanish War ground its way to its gruesome conclusion, and all over Europe people who had supported the Republic became truly cynical, despairing, without faith or enthusiasm for anything, I found myself looking forward more and more eagerly to conversations with Koltzov, journeys in his company, estimates from him of the course of affairs. He was a man who could see the defeat for what it really was, could assume that half the big slogans were empty, and a lot of the big heroes stuffed, or charlatans, and yet not let that bother him at all, or sap his energy and enthusiasm.

For a good many months before the end of the Spanish War I had been working chiefly in London, Paris and Geneva, and occasionally in Prague. It was strenuous, stimulating work, because my function, as I saw it, was to develop on the one hand the 'circle' influenced by *The Week* – to mobilize, scare and prod into greater activity all those people who could be so prodded or assisted in what was now, evidently, a desperately critical phase. These 'friends of *The Week*' were, for the most part, very far from being communists, and many of them were Conservatives, or their equivalents in the various capitals where *The Week* still circulated. To command even a little of their attention *The Week* needed the most sensational kind of 'inside news', but above all it needed to present the news in a particular style and pattern, so that even when there was really no available 'inside news' people felt that they were reading something new, getting a fresh and more exciting picture or story than they got from the newspapers, and getting it in, so to speak, a tone of voice such as they were accustomed to hear in their clubs. On the other hand, I regarded my work as diplomatic correspondent and reporter of the *Daily Worker* as equally – perhaps more – important in the business of bringing to bear against Nazism and the forces making for war such pressures as could be brought. But the effective style for the *Daily Worker* was entirely other than that required for *The Week*, so that it was necessary to develop, stylistically, a double personality. This, as I have said, is strenuous, because if you lose for a moment a vivid awareness of either of these two so different audiences, the story will fall to bits.

In Prague at the height of the Munich crisis, it seemed as though half the international figures one had known in Madrid had assembled there, and the sight of them seemed to be ominous. You felt that soon there would have to be shells cracking against the hotel to complete the picture. (It reminded one of the story of the famous Hearst reporter, specialist in political disasters, H. R. Knickerbocker, when he came to Vienna at some moment of crisis. 'Good God!' cried the hotel manager. '*You* here, Herr Knickerbocker? Is it then already so bad?') It looked like the end of an act, and it was.

I spent a lot of time with Koltzov at the Russian Legation, for that was the place where, if anything decisive were to happen, it would happen. And I knew that Koltzov was at least as important a figure on the stage as the Russian Minister, and perhaps much more important because of his double position at *Pravda* and at the Kremlin.

From this place of vantage I saw at very close quarters what really was the last scene of the act – everything that happened after that was anticlimax.

It was the moment when there still seemed to be an outside chance that either the League of Nations, or at least Britain, France and the Soviet Union, would stand together on behalf of Czechoslovakia against Germany.

The Czechoslovak army was in position on the frontiers, and at the headquarters of the commander-in-chief in the field there was no doubt whatever that war was a matter of hours. In the same belief, the Soviet Union had dispatched to Prague a force of fighter planes and bombers – an advance force which was to be massively reinforced at the moment of war. For obvious reasons this advance Soviet force was not officially there at all, and there were a good many people in the Czechoslovak Government who did not care for its presence – they thought Hitler would use it as provocation.

As the tension grew almost intolerably, a message from President

Benes urgently summoned the Russian Minister to the Palace. The message said the President wanted to put some urgent questions.

In the circumstances, it seemed likely that this meant that the forces in Czechoslovakia demanding resistance to Hitler (even if it meant that the Red Army would have to occupy Czechoslovakia in Czechoslovakia's defence) had won the day.

The Minister rushed off. When he got there, he told Koltzov afterwards, he found the President looking, as he said, 'like a photograph of himself'.

'If,' said Benes, 'the League of Nations declares for resistance to Hitler's demands upon us, even at the cost of war, what would be the Soviet attitude?'

The Soviet Union, said the Minister, would in those circumstances certainly fight. He could hardly keep the impatience out of his voice as he answered so otiose a question.

'If,' said Benes, 'the League does nothing, but Britain and France declare themselves ready to stand by us, even at the cost of war, what would then be the Soviet attitude?'

The Minister was impatient to get this question settled quickly, too. Of course, he said, the Soviet Union would fight.

He waited confidently for the next question – the third, the vital question. He wanted Benes to ask what would happen if neither the League nor France and Britain acted, and if, nevertheless, Czechoslovakia resisted Hitler's demands at the cost of war. For he was authorized to state that in that case, too, the Soviet Union would fight.

There was a long pause. Neither of them moved. At last the Russian, disregarding diplomatic discretion, broke the silence. Was there not, he said, a third question which Benes would care to put? A third potential situation?

Benes sat absolutely still for several minutes.

'No,' he said wearily, at last, 'those are the only two questions I have to ask.'

Gloom and a sense of futility enveloped the Legation when the Minister returned with his report. It could only mean that after all there would be no resistance, because neither the League nor Britain and France would carry resistance to the point of war. Glumly orders were sent to the airfield to tell the Soviet flyers that their mission was over before it had begun. All they could do now was to go home. Even Koltzov at this moment seemed to have lost resilience. And then, it must have been a couple of hours later, came an abruptly urgent call from Benes.

Would the Minister secure immediately from Moscow an exact, up-to-the-minute verification and reassurance of previous estimates of the pace and volume at which Soviet air power could get into action from Czechoslovak air bases? The Minister said he could get the required facts within an hour, and would rush them to the Palace.

The Legation was wild with excitement, Koltzov dancing and kissing people and hurling his beret repeatedly into the air. Counter-orders were rushed to the flyers at the airport. Two or three of them had just taken off, and one officer was so excited at the change in the news that he actually loosed off an anti-aircraft gun at them as the most emphatic possible signal.

And then – things were moving so fast now that policies were being made and unmade almost by the half-hour – the plot twisted again; someone, some force somewhere, intervened. The Minister dashed off to the Palace once again with the required information. And when he got there he was not even admitted to Benes's presence.

'The Czechoslovak Government,' he was informed, 'is no longer interested in the reply to this request.'

With that, it was once again a certainty that Czechoslovakia would not act with Russia alone as her ally. The shape of the next act was certain. Hitler's next triumph was assured. It was the hour, too, in which the Russo-German Pact became inevitable.

Sadly, Koltzov reminded me of the story I had told him about M. Claudel in Washington.

'Once again,' he said, 'the only thing to say is that in the little moment that remains to us between the crisis and the catastrophe, we may as well drink a glass of champagne.'

14 The Cliveden Set

ODDLY – or perhaps not so oddly, because I have always liked Americans, and the sort of man that likes Americans is liable to like Russians – a prominent light in my part of the gloom in those days was my old friend Mr Vladimir Poliakoff, formerly diplomatic correspondent of *The Times*.

With the head of a Slav generalissimo, and a get-up vaguely suggestive of Homburg about 1906, this Vladimir Poliakoff strode and occasionally tiptoed around and about the diplomatic world of the twenties and thirties like a panther, which duller creatures deem merely picturesque or bizarre until they note what a turn of speed he has. Among his other notable qualities was an infinite capacity for taking pains to do everyone, from Ambassadors to train conductors, small but unforgettable favours. A colleague, who regarded the very existence of Poliakoff with jealous disapproval, declared that there was not a Foreign Secretary in Europe whose mistress's dog had not been smuggled across one or other frontier by Poliakoff.

I met him for the first time in 1929 when I was tenuously attached to *The Times* office in Paris. The atmosphere in the office that day was sulphurous. The chief correspondent, on calling to see the Minister of Foreign Affairs, had been informed by the *chef de cabinet* that 'Your chief has just been with the Minister for an hour.' The correspondent was at first merely amazed that the editor should have come over from London without informing the office. Later, to his disgust, he learned that the supposed 'chief' was the peripatetic Mr Poliakoff on a quick trip to Paris. By virtue of a certain manner he had, he was quite often taken by foreign statesmen to be the 'man behind' everything from Printing House

Square to Whitehall, and his sincere denials merely confirmed their belief.

Furthermore, the assistant correspondent had been apprised by friends in London that Poliakoff was accustomed to refer to him slightingly as 'the office boy with the silk moustache'. As a result of all this, the chief correspondent shut himself up in his room, his assistant put on his hat and walked out, growling, and I, to my alarm, was left alone with the internationally distinguished Poliakoff. I saw him examining me with attention, and feared he would ask me high diplomatic questions which I should be unable to answer, and thus become discredited.

He said, 'What you have is the grippe. Your temperature – I am not accustomed to be wrong about such things – is a little over a hundred.' Astonished, I admitted that this was precisely the case. The tails of his grey morning coat flapping suddenly behind him, he bounded from the sofa.

'A-ha!' he shouted. 'I am the one to cure that. A special remedy. Ordinary ones are futile. I proceed at once to the chemist on the corner to give my instructions. Relax. I shall return.'

In ten minutes he was back and, seating himself beside me, took from his tail pocket a small clear-glass bottle from which he poured a few drops of liquid on to a huge silk handkerchief.

'Breathe deeply. Inhale the remedy of Poliakoff.'

He had his arm round my shoulder and held the handkerchief to my nose with the air of a field-marshal succouring a stricken private. The result was immediately beneficial. But I noticed, too, that the smell and general effect were exactly those produced by a well-known, widely advertised popular remedy, the name of which I have forgotten. I was sufficiently curious to inquire later from the corner chemist whether a certain gentleman – Poliakoff was easy to describe and unforgettable – had, a little earlier, bought a bottle of this well-known product and arranged for it to be specially decanted into a plain bottle. Such had, the chemist said, been the case.

I found this little manoeuvre, this taking of so much trouble to please, both impressive and endearing, and years later, when I had left *The Times*, was delighted to renew acquaintance with Mr Poliakoff at some diplomatic reception in London or Paris. He had a house in a square in South Kensington and there I used to drink Russian tea or vodka with him, or walk round and round the gardens while he exercised his two small Afghan hounds and talked to me derisively, in his harsh Slavonic accents, of the international situation. Even when he later brought a libel action against me our walks and talks continued amicably.

Being a supporter of what was called 'the Vansittart line' – the notion that by a friendly policy towards Mussolini it might be possible to split the Axis and isolate Hitler – he was fervent in denunciation of those powerful personalities in England who, on the contrary, saw in Hitler a bulwark and potential crusader against Bolshevism and thought friendship with the Nazis both possible and desirable. The vigour of his campaigns and intrigues against such elements was naturally heightened by his knowledge that some of them lost no opportunity to convince everyone that he himself was a hired agent of Mussolini.

His sources of information from anti-Nazi factions in the British and French Foreign Offices were thus first-rate, and the stories that came from them had that particular zip and zing which you get from official sources only when a savage intra-mural departmental fight is going on.

I rushed about between London, Paris and Brussels, supplementing and checking such stories from other sources. Vigorous anti-Nazis in the City, too, and on the so-called Churchillian wing of the Conservative Party were also very ready with 'inside information'.

At length I thought I had enough and more than enough to write in *The Week* a longish 'think piece' about the nature and aims of those in high places who were working, sincerely perhaps, but as it seemed to me disastrously, for the 'appeasement' of Adolf Hitler. There were, of course, several references to gatherings at the Astors' Thames-side house at Cliveden. When I published the story, absolutely nothing happened. It made about as loud a bang as a crumpet falling on a carpet. A few weeks later, I ran the whole thing again, in slightly different words, and with similar result.

And then about a month later I did it a third time. There were only trivial additions to the facts already published but the tone was a little sharper. But it happened that this time it occurred to me to head the whole story 'The Cliveden Set' and to use this phrase several times in the text. The thing went off like a rocket.

I think it was *Reynolds News*, three days later, which first picked up the phrase from *The Week*, but within a couple of weeks it had been printed in dozens of newspapers, and within six had been used in almost every leading newspaper of the Western world. Up and down the British Isles, across and across the United States, anti-Nazi orators shouted it from hundreds of platforms. No anti-fascist rally in Madison Square Gardens or Trafalgar Square was complete without a denunciation of the Cliveden Set.

In those days, if you saw cameramen patrolling St James's Square at lunchtime or dusk, you could be nearly sure they were there to get a picture of the Cliveden Set going in or out of the Astors' London house. Geoffrey Dawson, whose position as editor of *The Times* gave him a particular prominence in the 'Set', comments petulantly on this nuisance in his diary. If you talked to American special correspondents, what they wanted to know all about was the Cliveden Set. Senators made speeches about it, and in those London cabarets where libel didn't matter, songsters made songs about it. People who wanted to explain everything by something, and were ashamed to say 'sunspots', said 'Cliveden Set'.

And throughout it all the members of the Cliveden Set, furiously, wearily or derisively, maintained that they were not members because there simply was not any Cliveden Set to be a member of. It was a myth.

And the fact was that, however it started, it presently became a myth. Within a year or so, the Cliveden Set had ceased to represent, in anybody's mind, a particular group of individuals. It had become the symbol of a tendency, of a set of ideas, of a certain condition in, as it were, the State of Denmark. It had acquired a powerful and alarming significance for people who could hardly have named three of those who frequented Cliveden. The phrase went marching on because it first had dramatized, and now summarized, a whole vague body of suspicions and fears.

Occasionally, moderate-minded intermediaries who felt the story was stirring up dangerous thoughts urged me to tone it down in some way – curb the monster I had set loose. I had to reply that in the first place I thought the picture essentially a true one, doing more good than harm. In the second place, even supposing that, contrary to my own convictions, I were to get the B.B.C. to permit me to announce personally to the listening millions that the story had no foundation, that I had invented it, no one would pay the slightest attention. People would come to the conclusion that I had been nobbled by the Cliveden Set.

I was certainly taken aback by the wild improbabilities which some correspondents were writing about the Cliveden Set. It looked as though quite a lot of people were getting involved, were being branded as subtly scheming political intriguers, who would not have known a plot if you handed it to them on a skewer, and quite possibly had gone to Cliveden simply for a good dinner. But then, I reflected, if one is as ignorant of political goings-on as some of them claim to be, is it very wise, even for a very good dinner, to go at all?

I am prepared to believe that a lot of people I had cast as principal figures were really mere cat's-paws. But then a cat's-paw is a cat's-paw and must expect to be treated as part of the cat. Or, as the Chinese proverb puts it: 'Do not tie up your shoes in a melon field, or adjust your hat under a plum tree if you wish to avoid suspicion.'

What ultimately interested, and still interests, me about the entire affair were not the facts about the Cliveden Set but the journalistic detail – the way in which a phrase can 'trigger' to explosion a lot of facts which, for the most part, were already known to hundreds of people, but remained, as it were, inert.

'Newspaper writing,' said the great Thomas Barnes, mid nineteenth-century editor of *The Times*, and its true creator, 'is a thing *sui generis*; it is in literature what brandy is in beverages. John Bull, whose understanding is rather sluggish – I speak of the majority of readers – requires a strong stimulus. He consumes his beef, and cannot digest it without a dram; he dozes composedly over his prejudices which his conceit calls opinions; and you must fire ten-pounders at his densely compact intellect before you can make it comprehend your meaning or care one farthing for your efforts.' A newspaper story, he concluded, 'wanted a little devil in it'.

Poliakoff was a good man to help one put 'a little devil' into one's stories. Staid people naturally loathed him, as being an adventurer, a rapacious semi-oriental pirate upon the English seas. They had loathed in the same way the incomparable de Blowitz – and, indeed, one of the aspects of Poliakoff which gave me great pleasure was that his mind and personality, even his clothes, seemed in some way to connect the world of Henri de Blowitz, of the Second Empire, of Bismarck, and the Dreyfus case, with our own.

Probably this, too, was in part, at least, a courteous trick, a stage-show put on for my benefit, since he was always alert to note what people wanted, and then, if possible, give it to them.

'You,' he warned me several times, 'are a romantic. It is dangerous. On the other hand, it cannot be helped. Every man should be allowed to choose the brand of razor he cuts his throat with. A minimal human demand.'

As a result of this intense attention to other people, he learned, almost before I knew it myself, of an occurrence of great importance in my life. On a gusty morning in February, 1939, we were in his study, drinking a little vodka, and talking partly about the government and partly about the unaccountable *malaise* of one of the Afghan hounds, when he said suddenly and angrily, 'Pointless to talk to you this morning. Of what use the wisdom and experience of

132

Poliakoff? You are addled. You have fallen in love.'

And it was, oddly enough, the morning after the party at which I had for the first time met Patricia. I agreed that his diagnosis was correct.

'English?' Poliakoff asked. 'You would never understand an English woman.'

'Not at all. A glorious Irish girl who has just come out of gaol in Uzhorod, Ruthenia.'

'Excellent,' said Poliakoff. 'I advise you to press forward. The omens seem favourable for your happiness.'

He was right. Happiness – which includes excitement, and an appalling extension of terrifying responsibility – stretched all the way from that encounter to the moment of writing.

But it needed so percipient an observer as Vladimir Poliakoff to see that the omens were favourable. To anyone else examining the entrails of the situation they would have appeared bad, even stinking.

We were on the eve of 'der Pakt'. It was the eve of the dark day when the tickers confirmed that Herr von Ribbentrop, tool of the fascist hyenas and murderers, had arrived in Moscow. In a soap-opera repetition of the first Rapallo he had shaken political, economic and perhaps spiritual hands with Molotov the Hammer. Hammer of what? Hammer of the world proletariat against the fascist hyenas.

When that happened I thanked History for the Irish. For the fact, that is to say, that Patricia, being an Irish woman, had been brought up in an atmosphere in which the particular hypocrisies of imperial Social-Democratic England, never prevailed. Neither she nor her family were ever so self-deceived as to suppose that what was good for the Anglo-Irish was good for the Irish peasantry. Nor that what was good for the Anglo-Irish was necessarily good for the British. Centuries before, that sort of people had been denounced as being 'more Hibernian than the Hibernians'. They were people with a singularly realistic view of politics. A gun, one might say, is a gun is a gun is a gun. But if you want to win, what you have to do is have a gun in the right place in the hands of the right man.

'Right man' in this case means someone who – like the rebels of 1916 – will fire his gun for ideological reasons long after it is apparent to the damn-fool realists of the world that the cause was hopeless from the start, and is now visibly and irretrievably lost. Some years before he became Prime Minister of Ireland and President of the League of Nations Assembly, De Valera was about as gone a coon as you could find in international politics.

General de Gaulle in 1940 was another gone coon. He had no money, about thirty men, and an ideology which hardly anyone outside Carlton House Gardens and the Connaught Hotel understood. When they did understand it they were opposed to it – notably Roosevelt, and, in a more openly violent but less subtly corrosive way, Churchill. The silliest remark Stalin ever made – supposing that he made it – was his question, 'How many divisions does the Pope have?' If he ever did say so stupid a thing, it would indicate a strange lapse of memory on the subject of ideologies.

How many divisions did the Bolsheviks have at the London Conference of 1905? And as a theological student at Tiflis, Joseph Stalin, then Joseph Dzhugashvili, must have encountered somewhere the news of another ideological movement which started with no divisions at all and in no very long time controlled the Army of the Roman Empire.

It was the fact that she had been brought up right in the midst of the guns and the fertile – sometimes crazy, sometimes sublime – ideologies of Ireland that enabled Patricia to view the world into which she now jumped in an exhilaratingly realistic manner.

Once, in a conscientious moment, I was trying to explain to her the probable dangers and difficulties of being married to a man of my convictions and activities. She said, 'You must remember that during most of my childhood I was never allowed in the streets because there was supposed to be a danger of my being kidnapped or shot by politically interested people. Also, during most of that period, the outer gates were locked from dusk until dawn, armed gardeners patrolled the grounds, and they had instructions to shoot at sight any person seen moving in the grounds.' 'I suppose,' I said, 'that they challenged them first.'

Patricia was quite indignant at my naïveté. 'Nonsense,' she said, 'that would have given away the position of the gardener.'

With further naïveté, I supposed that what the armed men were defending that old house against were Sinn Feiners, Irish nationalists, anti-Raj types of every kind.

Not so. Patricia's grandmother had been a member of the organization of Irish nationalist women started by Parnell. Her mother had deep sympathy for De Valera. The house was all along in as grievous danger from the Black and Tans and the Auxiliaries as it ever was from the Sinn Feiners.

It was a house which, in its time, had taken a lot of defending. Sir Walter Raleigh, when he was Mayor of Youghal, and – temporarily –

owner of most of Munster, lived in it. One of the things he did while
he was there – apart from planting the potato and smoking tobacco
under the aged yews which today people sit under arguing about
cigarettes and lung cancer – was to invite the poet Spenser to stay
with him and write.

As is known, Spenser had the devil of a long thing to write, and I
have been told since that the climate of the Blackwater valley is not
a stimulus to writers. Soothing, soporific, are the words used about
it.

But Spenser did at least get so far as to enable Raleigh to
announce that some cantos of *The Faerie Queene* were written
from 'my Oriel Window in Youghal'. I have sometimes sat at that
Oriel window. It is perhaps sentimental, possibly even fatuous, to
find a particular pleasure in reading a canto of *The Faerie Queene*
while looking out of the window the man sat at when he wrote it.
But perhaps it is legitimate to allow oneself from time to time the
luxury of these sentimentalities, these fatuities.

What Raleigh esteemed about the house – not that it did him
much good in the end – was that it had the town wall around it. This
very same amenity appealed, a couple of centuries later, to Patricia's
grandfather, Sir Henry Blake. He, lifting himself by sheer energy
out of the backwoods of County Galway, had been Governor
successively of the Bahamas, Newfoundland, Jamaica, Hong Kong
and ultimately Ceylon. When he finally retired, the situation in
Ireland was such that it must have been obvious to a man of such
experience that – whatever his own views might be – he could be
ignorantly deemed a symbol of the Ascendancy and have his head
shot off as he walked his fields.

The wall provided a partial and prudent answer to the question
of how to have a big house and security too. It was also, in later
days, a persistent reminder to his grand-daughter of the 'realities'
of life. Statements about the 'realities of life', together with such
allied phrases as 'politics is the art of the possible', are repeatedly
mouthed by the mean-spirited to insinuate that the 'realistic' thing
to do is simply to put up with what we have, to regard all theories of
possible betterment with suspicion and deride them as dangerous
'messianism'.

The conclusion that Patricia drew from the 'facts of life' represented by the wall and the armed gardeners was different. If you
find yourself in a position where, without them, you may get shot or
burned out, then you must have them. But you tolerate that wall
and those guns on the understanding that you are applying your

best exertions to changing such an abominably uncivilized condition of life.

In the case of Myrtle Grove the physical defences were supplemented by a spiritual one – the fact that her grandmother was supposed to have the power of the evil eye. When the old lady sat in the library, the garden boy used to creep past the window on hands and knees for fear of accidentally encountering that eye and being blasted. At the age of seventy or thereabouts she learned Hebrew, the better to study the Scriptures and compare them with other historical or mythical writings in which she was interested. As a child Patricia hunted half the day and in the evenings, supine on a board for reasons of deportment, lay drinking madeira wine and reading *The Golden Bough*.

If she complained from time to time that she had 'nothing to do', her grandmother was likely to ask her exactly how many petals there were on a rare flower in the garden. 'You don't know? Then go and count them. There's always something to do.'

Inspired by the energy and curiosity of this grandmother, and of her own mother too, before she was twenty she had ridden across the Rockies, lived for months in a hut in Tahiti, and walked right across Central Africa making a 'language map' for the Royal Geographical Society. She had also, as I have said, got herself gaoled – as the traditional Beautiful Spy – in Ruthenia. It was a common love of that neck of the woods which brought us together at the party in London where we met.

For a person with that kind of background, the rocks and rapids of politics on the British left in 1939 were less intimidating than they would have been to a properly brought up English girl – to, for instance, most of those who had been debutantes along with her at the time when debutantes still existed and were presented at Court with absurd formalities amid thickets of ostrich feathers.

Nevertheless, when the news of the Soviet-German Pact came in, I could not help wondering whether the rocks might prove more dangerous than any even she could have imagined.

15   Katz Cradle

I HAD recently resumed my habit of travelling at least once a fortnight to Paris, partly because news of the kind I wanted to get was more 'available' in Paris than in London (where one would so often spend hours seeking to penetrate what one supposed was the discretion and 'English reticence' of some leading figure, only to discover that he knew nothing anyway) and partly – and more particularly – to consult and exchange information with such old friends and fellow-workers as Otto Katz (then operating under the name of André Simone), and that revered genius, Egon Erwin Kisch.

Though he died abruptly at the end of a rope, pronouncing me responsible for his misfortune, historians ought not to forget Otto Katz. No portrait gallery – rogues' gallery, some would say – of the period would be quite complete without the putty-coloured visage of that most talented propagandist and intriguer.

Pretty soon every schoolboy will think he knows all about that time, certified as having been full of starry-eyed do-gooders with pink illusions which, when darkness came at noon, blew up in their faces and turned them a neutral grey or else deep blue. Not so much, probably, will be heard of the late Katz – a man, nevertheless, reeking of eighty-five per cent proof *Zeitgeist*, and producing some pervasive practical effects upon events. Manuals of journalism for schools should have a bit about him, too.

He had sidled into my life in the summer of 1932, when he was acting as a kind of assistant director of the great anti-war congress of that year at Amsterdam. After the closing session, I found myself at midnight sweating horribly in a hotel bedroom, helping to translate the official German text of the congress manifesto into

137

English – which must be, as all agreed, as jolly and popular in style as the *Daily Mirror* and as rigidly exact as the Athanasian Creed.

Every so often, a grave smile and a light sigh floated in from the corridor, both brought to us by a smallish, light-footed man with a big head and abnormally broad shoulders hunched in a way to suggest that his burdens were indeed heavy, but he could bear them, and yours, too, if you cared to confide them to him. His smile said that whatever might be the faults of others working for peace that night, our little group was the salt of the earth – so brilliant and devoted that we should certainly produce splendid results, dead on time, if it killed us. He had the air of a stage manager going round the dressing-rooms of a troupe on the verge of hysteria.

When I asked who he was, they said, 'You don't know who Otto Katz is? Oh!'

After the sleepless night, he invited me at breakfast-time to drink brandy with him on the terrace, and we talked about the congress. I spoke with enthusiasm. He ascertained that I had been, until recently, a correspondent of *The Times* in the United States. Presently he went about his business, which, as it turned out, was to prepare and issue to the continental news agencies an interview with 'the distinguished former foreign director of *The Times*', who heartily endorsed all objectives of the congress, and had some sharply disobliging things to say about the British Government.

I protested to Katz, demanding corrections and denials of the story. People, I said, would think Wickham Steed had turned red in the night. He said: 'But as a sincere supporter of our cause and an experienced journalist, you appreciate that any retraction could be damaging to the excellent effect already obtained. *The Times* will doubtless issue any denials necessary. It will help to stimulate discussion.'

'But it's preposterous to describe me like that.'

'I felt the phrase made a clearer impact. In journalism,' he said, fluttering his hand in a stagy gesture, 'one should try for clarity of impact.'

His staginess had a basis in experience. He had worked in various capacities for provincial theatres in northern Bohemia. Almost the only way to anger him was to doubt his story that at some time during that period he had been married to Marlene Dietrich. You could abuse him with impunity, but, if you doubted these nuptials, he became passionate, challenging you to go to Teplice, or wherever it was, and examine the records.

Along some political or journalistic channel – it was certainly a career open to talent – he had moved into the tumultuous Berlin entourage of the late Willi Muenzenberg, whom many people took to be the main dynamo of the German Communist Party. Whatever may be the truth about all that, Muenzenberg – who claimed to be an illegitimate nephew of Kaiser Wilhelm II – had made a vital impact upon the political life of Europe. He had snatched the journalism of the extreme left from the hands of the pedants, insisted that a modern revolutionary newspaper could be as 'popular' in today's terms as an old-time revolutionary broadsheet, and that the technical tricks, skills, and 'appeal' of the stunting, pandering, sensation-mongering capitalist press were to be not despised, but learned. His success, particularly with the picture paper *AIZ*, which for a time was the largest-circulation weekly in Central Europe, had important consequences in Italy, France and Latin America. Muenzenberg's offices in the Wilhelmstrasse, across the way from the Foreign Office, were also the centre of those numerous international organizations (the League Against Imperialism for example), which, while the communists supplied the inspiration and driving force, did at moments of crisis rally many sorts and conditions of non-communists and anti-communists who wanted to get moving and found no other bus going their way.

In all this, Otto Katz was first the pupil, later the right-hand man and, ultimately, it was often asserted, the inspirer of Muenzenberg; he was certainly the chief engineer of the Muenzenberg machine. After Hitler moved in on both sides of the Wilhelmstrasse, Katz, who now called himself André Simone, operated from a series of headquarters in Paris. He padded about Paris, Geneva, London, New York and Chicago, exercising and developing an almost necromantic capacity for getting people who naturally loathed and suspected one another organized for joint action. The nature of the – so to speak – material he worked on seemed not to interest him greatly: he was as happy welding mutually hateful novelists and poets into a literary League for the defence of this or that, as he was arranging for a couple of Tory Lords and someone from Transport House to turn up on a platform with the editor of *l'Humanité*. The more improbable the *combinaison*, the more it charmed him. Indeed, after a visit with him to the United States, the Roman Catholic Prince Loewenstein told me that, though prepared for anything, he had, after all, been startled when he saw Herr Simone-Katz 'genuflect three times and kiss the ring of a cardinal to whom he then presented a Marxist professor just out of jail in Rio de Janeiro'.

All this time Katz was busy, too, as a very sharp-shooting press agent and public relations counsellor for the organizations in which he was interested. Almost weekly he brought off the tricky shot of planting a damaging anti-fascist story in a pro-fascist newspaper, and under his original impulse his stories ran about the world like snooker-balls. They certainly had an 'impact'. He regarded journalism simply as a means to an end, a weapon. In this I found him sympathetic. Long before, in New York and Washington, I had come to the conclusion that the real humbug of the press begins only when newspapers pretend to be neutral, impartial fact-purveyors, 'servants', so help me, 'of the public'.

Arriving in Paris from Spain unexpectedly one day during the Spanish War, I telephoned Katz at the office of the *Agence Espagne*, the news agency of the Republican Government which he organized and directed. As was usual when one telephoned any office run by Katz, an excited voice said, '*Si, si, mais, s'il vous plaît*, be so good speak *deutsch, bitte schoen, momentito*,' and then Katz came on the line shouting, 'Thank God you're here, come at once, urgent.' He plunged immediately into business. 'Have I ever told you that you are considered by many, myself included, the best journalist in the world?'

'Often, when you wanted to get something for nothing out of me.'

'Well, what I want now is a tip-top, smashing, eye-witness account of the great anti-Franco revolt which occurred yesterday at Tetuan, the news of it having been hitherto suppressed by censorship.'

I said I had never been in Tetuan and knew of no revolt there.

'Not the point at all,' he said impatiently. 'Nor have I heard of any such thing.' The point, he explained, was that a crucial moment had been reached in the supply of arms to the battling Spanish Republicans.

Occasionally, despite non-intervention, the government of Léon Blum, under pressure from the left, agreed that all concerned should shut both eyes tight while the military supplies were rushed across the Catalan frontier. At this moment a major battle was being mounted in Spain. On the frontier a big consignment of field guns was ready. The outcome of the battle might depend on its getting through. Next morning a strong deputation of communist deputies and others was to call on Blum, asking for a little shut-eye. Blum, naturally, was always more malleable when anything happened to suggest that Franco might, after all, lose the war. It was thus essential, Katz pointed out, that a jolt of that kind should be administered now. Something with a clear psychological impact. What better for the purpose than news of a sudden revolt against Franco at the very origin and source of his first onslaught, Spanish Morocco? Why not, for instance, Tetuan? That, he said, would have impact.

There seemed to be just a chance, and we worked on that story at a high pitch of anxiety and excitement. Our chief anxiety was that, with nothing to go on but the plans in the guide-books, which were without contours, we might have democrats and fascists firing at one another from either end of an avenue which some travelled night-editor would know had a great hump in the middle. The fighting, accordingly, took place in very short streets and open squares. As we saw it, an important feature of the affair was that sections of the Moorish soldiery, sickened by losses in Spain, had joined with civilian victims of colonial oppression and Spanish anti-fascists in united, if desperate, action. It meant that the same thing might happen in Spain itself. Katz was insistent we use a lot of names, of both heroes and villains, but express uncertainty over some of them – thus in the confusion of the struggle outside the barracks it had been impossible to ascertain whether the Captain Murillo who died so gallantly was the same Captain Murillo who, months ago in Madrid . . .

In the end it emerged as one of the most factual, inspiring and yet sober pieces of war reporting I ever saw, and the night-editors loved it. When the deputisation saw Blum in the morning he had been reading it in newspaper after newspaper and appreciating its significance. He was receptive to the deputation's suggestions. The guns got through all right, and the Republicans won that battle.

(I should say here that when, later, I published part of this story in New York, a defender of Blum wrote a furious denial that such could have been his attitude. He purported to know – I have no idea how – that no such motives could have actuated Blum. He may, of course, be right. Perhaps, for instance, Blum was interested because a revolt in Tetuan would shake the faith of betwixt-and-between Franco supporters in France, who thus would be less liable to make a scandal about the dispatch of arms to the Republicans. The defender I refer to wrote with such assurance that one is forced to suppose it is at least possible that he really did have some knowledge not available to other people. The supposition is at least strong enough to make it seem only fair to put his view – which I still think quite mistaken – on record here.)

Many people to whom I have at one time and another told this little story of the Tetuan revolt have been themselves revolted, profoundly shocked. Or at least they said they were. When I first published it as part of an article in a weekly paper, the late Dick Crossman referred to it with disgust in a piece he wrote for the *News Chronicle*. Aware that Mr Crossman had himself played a considerable role in British wartime propaganda, I was in turn taken aback. Was it, then, possible that throughout the life-and-death struggle with Hitler our propagandists had all along taken the view that their paramount duty was to be gentlemen, and not to tell lies, however damagingly misleading these might be to the enemy? What about, I thought as I noted Mr Crossman's disdain for the Tetuan trick, the 'Man Who Never Was' and suchlike episodes?

Reading on, I was fascinated to find that what fretted Mr Crossman was not that the thing had been done, but that I seemed to be quite happy, retrospectively, to have had a hand in it. According to him, it was true that he and colleagues had done that sort of thing during the war, but they had done it with gentlemanly distaste. '"Black" propaganda,' wrote Mr Crossman, 'may be necessary to war, but most of us who practised it detested what we were doing.'

A comfortable ethical position, if you can stop laughing. To me, at least, there seems something risible in the spectacle of a man firing off his propaganda-lies as, one presumes, effectively as he knows how, but keeping his conscience clear by 'detesting' his own activities. After all, if he does not think the cause for which he is fighting is worth lying for, he does not have to lie at all, any more than the man who sincerely feels that killing is murder is forced to shoot at those enemy soldiers. He can become a conscientious objector, or run away. *'Paris vaut bien une messe'*, and I do not recall that Henry of Navarre ever claimed that he had detested his own 'cynical' behaviour.

At any rate, Katz had none of these inhibitions and did his work *con amore*. He had, of course, his failures, most of them, so far as I could observe, resulting from a quality rather often found in people of his background, namely a tendency to get in a muddle about the English. I do not have that background, but I am conscious of being in a muddle about them too. He could simultaneously attribute to them almost super-human cunning and intelligence, and sub-human stupidity and credulity. He would thus sometimes spend time shooting, so to speak, at gun-emplacements which did not exist, and at others imagine that he had duped people by some manoeuvre which the simplest could see through.

He was very proud of having secured for whatever office it was he was finally running in Paris – I have forgotten what name it went under – the services of a young Czech who, Otto claimed, could pass anywhere as an absolutely typical young Englishman. I forget, too, just what benefits were supposed to accrue from this – perhaps the idea was that in this role he could better effect contact with voyaging V.I.P.s, make friends and influence people. A little difficulty was that, for reasons no doubt sufficient, the young man would have had trouble in getting a visa to go to England to get the 'tip-top' English clothes which Otto, by now quite intoxicated with his particular Pygmalion act, thought desirable. However, a Paris tailor was found who claimed to understand, more or less, what was considered correct for business or *le sport* by English chic (in both senses of the word) types. And they rigged that poor young Comintern-commando up in an outfit of which it could be said that anyone who did not immediately discern on seeing him coming that this must be some Czech dressed up in a Frenchman's idea of an Englishman would have needed his eyesight tested.

I said as much to Otto, who was offended and became moody. Then a fine idea cheered him.

'Are you quite sure,' he said gently, 'that you yourself understand quite what is the correct thing in England? After all, my friend, you have lived so much of your life in Central Europe, in the United States. And even in London, do you see a great deal of the right people, socialites and such? It is easy to lose touch with English Society. It is not,' he added kindly, 'your fault. All the same, in my view Tommy looks absolutely . . . what is the word? . . .pukkah.'

He laughed, repeating 'pukkah' with pleasure.

'Tommy?' I asked, incredulously.

'I want,' said Otto, 'us all to get used to calling him "Tommy". A good, non-committal name.'

Irked, I could only remark that the address of his new office was, in every sense, a good one – it was in the Rue de l'Ancienne Comédie.

I never knew just how Otto Katz got out of France a little while before the twist of events which produced in turn the Nazi-Soviet Pact and the supression of the French Communist Party. He escaped the fate of those refugees who were first arrested by the French and then killed by the Germans. He spent the greater part of the war, I think, in Mexico, returning later, after the German defeat, to Prague, where he became a kind of foreign or diplomatic adviser to the official communist newspaper *Rude Pravo*.

Some years later he was hanged by the communists, and just

before he went to the gallows made a confession saying that he would have done well enough had he not, at an early date, been misled and recruited by me as an agent of the British Intelligence Service.

16   Pop Goes the Weasel

A MAN who claims to have been present at the time told me recently a poignant story of a discussion held in the Kildare Street Club, Dublin, in the last week of August 1939. I suppose if you amalgamated the London Carlton Club and the Athenaeum and then stuffed the end product with moth-balls, you would get something resembling the Kildare Street Club. It is, for instance, the place where two men quarrelled for life because, due to acoustics and confused mentality, while Mr A was making bitter comments on the coldness of the bath water, Mr B understood him to be aspersing, as frigid, Mr B's daughter.

However, by the late August of that year the news that some kind of international conflict might well be brewing was already known at the Club. The late Earl of Wicklow, mulling over the situation with friends, said they could take it from him that the whole idea of war was nonsense.

'Austria-Hungary,' said he, 'has learned her lesson from the last war. If Hitler were to attack, Austria-Hungary would take him in the rear, and he knows it.'

With regret, his friends reminded him that Austria-Hungary, as such, no longer existed, and that its disparate portions were, directly or indirectly, under the control of Hitler himself.

The Earl reflected briefly and then said, 'Well, be that as it may, Hitler will still not dare to act. He has to reckon with the Serbs. The Serbs, and mark my words, the Serb is a good fighting man,' said he, 'hate the Boche. Serbia will take Hitler in the rear, and he knows it.'

Sadly they told him the situation regarding Serbia – how it had ceased to exist as a separate nation, been merged into Yugoslavia, and how, for various reasons, Yugoslavia was in no sort of shape to be conducting decisive attacks upon Hitler's rear.

'In that case,' said the Earl of Wicklow, 'the whole thing is reduced to an absolute farce.'

The idea that the whole thing had been reduced to an absolute farce was, with more or less justification, according to your view-point, the first reaction of millions of honest Britons to the news that 'Hammer' Molotov and champagne merchant Ribbentrop were together in Moscow, arranging to be friends for evermore. Witty, encouraging and inaccurate to the last, the British Foreign Office spokesman said, 'All the Isms are Wasms.'

No one old enough to have been politically conscious at the time is likely to forget the bubble of passions, the frantic accusations and counter-accusations, the 'agonizing re-appraisals', the re-affirm-ations of faith, the hubbub of emotions, which thereupon broke out. And, of course, people too young to have been there must by now find a lot of the excitement irrelevant and incomprehensible. It was real enough that night.

After seeing the news on the ticker I went home and brooded much of the night, and in the morning took the telephone off the hook – it was sufficiently evident what the various people who would ring one up would, respectively, and in contradiction of one another, say. And indeed they have been saying it ever since.

I went down to the *Daily Worker* deliberately rather late – I had my own mind made up and I thought it would be tedious to have to watch a lot of other people making up theirs.

At that time, the paper, after being evicted from the Dickensian barn it originally inhabited in Tabernacle Street, where the electric light was constantly failing and much of the work had to be done by candle light, was housed in the City Road, and the public house we used, just across the road, was the original Eagle where the weasel went pop.

Naturally, being so situated, we had done a lot of research into the origins of the rhyme and what exactly the weasel was. Our consensus, for what it is worth, was that the 'weasel' was one of those big tailor's irons. A hundred and fifty years ago, the City Road was a road leading through fields and open countryside to pleasure gardens somewhere in the neighbourhood of what is now Camden Town – or perhaps still farther out. In any case, to go 'up and down the City Road' was a practice indicating dissipation and extravagance, and the expense was increased by the habit, fashion-able it seems among the City apprentices and their masters, of breaking the journey by a halt for drink at the Eagle. And the outcome was that the out-of-pocket tailor had to pawn or 'pop' the principal tool of his trade, the weasel.

The public house was lavishly decorated with drawings by the *Daily Worker* cartoonist Rowney – formerly of the army in India and later killed in Spain. He had a strong, rough line, very suitable for harsh political cartooning and seen to great advantage on the walls of a profoundly cockney public house. There was a large one of a tailor actually popping his weasel which was particularly admired by the proprietor, who had rubbed Rowney's slate clean of heaven knows how many unpaid drinks when the drawing was delivered.

The place did good business in those days – partly because the *Daily Worker* staff and people from King Street who had come along to advise and supervise, and people from all over who had come to wheedle from the paper free publicity for their bazaar or protest march, all used it, and partly because, in consequence, there were rarely less than three plain-clothes men from the C.I.D. putting their whisky down to expenses inevitably incurred in the pursuit of important political secrets such as might be expected to drop from the lips of the subversive types regularly there assembled.

I remember remarking, as we sat that August morning in the gritty sunshine that came in from City Road, that it certainly looked like being a hard winter. For it was already evident that, however necessary the Pact may have been to the Russians, by signing it they had effectively dynamited everywhere all the Popular Fronts, the vague but comforting alliances between Reds and anti-Nazi Conservatives. We were out, from now on, in a very cold cold.

I was, it goes without saying, powerfully and instinctively moved to take that opportunity to break with the communists there and then and brigade myself with the 'Churchillian Tories'. Personal considerations swayed me in that direction, not least among them the fact that Patricia had just run away with me and I felt that now, as a result of the latest turn of events, I was getting her to jump into a much deeper hole than she could have foreseen a few months before. On the other hand, quite apart from the high political rights and wrongs of the matter – and I was uncomfortably undecided as to who was right and who wrong – I was dominated by the feeling that I had, of my own free will, joined, so to speak, a regiment and that I had better soldier along with it, particularly at a moment when it was obviously going to come under pretty heavy fire.

It seemed to me that in those dead days of the Popular Front I had had a rather easy time being a communist, and it would be, to say the least of it, shabby to quit now.

And, of course, there were other powerful reasons in favour of fighting things out on whatever line the communists might finally determine to adopt. You cannot work closely with people for years without enmeshing yourself in a network of personal – sentimental, if you like – loyalties and affections.

Nevertheless, the fact that a person is swayed by his 'group' does not answer the question how and why – assuming that he had a choice in the matter – he got into the group in the first place. And in this matter I think that a good many people in England whose business it should be to understand why people become communists are the prisoners of their own propaganda – always a dangerous situation and, in this case, useful only to the communists themselves.

For years people have been going around and about saying that in Britain communism is an alien thing, that it is repugnant to all but the physically starved or the mentally distorted or those who may imagine that they are going to float on a high tide of roubles.

Such an account of the situation is patently untrue, or at least miserably inadequate, and therefore, as I say, dangerous. The reality – and it is a serious matter – is that communism can and does have deep affinities with British radicalism. Manchester and London did as much to shape Karl Marx and Marxism as did the Rhineland or the Paris Commune – perhaps more. And, paradoxical as it may seem, communism has – or at least very often has – a particular appeal to people brought up in the British public schools and universities, especially people with a classical and Christian education. The Greek dramatists and both the Testaments smoulder with passages which, at any rate to a young man, are incitements to revolt against orthodox society, to throw in his lot with the 'have nots' against the 'haves'. And if you ask me what first – long before I experienced Central Europe in the inflation time, or attended the American crash of 1929 – 'conditioned' me to be susceptible to the appeal of communism, I should have to say that it was, for example, the Magnificat I listened to every Sunday at evensong in the village church, and Antigone's defiance of Creon in Sophocles' play.

To draw attention to the putting down of the mighty from their seats is by no means an innocuous proceeding – unless, of course, the congregation is asleep at the time and does not notice what is being said or sung.

All the same, it was somewhat melancholy to sit there in the

Eagle and reflect that at least half one's friends were soon going to stop speaking to one, perhaps for ever. I recalled a sentence written by my great-grandfather, then Lord Cockburn, who was a young Whig in the Edinburgh of the early nineteenth century, a time when, as he says in his memoirs, 'even in private society a Whig was viewed somewhat as a Papist was in the days of Titus Oates. Very dear friendships were in many instances broken, and although the parties may have survived till age and changed times made longer severance absurd, the reconcilement was always awkward and never true. This incompatibility of public difference with private cordiality is the most painful recollection that I have of those days, and the most striking evidence of their hardness.'

It occurred to me that world events were conspiring to make a lot more difficult even than it had looked at the outset any reconciliation between Patricia and her parents, of whom she was profoundly fond.

On the news that she was running away with me, her mother had said, 'Do you realize that, if your brothers were in the diplomatic service, a scandal of this kind would force them to resign?'

Patricia said, 'But in fact they are not in the diplomatic service.'

'That,' said Mrs Arbuthnot characteristically, hammering the floor with her stick, 'is not the point.'

Major Arbuthnot voiced a different objection. He had been proud, he said, of holding a certain record at the Carlton Club – he was the only member who had three sons and a son-in-law, all of whom were members too. Now, though Patricia's first husband would no doubt remain a member, he would cease to be the Major's son-in-law, and the record score would have to be wiped out.

Though endearing and nostalgic, these reactions seemed, at first, those of people imprisoned on the stage of a period piece. I soon found that the contrary was the case. Regretting the ruins of their Edwardian period – including the loss, first gradual, then sudden, of the greater part of their fortune – they yet managed a singularly lively and alert existence in the present. Like all honest and lively elders, their attitudes were annoyingly unpredictable to contemporaries suffering from arrested development. Major Arbuthnot, indeed, who could take pleasure in quite contradictory ideas at the same time, considered it his congenial duty to *épater* people of pompous or rigid mind wherever he found them. Mrs Arbuthnot, who superficially seemed the archetype of the Edwardian *grande dame*, was in profound sympathy with Irish nationalism, detested 'colonialism' and 'racialism', and first warmed to me when she learned that I had actually fought against Franco whom she despised as a disloyal officer and a puppet of the disgraceful Hitler. Both of them had that warmth and openness of heart which is the product of a deep inner self-assurance.

17 Unnatural Break

WHEN I was at the *Daily Worker* the paper was more or less continuously on the verge of financial ruin – except during a short period at the very end of the war and in the first months of the peace, when, chiefly as a result of the battle of Stalingrad, communists everywhere could enjoy some reflected sunshine.

Pay-day was something like a game of hoop-la, with a lot of players and not enough prizes. Rarely indeed was there enough in the cash-box on Friday to enable everyone to get paid his full weekly wage – which was grimly meagre anyway. The total was shared out by the manager, a humorously tough type from the Elephant and Castle district who later was killed in Spain, on the basis of a kind of inverted means test. Staff members whose wives were about to give birth, or the ceilings of whose kitchens had caved in and had to be repaired at heavy expense, got a bit more than others.

Once, after that manager had been killed, I found a new, temporary manager sitting in his office on a Thursday morning apparently half dead of apprehension. He had looked at the available funds, and their low ebb had scared him. He felt it would be terrible to have to face the staff on the morrow with such more than usually bad news. And just as he was feeling like that, a man – sent he thought at the time by Providence, but by this morning he feared it might have been the Devil – had come in and given him a sure-fire tip on a 20-1 outsider running on Thursday at Haydock Park or wherever it was. And the temporary manager had taken half of all the money available for the wages and backed that horse with it.

'Should that animal fail,' he said, trembling – the tension was such that he felt he had to confess his rash act to someone – 'the lads'll about kill me.' However, the tipster had not been the Devil but Providence, and that week everyone got full pay and even some arrears.

Fairly soon, however, the government put an end to our political as well as our economic troubles by suppressing the *Daily Worker*. There came an afternoon in 1940 when one of those C.I.D. men who had so often and so attentively watched us playing the pin-tables at the Eagle came across the road and presented us with the notice of suppression. Noticing me among those present, he displayed a certain embarrassment, and presently revealed its cause.

He was a busy man. On that same afternoon he had another paper to suppress – namely my weekly newsletter, *The Week*. But it appeared that, under some British regulation attached to the Act which enabled them to suppress at all, there was also an obligation to serve the notice upon the owner or responsible publisher in person, and in that responsible person's own place of business. That, at least, was the policeman's interpretation of his duty, and so what were we to do? Here was I – also a busy man, and due to be busier still when we had to deal with the situation that would arise from the suppression – and we were in the City, and the offices of *The Week* were literally miles away in Victoria Street.

Asked, courteously enough, by the policeman whether I would engage myself to meet him a little later in Victoria Street for the sake of being put out of business a second time, I pointed out that I was likely to be working pretty hard in the next little while. It was an allusion which he perfectly understood, for it was obvious that the moment the *Daily Worker* was suppressed we should all be getting busy issuing illegal versions of it, which was going to be a dangerous and time-absorbing business.

Finally, the Inspector asked me whether I would care to have him drive me down in the police car, so that *The Week* could be suppressed with a minimal loss of valuable time. I thought for a moment that it could be considered unseemly for me to go cruising on such an errand at the expense of Scotland Yard. But, after a moment's reflection, I accepted the offer and we shot across the town in the police car, making excellent time between the suppressed *Daily Worker* and about-to-be-suppressed *Week*.

Within the hour, they had shut up *The Week*, and as they did so I had that peculiar sense of relief one sometimes has when they finally tell you you have to take to your bed, or go to hospital. You may be in pain but the administrative side of things, the awkward decisions, are their pigeon now.

For a little while we did run an illegal *Daily Worker* – a tiresome business because one was aware that in fact the thing was a mere gesture, the publication reaching hardly anyone. And yet you could get five years hard labour if you were caught at it, just as though you had been pouring criminal incitements into the ears of millions.

I dare say the affair was almost as annoying for the Special Branch of the C.I.D. as it was for us – for in this strange charade they too had to pretend that whatever we were doing was of vital importance, and during that nasty butt-end of winter they had to follow us about in all weathers.

During that time of relative isolation you needed not only lights in the darkness (there were really quite a lot of them) but barometers to tap and thermometers to read, so that you could feel you knew rather more about the state of the weather than you could learn from the newspapers or the meetings of the faithful.

In this respect I found much pleasure, comfort and utilitarian advantage in the society of a Mr Harry, who kept, in our neighbourhood, a big public house which combined a rich Edwardian cockney flavour with a faint element of up-to-date garishness, according well enough with the big motor-cars of military men in his yard by day, and the aircraft overhead dropping incendiary bombs into the roadway by night.

Apart from keeping this public house Mr Harry was a member of a family vaguely connected with what might be called the down-to-earth side of cockney entertainment. Through a cousin he had an interest in a boxing establishment or prize-ring somewhere, and another cousin had a piece of a music-hall, and someone else of the clan was promoting some other little show in the provinces. In token of all this, Mr Harry himself wore spectacularly expensive suits, had a carnation regularly in his buttonhole and smoked – right through the worst of all the shortages so far as I can recall – big cigars.

He was a man who felt that the first business of an inn-keeper is to be tolerant to all who do not actually disrupt by their conduct the harmony and comfort of the inn – and in time of war, and savagely aroused political feeling, to maintain that kind of balance is a considerable achievement. Mr Harry liked to achieve it, so that without much danger of being suddenly assailed by a fellow-drinker as a Moscow-minion, a fifth-columnist and probable Jew-baiter in disguise, I could spend a couple of hours there taking the temperature and tapping the barometer of what people were really saying, sometimes in the saloon bar, sometimes in the public. It was understood that I was an eccentric who refused to be 'typed' as an unfailing *habitué* of one or the other.

Mr Harry himself liked to make people at home. But he was also a busy man, and often did not take time to find out whether some vague rumour he had heard about one of his clients was true or not. Thus, when I first took to going there, he had picked up from somewhere or other a report that I was a former diplomat currently doing hush-hush work of a military nature. He at once told me that, at an unspecified period of his early youth – at the time I speak of he must have been in his late forties or early fifties – he had been in the Indian cavalry.

'Had my white charger, old boy,' he said, drawing luxuriously on the cigar, 'and rode all over India on it. Glorious. Never mind about the bombs – the old Empire will come through.'

Learning, a little later, that his earlier assumptions had been mistaken, and that I was something to do with 'the literary game', he told me, at a rather intense period in the blitz, that he himself had been, until very recently, a 'great reader'.

'Used,' he said, 'to like nothing better than settle down with something good.'

'What sort of thing did you read?'

'Well,' said Mr Harry, 'Thucydides, Dante – that sort of thing. But d'you know,' he said mournfully, listening to the sirens, 'this sort of thing's got on my nerves. I can't settle to that sort of thing nowadays. It's changed my reading habits altogether. Can you imagine what I read now?'

'Dickens?' I guessed. 'Or some of the modern novelists?'

'Nao,' said Mr Harry, his cockney broadening in disgust at my naïveté, my underestimation of the nerve-shocks he had received. 'Nothing but the back numbers of *Men Only*.'

'The *back* numbers?'

'Yus. Just the back numbers. The up-to-date ones get on my nerves. Too much of all this around us. Too much war.'

When Mr Harry admitted to himself, as he must have known with one half of his mind almost from the outset, that I was in some way mixed up with the communists, I knew that the political climate of Britain had considerably changed. It must have been a month or two after Hitler's attack on Russia that he mentioned to me that he had always been a close student of politics, and that he had always felt 'some sort of socialism or communism' to have a particular appeal.

154

'After all,' said he, 'you have to consider elementary human justice. Don't forget that, Claud, old boy.'

Because it was sometimes used by groups of fire-watchers the public house could on occasion, without interference by the police, stay open half the night. In an unusual upflare of common sense it was thought better that an incendiary bomb should be dealt with by a man who had been notably infringing the licensing laws than that it should be left to burn the neighbourhood. At one such moment Mr Harry and I were standing alone in the bar, very late, and he said to me, 'I can see it coming, Claud. The communists are going to take over the country when this little lot's finished with. And I don't say they shouldn't. I don't say you haven't common human justice on your side, Claud. All I ask of you is just one thing.'

'What's that, Harry?'

'All I ask, Claud, when you and your pals take over and make that great revolution, that you'll just leave me my King, my constitution and my country.'

He had tears in his eyes, and it was hard not to be able to offer him a binding guarantee.

A year or more after the war was over, Mr Harry took a trip to the Channel Islands – the only bit of the British Isles actually occupied by the Germans during the conflict. He was enthusiastic. He described some huge beer cellar which the German military had remodelled and decorated in the Munich manner – a magnificent place, which, by its existence and the amenities it could offer to the English visitor, showed that out of evil some good could come.

I made some disobliging remark to the effect that I had read somewhere that a good many of the Channel Islanders had made quite a good thing out of the war – had collaborated with the invaders 100 per cent, giving them lists of local Jews so that they could be deported, and so on. Mr Harry said he had heard similar reports in the islands, and judged them to be well-based.

'But you don't understand, Claud old boy,' he said, 'at the time they did that, those people thought the Germans were going to win.'

Within a couple of weeks of the German invasion of Russia, Mr Rust had begun to organize what turned out to be one of the most remarkable 'mass campaigns' in the history of the British left – the campaign to lift the ban on the *Daily Worker* and, incidentally, *The Week*. With extraordinary skill he fused the enthusiasm for the Russian fighters, the general belief of millions of British working people that now a lot of real tough friends had come to their senses and were fighting shoulder to shoulder with them, with the immediate objective of getting the ban raised. I was told at the time that, from quite an early date, Mr Churchill had expressed himself as in favour – or at least not opposed – to such action. But, as a result of what could seem a paradoxical structure of British politics ever since approximately 1924, it was the leadership of the Labour Party which most strenuously resisted the move, and used all its influence and knowledge of left politics to dissuade the rest of the government from doing anything of the kind.

It was not until, to the visible and aghast astonishment of those on the platform, the Labour Party's own conference at Central Hall, Westminster, in the winter of 1942–3, voted against the ban by a small but respectable majority, that the final event became inevitable.

The Week was told it would be allowed out, too.

At this moment a curious episode occurred. Half casually, half intently, Mr Rust asked me whether I did, in fact, propose to restart *The Week*. I was astonished. We had been campaigning for the freeing of both papers for months. He then said that there were some people at King Street who felt, or might be expected to feel, that *The Week* constituted an anomalous phenomenon – one which could even be embarrassing. I inquired in what sense that could be so? He explained that what was anomalous was that on the one hand, as a result of recent events, *The Week*, which hitherto had, so far as a lot of its subscribers were concerned, been seen as merely radical, and even anarchist, was now rated as an organ of the Communist Party. Yet, except in so far as its editor was associated with the *Daily Worker*, the Communist Party had no real say-so about *The Week*, no editorial or financial control. He made it clear that this was a situation which gave many people at King Street nightmares. And I could see, in a way, why. It was made clear to me that nobody would take it amiss if I just failed to take advantage of the lifting of the ban and devoted myself in future exclusively to the *Daily Worker*.

In some ways the notion was attractive, for I could see that the situation, which was so entirely different from that which *The Week* had been founded to exploit, and of which it had so successfully taken advantage in the 1930s, no longer existed – and had not, in fact, existed since, at the latest, the end of the 'phoney' war.

Yet the cool suggestion now being made irked me and caused me uneasiness. I had a feeling it might be better to keep my tiny boat in seaworthy condition.

18   The Long Train

IN the latter part of the war, communists were suddenly so popular that it nearly hurt. Every district organizer seemed to carry the Sword of Stalingrad in his brief-case. And I think it can hardly be denied that the communists, by their wholehearted – one could almost say reckless – devotion to 'the war effort' during that period, really did constitute themselves a factor of serious importance in the maintenance and increase of production, in the elimination of industrial conflict or friction, and in the combat against 'war weariness' and apathy. They were, after all, the most highly organized and efficient body of militants in the country. It was a curious experience to shift so suddenly from membership of a hated sect, to a position on a quite high-powered bandwagon.

Although, politically, I naturally welcomed the turn of events and the end of the nerve-racking period between the signature of the Nazi-Soviet Pact and the outbreak of the Nazi-Soviet war, from a strictly personal viewpoint the new situation, as it developed during the following couple of years, left me feeling increasingly at a loose end. Things were suddenly so cosy that one had the sensation that nothing one might write was really necessary – everyone was rushing in the right direction anyway.

It was naturally irksome to keep writing so much, so encouragingly, about the war effort without oneself getting into battle. We applied over and over again to get me credentials as a war correspondent. But Labour leaders opposed that, on the ground that having a war correspondent would increase the prestige of the *Daily Worker* – and anything was better than that. And the War Office objected, too – on the ground that a communist war correspondent would be either a Russian spy or an agitator, fomenting grievances among the troops.

Aware of this last objection, I suggested to Mr Brendan Bracken, Minister of Information – whom I had often occasion to attack, but always esteemed – that the difficulty might be circumvented. I could be a correspondent with the bomber squadrons over Germany, held, if necessary incommunicado on the base between missions. And the risk of my subverting a bomber crew must, I thought, be regarded as nugatory compared to the havoc I might wreak amid the infantry. Mr Bracken was sympathetic, and I believe supported my request with vigour. But nothing came of it.

I was thus almost exaggeratedly elated when, in April 1945, I found myself in San Francisco for the first gathering of the United Nations. We British, a pack of journalists, some pundits, and a mutter of diplomats, assembled in the bar known as the Top of the Mark to pay our respects to V.E. Day, the end of the war in Europe. It was a heavyish payment, because it consisted of listening to a speech lasting for forty-one minutes (I timed it) by Anthony Eden, British Foreign Secretary, a perpetually young man who spent a long life trailing a brilliant future behind him.

He made the ritual remarks about San Francisco, our host city: statements to the effect that just as San Francisco had recreated itself after disaster, so the world was going to do the same thing, through the United Nations. As he skied away expertly down the platitude slopes, there was time and leisure to look around.

So I looked down from this twentieth floor at Alcatraz and thought all the sad thoughts one had about a place like that. I told myself that oppressive as it was to be cooped up here, captive audience for Anthony Eden, it was a lot better than being cooped up in Alcatraz. Count your blessings.

Right through those foundation meetings of the U.N. I kept asking myself just how much influence the *locale* was having on the minds and emotions of that whole bizarre and powerful gathering.

An unanswerable question. But it was the kind of question we used to ask in Geneva, Switzerland, when the doomed predecessor of the U.N., the League of Nations, met in that city, reeking with all the fury of old European conflicts, and Mont Blanc slumbered aloofly above it all.

We had come across North America on what was called the Peace Train. It should have been exhilarating. But it was sad, too. The heads of delegations had flown out. But there were not enough planes to accommodate all the second echelon diplomats, the mob of politicians who thought their visible presence in San Francisco would roll up some votes for them back in Lyons or Liverpool, and

national and international spies disguised as diplomats, politicians
and journalists, and the genuine journalists, dozens of us, with a
general briefing to report to the world on the new dawn.

The tracks were cluttered with wartime traffic, so the train made
repeated stops at smallish towns along the way. And at each town,
there were crowds of people reverently watching the Peace Train
and hoping, expecting, that this time everything was going to be all
right. We were going to ensure the peace of the world, for ever and
ever. Once in Iowa and twice in Wyoming, I saw people move
forward and touch the train with their fingers. At one of the
Wyoming halts a woman cradling a baby in her arms brought the
infant close up to the train and had him touch it. That touch, she
felt, would help him grow up in a world at peace.

Some people on the train looked upon this as evidence of peasant-
type superstition prevailing in the Midwest. It couldn't, they said,
happen in Europe. As for me, I felt humble and, as I say, sad. All
that great faith and hope out there, and we inside in the Pullmans;
not, I thought, a bunch that was really going to live up to the
advance billing.

But we made it to San Francisco's lovely Opera House, much
tarted-up and rearranged for the opening session by the State
Department. A spokesman for the Department, looking round,
said, 'We want it to be worthy of the occasion. And if it isn't, all I
can say is it cost a whole wad of money.'

There they all were: Secretary of State Stettinius (hosting chair-
man of the conference); British Deputy Prime Minister Attlee plus
Anthony Eden; Foreign Affairs Commissar Molotov; T.V. Soong,
Chinese Minister for Foreign Affairs; and Secretary General Alger
Hiss. Also delegates from the whole wide world from Chile to
Ethiopia, going either way around the planet.

The sessions shuttled about between the Opera House and the
Veterans Building, and the people who wanted to know what was
happening shuttled about between the bar of the Palace Hotel,
where a lot of delegates plus Orson Welles and Rita Hayworth were
in spate, the bar of the St Francis, where similar goings-on were
going on, and, naturally, the Fairmont and the Top of the Mark.

Shuttling like that I found the ride through the city more excit-
ingly rewarding than anything that was likely to happen when I
reached destination. I had moments when I wished I could be just
travelling hopefully through that astounding town for ever, and
never arrive at wherever I was, in the cause of world betterment,
supposed to be.

The whole thing presented a problem.

You could go to the public sessions and be bored to tears listening to statesmen saying at length what you knew they had to say anyway. Or you could stick around where the action was. If you repeatedly failed to attend a public session, people who had subjected themselves to that ordeal accused you either of frivolity and lack of appreciation of the occasion and the gravity of the situation, or else of slinking off and conspiring somewhere. If you spent too much time at the public session, you lost touch with all the conspirators, and they treated you as a starry-eyed ninny, taking all that verbiage and show-off over there seriously.

But at the end of the day, the thoughtful conspirators, the lobbyists from all over and the long-eared journalists had a chance to meet up with the talking delegates, and those worthy men and women who had felt it their duty to hear the talk right off the vocal chords rather than scanning it through the prepared handout. Every evening some public-spirited organization such as the San Francisco Chamber of Commerce and a long list of other dedicated organizations laid on cocktail parties. Enormous affairs, where, through the roar of the decibels I once heard an American senator roaring to Lord Cranborne, British Secretary of State for Dominion Affairs:

'Strictly between these four walls, Viscount Cranborne, I want to tell you the entire clue and rationale of our policy. . .'

I tried to hear above the din what this momentous communication was going to be. Lord Cranborne, as was his manifest duty, tried to hear. But the decibels howled over us before either of us could get even the gist of it.

Possibly a big diplomatic opportunity missed.

But, in the meantime, there was San Francisco, full to bursting with its tight-packed history, so that on one street you thought you were back in the days of Crocker and the railroad boom, and on the next, that here was the kind of city of the future that Europeans used to dream about. Rightly, I did all the things residents tell you not to bother with, because they are the things tourists do. I went to Fisherman's Wharf and Chinatown and that place on the cliff where the sea lions jump. Somebody had produced, for the occasion of the conference, a little brochure called 'Where to sin in San Francisco'. Europeans bought it furtively, thinking it might be a guide to brothels. They found themselves disappointed. You could have taken your aunt to all the places listed, which were no more sinful than a dry martini.

But the air sparkled by day, and the fog and clouds came in off the ocean at evening, right on cue, the way everyone had said it would be. It was a lot more impressively head-turning, adrenalin-squirting, than Geneva. And I still kept wondering what impact all this was subconsciously exerting on all those men from all over. (A lot of them have been shot or gaoled since in their numerous homelands, but they were powerful then.)

When I was bored to near suffocation by their orations and perorations, I played a game. I forced myself to imagine all those fellows, from Stettinius, to Eden, to T. V. Soong to Molotov, the way they must have been when they were little kids in short knickers, with their chubby knees muddy from playing around in their yards. I thought how their mothers must have loved them, and have foreseen for them a fine future, doing good to the neighbourhood and perhaps all humankind. I compelled myself to identify with those mothers, and to offer thanks to the Almighty for the fact that those mothers were now dead, and could not witness what had really happened to those kids.

19   Emergency Exit

IT was an auspicious day to be cross-examined on one's reasons for approaching the Communist Party. I had just returned from my first visit to Ireland where I had been driven into a dock thigh-high with mud by Belfast dockers who believed me to be an agent of the Pope because I was selling the *Daily Worker*. That afternoon, arriving in Dublin, I had been chased down O'Connell Street by Catholic novices masked with white handkerchiefs and carrying razors, threatening to castrate me as an agent of Antichrist, also on the grounds that I was trying to sell the *Daily Worker*. At the same time on that same day I speak of, early disciples of the British fascists were smashing up Jewish shops in the East End of London a couple of miles from where R. Palme Dutt and I now sat, discussing why anyone like me should seek to join the Communist Party – unless of course he were a spy from the other side cunningly infiltrating the organization; having secured his credentials by ostentatiously resigning from *The Times* allegedly on the grounds of leftist hostility to the politics of that newspaper. That was a version of events which, I was well aware, must be prominent in the minds of the leaders of the British Communist Party.

Rajani Palme Dutt was one of the most brilliant thinkers I have ever encountered. He had that kind of luminous intelligence which enables a man to follow the exact minutiae of dogma while retaining the fullest flexibility in relation to reality – a mind in fact similar to that of Karl Marx himself. Sitting across the table from me in a typically horrible London tea-shop which, for obscure reasons, he preferred to the more cheerful surroundings of a pub, he wanted to know whether it was at Oxford that I had first been attracted to communism.

I should record that this conversation took place in the early 1930s, when communism was having a vigorous impact on Cambridge undergraduates (as we have all recently been reminded), and that Dutt, though an Oxford graduate, had been brought up in Cambridge, where his father was a doctor. I explained to him that the Oxford of my day was virtually innocent of any kind of serious class politics. The political battles, such as they were, were between the supporters of the Conservative and Labour Parties, and perhaps still more vehemently between the two wings – Asquithian and Lloyd Georgian – of the Liberal Party.

For myself, I regarded life in Oxford rather as a person regards a moving picture in relation to the real world outside the cinema. As I have already indicated, the real world for me was Central Europe, and my life in Budapest – where I spent the long Oxford vacations – was real life, and more especially real political life.

I explained to Dutt, who was some years older than myself, how the natural reaction of people of my age to the immediate post-war situation was one of revulsion from what we saw as the criminal imperialism and murderous warmongering of our elders, culminating in the equally criminal 'Carthaginian peace' imposed upon the defeated peoples of Central Europe. In fact I became at that time a starry-eyed and grossly romantic Hungarian nationalist, my enthusiasm for that cause only occasionally checked by the insane demand of some of the Hungarian nationalist leaders that the crown of Hungary be offered to the first Lord Rothermere. (He on his side repeatedly indicated his willingness to accept this offer if it would do anything to stem the tide of Jewish Bolshevism threatening, as he believed, to overwhelm Europe.)

So then what? Dutt wanted to know.

So then I went to Berlin and met, as I have recounted in this book, the great German nationalist Foreign Minister Herr Gustav Stresemann. Very few encounters with that devious politico were sufficient to convince me that sentimentalist sympathies with the defeated powers, fuelled as they were by the arguments of Maynard Keynes's *Economic Consequences of the Peace*, were mistaken and dangerous illusions. As I have also recounted, I was at this time introduced to the works of Lenin and from there went on to read first Bukharin and then Marx. It was at this point that I began to realize that the divisions were not, so to speak, vertical between nations, but horizontal, between the class strata of society. But at this time in Berlin all Marxists and incipient Marxists like myself were constantly subjected to lectures demonstrating that the development of

American capitalism – Der Fordismus – had rendered Marx a laughable back number. The problems of capitalism had been solved in Detroit without need of any nasty detour through Moscow. It was for this reason that when I at last joined the London *Times*, I did so on condition that I be appointed to New York.

'And when,' Dutt asked, 'did you arrive in New York?'

'In July, 1929,' I said.

Dutt's loud laughter shocked the decorous little tea-shop.

It became obviously unnecessary to spell out to him the experiences of the Great Crash and the horrors of the depression which followed. He knew all that as well as I did although he had not seen, first hand, the unemployed fighting for the garbage in the dustbins of hotels on Chicago's Michigan Avenue, had not seen General MacArthur's troops bayoneting the starving Bonus Marchers on Pennsylvania Avenue, Washington, had not heard Al Capone's eloquent defence of the capitalist system as one which made a career like his possible and profitable.

Dutt then, with some caution, approached a final point. As politely as possible, he explained that quantities of Englishmen had briefly scanned the works of Marx and Lenin, had even been revolted by some of the manifestations of the murderous quality of the capitalist system, but still believed that some form of liberal or social-democratic approach might be effective as a cure. I said, rather frivolously, that I was a Scotsman and therefore unaffected by the hideous evasiveness and lack of logic so common in the English character. For me, I explained, the communist approach seemed the only one likely to repair the situation, and, that being so, believing in the necessary unity of theory and practice, I considered it necessary for me to join the Communist Party both as a writer and as a worker in a street cell in Hammersmith to which I was assigned.

Taking a chance at being grievously misunderstood, I coined for Dutt's benefit a phrase which I still think basically true. 'I do not,' I said, 'believe that the communists will get us to heaven, but I do believe they are the only people who may prevent us going to hell.'

But that conversation had taken place twelve or more years ago. Now Hitler had been beaten and the circumstances were transformed. What was the role of the Communist Party in post-war Britain and what were my feelings about the contribution I was making to it?

It is always disconcerting, after long immersion in a particular kind of activity, to come up for air one morning and wonder whether you and your fellow-workers are getting anywhere at all. We ran faster and faster, and seemed to remain almost exactly in the same place. If Marx was right in noting that the crucial thing is not simply to understand the world but to change it, we seemed to be changing very little.

For example, to descend from the general to the particular, the circulation of the *Daily Worker* at about this period was not merely not rising, but falling. Well, of course, that was very easily explained – it was due to the war ending and the consequent change of political atmosphere. This was an explanation, all right, like another. But was it an excuse?

The size of communist representation in Parliament, fluctuating at that time, so far as I recollect, between one and two, could also be fully explained: the voters almost everywhere were certain the communist candidate could not win the seat, so to avoid wasting their suffrages they gave them to the Labour candidate instead. A very truthful account of the position. But just what *made* the voters so certain that the most sensational victory the communist was likely to achieve was the saving of his deposit? Worse still, what made the voters' prognostications ninety-eight per cent right?

A more personal feature of this depressing scene was my growing conviction that, although some British communists were doubtless proving immensely effective somewhere, my own effectiveness was sinking towards zero. Often I experienced that nightmare of the publicist in which he finds himself condemned to shout exhortations, warnings, funny jokes, and alarming disclosures down a telephone line with nobody at the other end of it. They have put down their receivers and gone to the pictures or a meeting of the Labour Party.

It was clear to me that if the circulation of the paper was falling, or at least failing to rise, the fault must be to a quite large extent mine. I was the most experienced writer there, I often wrote more of the paper than anyone else, and both before and during the war my writing had admittedly been effective, had had an impact – occasionally a major impact. I had a fairly clear idea of the nature of the fault. Just the same qualities, it seemed to me, which had made me an enthusiastic and effective commentator during, say, the period of hunger marches and anti-fascist brawls and riots in London, Paris and Marseilles; the period of the Spanish War; the electrically sultry period of Hitler's advance from Munich to the war; the period of the war itself – these qualities and dispositions appeared in some way to unfit me for what were called 'the tasks of reconstruction'. For the first time in my life I realized what people mean when they use the term 'maladjustment'. Hitherto I had supposed it was something that happened only to other people.

It is all very well to recognize the fault, but it is not really much use when you recognize at the same time that it is a fault which it is now too late to correct. I used to reflect that had I, for example, in years gone by, taken more trouble to study and steep myself in the history and essential character of the British Labour movement, had I exerted myself more vigorously to comprehend the British character, I should be better adjusted to the situation. But there was no time to start doing all that now.

I was thus in the unpleasing position of a man who has volunteered to help drive a car over rough roads and now finds that he has forgotten how to change gear and rather suspects that the car has taken a wrong turning anyway.

I had been in Paris attending some conference or other of Foreign Ministers, and Patricia had gone for a short holiday at her parents' house in Ireland. On the evening of our mutual return to London I told her suddenly – I had never even hinted at it before – that I was thinking about the possibility of dropping everything and starting an entirely new life. I had expected her to be startled. Instead she coolly remarked that she had noticed for months that for me the savour had gone out of things, and that as for her she had reached the same conclusion, but had not liked to mention it.

'The only thing is,' she remarked, 'what exactly would we use for money?'

It was undoubtedly a ticklish problem. The pay at the *Daily Worker* was still small, though, in contrast to the sort of thing that had happened in my early days there, it came regularly week by week. But it was possible to supplement it considerably by writing for communist newspapers abroad – notably in Poland and the Balkans. Also I could, very occasionally and under a plethora of pseudonyms, sell an article or short story to a non-political magazine, though my American outlets, which had been very profitable in the pre-war years when a known communist could still sell to non-communist publications in the United States, had clogged up at the beginning of the war and never reopened. Patricia had a small allowance from her father. I have forgotten what precisely our average income, including my earnings and Patricia's allowance, amounted to at the time – I suppose about £600 or £700 a year, which would be reduced to somewhere between £200 and £300 if I quit the paper and left London.

Furthermore, after years of more or less strenuous and somewhat specialized political journalism, I knew that it would take some time to develop, as it were, new muscles.

We had, naturally, almost nobody with whom we could discuss the position. Of course the people at the paper would have felt, quite sincerely, that the only proper course was for me immediately to go to them with my doubts and problems, so that a 'full and frank discussion' might be held. It would have been the correct communist way of doing things. Equally sincerely, I felt that it would achieve nothing useful whatever, and must inevitably produce exasperation and suspicion on all sides. I could not see myself successfully explaining the nuances of my attitude in acceptable terms. The nuances, so important to myself, would, like certain wines, 'travel badly' into strict Marxist territory. The fact that I did feel that way was incidentally a proof that, despite all those years at the paper, I had not, after all, become a very good communist. I thought that the more I kept my ideas and purposes to myself, the more I should be likely to save both myself and them a terrible lot of trouble. It was therefore impossible to take counsel with more than one or two intimate and truly reliable friends.

Nearly a year passed before Patricia and I made up our minds that, if we postponed the move until we had carpentered together some assurance of future financial security, we should perish of economic paralysis in London. We decided to sell the balance of the lease of our flat, which brought in a few hundred pounds, and take off for Ireland at the earliest practicable moment.

There remained a vital tactical problem to be solved. I was naturally anxious not to do harm to my old friends and associates at the *Daily Worker* by making any kind of spectacular exit. It would, I thought, be unbearable to become the centrepiece of a press furore in which I should inevitably be treated as a kind of Kravchenko, dashing out from the Iron Curtain to write *I Chose Freedom*. Maybe I really was 'choosing freedom', but, in my case, that seemed no good reason for biting the old comrades.

The easiest way of avoiding that undesirably spectacular exit seemed to be to fall gravely ill of a diplomatic illness. When you are in reasonably good health, there is a certain charm in the process of selecting which illness you are going, diplomatically speaking, to have. In earlier days the whole business was, I imagine, easy. If the worst came to the worst you could say you had brain fever – that undefined disease which so often hurried mysteriously to save the plots of so many Victorian novels. With the advance of modern medical science the thing becomes more difficult. In my experience, modern medical specialists do not worry unduly if you die, but they feel uneasy if they cannot record in some detail what you died of.

At this point a miracle occurred. I had (a strange thing for me) been sleeping badly, and used to take sleeping pills occasionally. One day I asked a friend of mine who, although not a doctor, was a distinguished chemist, whether he could recommend a pill which would induce sleep but would not, at the same time, give me an agonizing stomach-ache at the moment of wakening.

He inquired about the pills I had been using, inquired about the stomach-aches and said, 'I will get you some pills, but what you have to do is to get in front of an X-ray. What you have is a pretty severe stomach ulcer. The symptoms are unmistakable.'

He explained about some ingredient in my pills which, if you happened to have a stomach ulcer, touched it up and made you writhe.

It seemed too good to be true, but my friend fixed up an emergency X-ray for me in some laboratory, and when we got the pictures there it was – a genuine, entirely undiplomatic ulcer.

Just in case anyone thought this was a put-up job – which was of course exactly what everyone was going to think – I went to one of the big London hospitals and had another X-ray done there. The result was the same, and, this time, as it were, official. The doctor who told me the news was quite surprised. Possibly he had never before had the experience of telling a man he had a bad ulcer and seeing the man beam with pleasure and thank him warmly for the information.

In face of that neutral evidence, everyone agreed that a long rest was essential. I pointed out that as luck would have it I knew of a place which was ideal for the purpose.

In point of fact, Patricia, our eldest son Alexander and Andrew, our second son, still in his basket, had already flown to Ireland. The removal men had made preliminary arrangements for shifting as much of our furniture as had not been blown to bits in the house we had had before. And a few days later I was on the Fishguard–Cork boat, *en route* for the ancient town of Youghal, a town standing – like the poet Cavafy in E.M. Forster's description – 'at a slight angle to the universe'.

20 Seven-League Boots

Just once in a longish while you find you can write yourself an order for a pair of seven-league boots, and you travel inhumanly far in next to no time. It is only eight hours or thereabouts from Fishguard to Cork, but on the quay there in Cork I knew at once what kind of boots I had on. For whatever a person feels about Ireland – likes it, loathes it, or it merely blurs on him – it is a long way from England in all directions. Here and there it is a little nearer to America, but it is a long way from there, too.

In the car to Youghal that day I re-lived the sensations of being seventeen and travelling for the first time across Central Europe. Not, evidently, that there is the slightest resemblance, physical or otherwise, between Ireland and Central Europe. It is simply the 'other-ness', the difference between this or that new sort of life and whatever rut you have somehow jerked yourself out of, which brightens the eye of the beholder. And you can be in a dull rut at seventeen as easily as at forty-five.

We came into Youghal, running along beside the ocean where the thrust of the Blackwater's current fights the Atlantic tide. Here on the left, we had two neat new textile factories, claimed to be among the most up-to-date boxes of machinery in Europe, supervised technically by imported experts from Lancashire. A few hundred yards up the road behind them are a wishing-well and a magic tree where, surreptitiously, some people still hang rags torn from their clothes as they did before the Christians superseded the Druids. Some few hundred yards farther up the same road is the site where, in Ireland's last war with England, three men of the Irish Republican Army let off a land mine under the first truck of a British column. They had information that the truck was full of ammunition, but at the last moment there had been a switch and some boys belonging to the band were blown up instead.

At this end of town were the hotels, some with spacious names like 'Pacific' and 'Marine', and one called, with scrupulous honesty, 'Railway View'. It recalled a time when you could any day see an ocean, and a big river full of salmon and bass, and distant mountains, but to look straight out of the bedroom or dining-room and see a railway station was a worthwhile experience.

After that, the road narrowed to where the real Youghal lay, longitudinally squeezed, between the river and the hill; a beautiful, gnarled town where history smells as strong as blood.

It took us six weeks to find a house for ourselves, and more than two months to have it made habitable. For, as was natural in a country which had lived in a state of colonialism for centuries, there was a shortage of small country houses; everything seemed either too big, with hundreds of acres of land, or too small. And for equally historical reasons many, many houses were derelict. People got poorer and poorer, or emigrated, leaving the house to very poor relations, who could not afford to do otherwise than let the roof cave in above them.

The house we found, on a hillside a mile and a half from the town, had once been the summer residence of the Mayors of Youghal. Why, with so small a town around them, they needed a summer residence at all is not exactly known. It is supposed that in hot summers the open sewers and gutters stank and were deemed unhealthy. At other seasons, the house and its courtyard were used for the collection of tribute from the country. The tributary cattle were brought in and penned in the yard behind a gate with powerful stone pillars. A little above the house there was a square watch-tower. When I say 'was', it is still there, like the house, but in those days – the early sixteenth or late fifteenth century – when the house and tower were built, the tower was a look-out place for the soldiery who from there could give early notice of any move by the natives to attack the place and possibly recover their cattle by force of arms.

At right angles to this ancient house, which had thick, rough stone walls and small windows and a general air of sturdy prepared-ness for the worst, they built, in about 1740, another house, on the spacious and elegant Georgian pattern, with wide windows twelve feet high in all the ground floor rooms. Through doors on the ground floor or landing you step through a couple of centuries from the old part of the house to the new.

When we found it, the house, or rather a corner of it, was occupied by an aged man in a rusty black cutaway coat and a stetson-type hat. He was an energetic old man of great goodwill, but he was in no position to prop up the house. He lived, for the most part, in one room, where the ceiling was still intact, seated under an enormous crucifix, studying sacred books in Latin. The lower part of the house was invaded, not by neighbours now, but by fowl of many kinds, and sometimes by cows.

Very soon after we had taken the house, he died, and for a while it was hard to get anyone to work late around the place on account of his ghost. I never saw it myself, although I do not, in principle, disbelieve in ghosts. But I have never been able to understand why it is still so very generally supposed that ghosts are malign and therefore alarming. If the person who has now become a ghost was benign in life, why should he be sinister on his *post mortem* appearance? I used to argue thus with one or two of the workmen who seemed distressed at the thought of the old man possibly wandering about the passages. I convinced no one, and I think they probably supposed I was making up all this stuff about the benignity of ghosts for the purpose of getting them to work overtime.

21 Odd Jobs

In a fable of R.L. Stevenson, the old man says to the young man, 'Why are you weeping?' 'I am weeping for my sins,' says the young man. Months later, they meet again, and the young man is still weeping, 'Why are you weeping now?' asks the old man. 'I am weeping because I have nothing to eat.' 'I thought it would come to that,' says the old man.

During my long years as a red political journalist, all other connections with the journalistic and literary world had slowly but inevitably broken down. And it was not difficult to surmise that if I now appeared waving some kind of new leaf and asking to be paid to write on it, there would be considerable askance-looking by many. Every agent, publisher and editor will truthfully tell you how important it is to build up a name. But the two names I had built up reeked of politics and subversion. It was necessary to act as though one were twenty-one years old, just down from Oxford, and trying to break into, as the saying goes, the writing game.

Salvation came in the shape of Mr Richard Bennett, at that time editor of the monthly magazine *Lilliput*. He liked my writing, and had no political inhibitions. At the same time, he and I believed – we may, of course, have been wrong – that some backward individual on the business side of *Lilliput* might not like to have a person of my background writing for their paper. I became Kenneth Drew. The necessity for writing pseudonymously became still more apparent after I had made some financial calculations and reckoned that, at the rate *Lilliput* paid in those days, I would need to get at least two pieces into the magazine every month, and sometimes more. Without cast-iron pseudonyms that was going to raise a lot of eyebrows.

So I was not only Kenneth Drew but James Helvick and a man called Patrick Cork, and, I seem to remember, Hector Hamish or somebody of similar name, and a couple of others as well. Later, Hulton Press launched a new weekly called *Leader,* which was understood to be going to revolutionize British weekly journalism, and Drew – I think it was he – wrote a long series of articles for it. It was a good paper, and I dare say it would have revolutionized British journalism if given the chance.

But one of the curses of contemporary British journalism is the increasing power and influence of a lot of people who know nothing about journalism, but have persuaded numerous proprietors and shareholders that they are in possession of statistical gadgets and Geiger counters which, properly read, reel off the news of what the public wants. They conduct polls. They make surveys of 'representative groups'. They dip their thermometers into the water as assiduously as attendants at a thermal bath. Then they go to the proprietors or the advertising managers and report that three per cent of men earning more than £6,800 annually are allergic to science fiction, or crazy to read more about yachting or love. Naturally they get the right answer some of the time, though no more often than people using common sense and intuition instead of statistics and polls. But since everyone has an eerie awareness that he does not really know what the public wants, anyone who appears with a definitive and didactic statement on the subject is reassuring.

The result, all too often, is a kind of paralysis of the editorial will. An editor has no business to be worrying himself sick about what the public wants. He should be thinking about perfecting and producing what he wants and then making the public want it, too.

Somebody proved that *Leader* was appealing to the wrong income groups, so that despite the energy and ability of its editor, Sydney Jacobson, who fought hard to save the paper from needless extinction, and to give it at least a fighting chance, I learned in Ireland that they were folding it up immediately.

A guest at my house wrote, at this time, in the visitors' book, a description of what he called the Literary Colony at Youghal. He claimed to have met Frank Pitcairn, ex-correspondent of the *Daily Worker* – a grouchy, disillusioned type secretly itching to dash out and describe a barricade. There was Claud Cockburn, founder and editor of *The Week,* talkative, boastful of past achievements, and apt, at the drop of a hat, to tell, at length, the inside story of some forgotten diplomatic crisis of the 1930s. Patrick Cork would look in

– a brash little number, and something of a professional Irishman, seeking, no doubt, to live up to his name. James Helvick lived in and on the establishment, claiming that he needed quiet together with plenty of good food and drink to enable him to finish a play and a novel which soon would bring enough money to repay all costs. In the background, despised by the others as a mere commercial hack, Kenneth Drew hammered away at the articles which supplied the necessities of the colony's life.

Helvick wrote a play which kept being accepted by managements and then shelved for reasons good, bad and all inscrutable.

I thought that while awaiting further developments on the theatrical front, and keeping Kenneth Drew's nose to the grindstone, I might get somewhere by taking one theme from the play and turning it into a novel, *Beat the Devil*, by, of course, James Helvick. By the time the novel was written and published in Britain and the United States, it could be said that things were definitely not going so well.

Our house in Ireland began to look more and more as though it had been invented by Somerville and Ross. Since we had not yet finished paying for the earlier structural repairs we could scarcely get the contractor to embark on a new series. Odd job men did their best, but the task was too great to be handled on a 'do-it-yourself' basis, and rain poured through the roof and ceilings. The process-server, supposed link between Cominform and Freemasonry, was out to see me repeatedly. And the men wandering about the grounds were not guests or employees, but Sheriff's officers, mentally pricing the horses and threatening to drive them off and sell them.

By great good luck, we decided that since there appeared to be nothing we could immediately do about this situation, the sensible thing to do was to let the process-server and the Sheriff's men carry on as best they could, and accept an invitation to stay, for the Dublin Horse Show week, with Lady Oranmore at her house in the Wicklow mountains. It was a big house party, and my pleasure was particularly great when I heard that my old friend Mr John Huston, film director, was coming.

He arrived in Dublin very late one night, and joined our party at a Hunt Ball there. At about four o'clock or five o'clock in the morning, around the time people start stripping to the waist and jumping off the balconies blowing hunting horns, I started to talk to Mr Huston about my novel. At such a time, I was well aware, Mr Huston would prefer to talk, for instance, about horses in their many aspects: things to hunt foxes on, things to put your money on.

However, he is a volatile man and I was afraid he might suddenly get a telephone call from Beverly Hills and fly off to Hollywood before anyone was awake after the ball.

Something of the kind nearly did happen a day or two later, because after he promised to read it I found I had forgotten to bring a copy with me. At the last moment I found, and rudely snatched back, a copy which I had recently inscribed, in terms of the sincerest admiration and affection, to our hostess. She said it seemed rather sad to have been in possession of a tribute like that for such an unexpectedly short time, but surrendered the book for the good of the cause. It then struck me that Mr Huston – who was travelling without benefit of secretary – might very likely lose just one copy. Just as he was leaving for the airport, I found that there was another copy in the house – warmly inscribed to Mr Terence Kilmartin. He, too, acted for the good of the cause, and I threw the two copies into Mr Huston's car as it started up the driveway.

Mr Huston is a good friend and proved it when he started to read the book the moment he got to London. Two days later I had a guarded message from his secretary to say that he was so absorbed in it that he had had a fall as a result of reading it while walking downstairs.

A week later he was back in Dublin. Mr Huston is one of those blessed men who, if they like your work, say so clearly and repeatedly. Such men know that, like Wilde, an author can stand any amount of flattery provided it is gross enough. Nor was his praise inhibited by any niggling fear that he was putting the price up. His own affairs were, as I understood it, in a considerable financial tangle at the time – it was, I think, just before the enormous gamble he had taken on *African Queen* paid off. He and Humphrey Bogart had a company called Santana which could buy the film rights of the book and arrange major financing for it afterwards. He said there was an ideal part for Bogart in *Beat the Devil*.

Thinking of my experiences with the theatrical managers, I imagined that about now there would be a long pause during which, for weeks on end, nothing would happen of a character satisfactory to creditors and Sheriffs. Our enthusiastic conversation took place at breakfast in Dublin. While I was talking to his wife, he was scribbling something. It was, I found a little later, a long cable to Mr Bogart in Hollywood, speaking in glowing terms of the book, advising him to buy the American edition instantly, and assuring him that in Huston's opinion they should buy the rights immediately too.

Partly for the purpose of talking about the possibilities of the screenplay, partly because he wanted to ride in new country, we arranged that the Hustons should come down to Youghal at once and stay with us for a couple of weeks. From Mr Huston's hotel room, I rang up our home. The number was unobtainable. I became flustered. Mr Huston sat on the bed, watching me with sardonic sympathy.

'It's happened to all of us before,' he said softly.

At Youghal we had to keep our hats on part of the time as we talked about the screenplay, because of the leaks in the roof. Meantime, the local post office was handling some of the longest telegrams seen in those parts since the Easter Rising – cables between there and Beverly Hills. Finally a firm offer came – for a larger sum of money than I had seen for a very long time indeed, if ever.

'Look,' said Huston, 'this is a firm offer, but in Hollywood terms it isn't so damn big. Not so damn big at all. If you hang on, and especially if the book goes well in America, you can get three or four times that figure.'

I said, thinking of many phases of his career and of my own, 'Listen, we've both of us known times when ten dollars, cash on the barrelhead, now, is worth a whale of a lot more than a hundred the week after next.'

'If it's like that,' said Mr Huston – and considering the drip, drip from the roof it was not very difficult to note that it was just like that – 'what are we waiting for?'

If the hunters and ponies had known what was happening they would have danced in their stalls.

22 Du Côté de Chez Bouverie

I WAS constantly reminded of the ramshackle way in which quite considerable enterprises are conducted, when, round about the early fifties, I twice spent some time in London working – very profitably for myself – on newspapers which did not fold or fail for the reason that they never appeared at all. For a time I was co-editor with the late Maurice Richardson of a mighty new (intended) weekly called *Seven Days*. Not to be confused with another, and successfully published, *Seven Days* of later date. Even the advertisement manager approved the final dummy when he saw it, and the circulation experts said they could sell three million a week of a product like that. Then, according to the manager, the proprietor's wife vetoed the project on the ground that its 'tone' (acerbic to scurrilous) could injure her advance up the slopes of the upper classes and prevent her becoming a friend of Princess Margaret. Later, I was diplomatic editor of a costly affair called the *Sunday Star*. There was a large staff, headed by that journalist of genius, the merry yet very serious Reverend Marcus Morris, creator of *Eagle*. We produced a dummy every week for many weeks, and were very well paid for it. Then it emerged that the proprietors had forgotten to get an agreement about the distribution of the new paper. The retail newsagents wanted an increase in their commission on the amount they were getting from existing Sunday newspapers. The Newspaper Proprietors' Association stated it would expel the proprietors from its midst, and ruin the paper from the start by refusing it admission to the newspaper trains, if it gave in to the retailers. All this could have been ascertained before a penny was spent. As it was, the undertaking had to be quietly abandoned, and I returned to Youghal with a big increase in my bank balance, and

177

no loss of scepticism about the wisdom of those on high in our society.

A few months later, I got a letter which surprised me not a little – an invitation to write an artice for *Punch*, which I had not even dreamed of reading for years. Not only that, but it was signed by my friend Anthony Powell who, it astonishingly appeared, had become *Punch*'s literary editor. A pleasure of living in Ireland is that you can, so to speak, turn England on or off as desired, and at that time I had no knowledge of the volcanic disturbance which started to shake Bouverie Street with the appointment of Malcolm Muggeridge as editor of that publication. Furthermore, had I heard this bit of news it would certainly not have occurred to me that it boded me any particular good. True, I had no intention of writing for *Punch*, but if I had, the appointment of Mr Muggeridge would have seemed to me to rule out any possibility of successfully so doing. For although we had never actually met I had hated him for years. Those were, of course, principally my communist years when Malcolm Muggeridge had great prominence in our Rogues' Gallery of men who, for example, had gone to Moscow to bless and stayed to curse; of hardened, obstinate and vicious enemies of Truth and Progress; of particularly able, and, therefore, particularly detestable and dangerous journalistic and literary swordsmen in the ranks of wickedness and reaction. Nor was conflict with Muggeridge in those days restricted to the battle of the typewriters. For he was often deadly active in the affairs of the National Union of Journalists – his activity always directed towards frustrating or defeating some vital activity of our own.

Knowing nothing of his appointment to the editorship, I was still bewildered by the presence in the literary chair of Anthony Powell whom I had known since Oxford and whose novels, with their exquisite sinuosities and profound risibility, had enchanted me for years. What, I had to ask myself, in God's name was *he* doing in that *galère*? And what, admitting that he personally was aboard the sluggish old hulk, on earth made him suppose that *my* presence would be welcome? Just making the matter more mysterious was a note in his letter – he was asking for an article about Ireland – saying that he would like the piece to be 'somewhat astringent'. If he were simply trying to do me a good turn by arranging for me to get a small piece of money out of *Punch*, surely, knowing my general line of literary brew would he not instead have put in some cautionary note urging me to draw it mild?

After a few weeks of my astringent writing, Tony mentioned in a letter that if I chanced to be in London in the near future he would be particularly glad to have me call upon him at the *Punch* office. I had arranged a small 'bandit raid' on another quarter of the city, which made it convenient for me to go over almost immediately. I visited the *Punch* office, and spent an agreeable half-hour in the office of the distinguished literary editor. The *Punch* offices have a peculiarly solid, Edwardian air about them which is agreeable enough to the detached observer, but made me a little nervous. I was a great deal more nervous when Tony, who supposed I knew all about it already, incidentally disclosed that the enterprise was now under the guidance of Malcolm Muggeridge. To my further discomfiture, he made the suggestion that we now take a walk down the corridor and visit Mr Muggeridge in person. I positively babbled. I tried, in a few hurried words, to explain the relationship existing between this Muggeridge and myself. I tried to make clear that while it was already incomprehensible to me that Muggeridge should be publishing articles from me – it seemed to me that he must be imagining that I was a different, perhaps an Irish, Cockburn – it was certain that a personal meeting should at all costs be avoided. 'I have every reason to suppose,' I said, 'that he detests me as deeply as I detest him. Let us keep this whole thing as far as possible in the old boy net – let me deal exclusively with yourself. A meeting with Muggeridge can end only in bitterness and disaster.'

Pooh-poohing and laughing – idiotically, I thought – Tony insisted; in fact he actually held me by the arm and steered me down the passage and into the bugbear's den. Of that first conversation I remember very little, except that it was from the start tumultuous and at the end – hours later – hilarious. Neither of us, I imagine, was much inclined to revise or regret the opinions we had had of one another in the past. For neither of us, I think, enjoys wasting time wondering whether this or that thought or act perpetrated in the past was or was not mistaken. But it is a natural corollary of this attitude – the attitude I mean of a belief that one's past actions were not mistaken but correct – to acknowledge freely that life and situations are fluid, and that a position which it was correct to maintain then may be ludicrously erroneous now. There are, of course, people who believe that to accept this rich fluidity of life is to abandon principles. Many such people are sincere, although I have noticed that a good many who talk most rigorously of 'principle' are in reality too lazy, too nervous or too cold-hearted to recognize the moment when what they think of as their 'principles' have transformed themselves from vehicles of healthy, and even perhaps

179

beneficent, action, into notions about as useful to them or anyone else as a ball and chain round the leg. Certainly, as I remarked earlier, 'the copy-book maxims are true'; and there are times when the thing to do is maintain with the utmost rigour not merely the principle, but the outer – even the verbal – formulation of it. But it is also true, as everyone with any knowledge of religions and creeds well knows, that too often the formulation remains, an unburied corpse, a long time after the spirit, so to say, of the principle has left it and taken up its habitation somewhere else. In my own experience it has always proved a lot easier to stick to a principle than to know when to change it.

Within an hour of meeting Malcolm Muggeridge I was aware that there was the sort of man who, if he caught himself feeling comfortably convinced of anything for a longish period of time, would start ringing alarm bells in his own head and heart; a man who felt immediate guilt on discovering that he was taking anything for granted; that in fact to take anything for granted – even the truth if it were the truth – was more heinous than to spring up with a restless effort and, quite possibly, bound straight into an abyss or error. He was, in fact, an enemy of mental and spiritual placidity, one compared to whom many who believe themselves to have alert, inquiring minds, appear on the contrary sunk in comfortable complacency. Particularly during that early period of his editorship of *Punch* – coinciding with his advance to prominence on television – he was continuously attacked either for being inconsistent and contradictory in his opinions, or else having no genuine opinions at all. It is, I should think, true to say that he regarded all opinions as being necessarily in a state of more or less violent evolution; and I suspect, too, that he was a good deal less afraid of involving himself in truly frantic contradictions than of getting, as it were, bogged down in some sticky morass of opinion which real life had already left behind. It is this quality which puts him among the relatively few people – though I have been happy in meeting quite a number of them – with whom a genuine conversation can be conducted. For, taking this evolutionary view of the nature of opinions, he positively hopes and desires that the conversation or argument may change his opinions, and has the same hopes and desires about whatever opinions you may start out by expressing.

This quality, almost immediately apparent, took me agreeably by surprise. Dealing with editors and executives and such, I cannot help starting with an assumption that one is not going to be able actually to communicate with them at all. We shall both, I think, boom and babble away, sending streams of words past one another's ears, but it will all be quite irrelevant to what one is really going to do, or write. This has led me into some difficulties. A conversation of that kind must, for the sake of propriety, go on for a certain length of time, for if you sit with such a man for only five minutes and then quit, he feels you have wasted five minutes of his time and resents it. But if you can keep things humming along for a half-hour or so, he is inclined to think that something worthwhile must have been achieved. It can thus occur that, just for the sake of making a nice atmosphere, you say whatever comes into your head, you speak with seeming enthusiasm about some notion that entered your mind just that minute and will leave it again two minutes later, and next day you get a telephone call from the man saying that he had been thinking deeply about that thing you said and he would like you to get to work on it right away and develop it. If you ask him at that stage what on earth it was you were talking about he is chilled and disappointed.

Malcolm started, after a while, to speak of Jesus Christ. It is of interest that the figure of Christ can still act as a kind of catalytic agent or, so to speak, as a form of introduction between people who are of West European and Anglo-American background but are otherwise strangers or, as in this case, old enemies. A person's reaction to Christ, or the idea of Christ, can still often enough offer a convenient shorthand *précis* of his more general attitude to life and its phenomena. Christians are sometimes even vexed by the fact that this should be so among non-Christians or possibly anti-Christians. But in reality this fact simply emphasizes that the creation and elaboration of the Christ-myth (I use 'myth' in its exact and neutral sense), was a necessity for the Mediterranean, and subsequently European, mind, and was one of its most profoundly characteristic achievements, only equalled much later in its formative power by that of Marxism-Leninism. A person who was simply unaware of Marxism-Leninism – not just someone who had never read a line of Marx or Lenin, but one whose consciousness had been somehow sterilized in this respect – would have a difficult time making himself understood or understanding anyone else in the Western world now. This is self-evident. But it is a fact, too, that a similar unawareness of the Christ-myth would in reality though not so apparently inhibit communication. This is not always self-evident to non-Christians, who – sometimes thoughtlessly, sometimes as a result of anti-clerical wishful thinking – under-estimate the role of the Christ-myth in the consciousness of the Western world. (Equally wishful-thinking anti-Marxists, for their part, can make the same kind of mistake.)

Yet the co-existence of these myths in the Western consciousness is a fact of basic importance. For it is this which offers at least a possible prerequisite for the creation by the Western mind of a new myth, higher in the spiral of human aspiration. To overlook or deny this restless co-existence is to suggest that the Western mind has come to a dead end.

Despite my general nervousness, despite, too, the parquet flooring of the *Punch* office with carpets on it, all so very gentlemanly, and the thought that if they tired of the newspaper business the owners could sell this bit of Bouverie Street from right under our eager feet for millions of pounds, I began to have the feeling that with this fiercely gentle, chivalrously ungentlemanly man on the far side of the grandiose editorial desk, jerking and flashing his eyes and from time to time cackling out a cacophony of furiously raucous expressions like a sailor's parrot loose in the Mission Hall, something new and special in the way of clowning and satire might yet be made of this ancient publication, once so rowdy, later so often muffled nearly to the eyes in old school scarves. The room at large was as dead as a whited sepulchre, but you could feel some life crackling behind the desk, as though someone, for a joke, had thrown a fire-cracker into the mausoleum. There were some portraits on the walls, including some horrifying depictions of Edwardian and neo-Georgian *Punch* pundits, sell-outs, some of them, of the type who would suppress a joke or blunt a satire rather than be black-balled at this Club or thrown with contumely out of that one. But, as Malcolm pointed out with pleasure, by just twisting in his chair he could look down into the street half blocked a lot of the time by the great lorries bringing ton after ton of newsprint to the door of the *News of the World*.

What Malcolm had in mind at that time was the possibility – the bare, outside possibility – that the supposed 'revolution' in Britain (a supposition necessary to justify the existence of the Labour Party) really had produced some new ways of thinking, and with them some new hankerings for adult satire. A triviality? A mere 'marginal' demand? Perhaps. It was one of the things that had to be found out. There is no law that says people have to laugh. And there were times, sitting there in Bouverie Street, when it looked as though maybe someone had brought in a law telling people not to. Caution, good taste, helpfulness and discretion were all hall-marked on the bottom of the state as it was presented to Britain a few years after the Russians and Americans at last met on the Elbe. And yet, on the other hand, this could not be – it could not be that the British as a whole had gone down the drain with the British upper middle classes. Indeed no, for there they were, bowling up and down Fleet Street between the City and Mayfair in their big cars, richer and happier than ever – the men of the 1950s to whom if you said 'right' or said 'left' it was to them the same thing, which was nothing. And you had to remember that at that period there was a notable tendency among the intellectuals, too, to adopt this 'anti-ideological' position. (And, as is known, by the summer of 1959, the ideology of anti-ideology had become a near-creed of the Western intellectuals. They took whole suites of a German hotel to meet in and discuss it.)

Personally I thought that the trick could be turned, that there were enough people extant to make a living for a rawly satirical paper – a paper which (on the principle I have always held) would write the way people really talk. And if the customers were there at all, then there was no doubt the people at *Punch*, given the green light, were entirely capable of meeting the demand.

I think that for about the first two years of his editorship, Malcolm believed this to be a correct estimate of the possibilities. Believing that, he saw too that the prerequisite for success was to make a loud, nasty noise of the kind nobody associated with *Punch*. If the potential customers for a new kind of magazine were lurking anywhere, such a noise would alert them and they would come running.

Inevitably there was some heavy thinking – even among those who favoured the attempt to seek out this potentially existing new public – on the question of whether it was going to be possible to flush enough of the new customers before too many of the old ones cancelled their subscriptions. A good deal was said about the 'retired colonels in Cheltenham' who, traditionally, were supposed to be the *corps d'élite* of *Punch* readers, and on whose defection the entire position would crumple up in ruin. I argued that, first, there are no retired colonels in Cheltenham because this great British revolution we understand we have had has changed all that and, secondly, if there are they are lovers of Picasso, members of the Labour Party, and, in many instances, pansies. I was told that the circulation department actually sent a man down to those parts to find out whether this was or was not the case. It may – given the way things are in Fleet Street – have actually happened. I was pestering the Old Guard with my attacks on the Cheltenham syndrome, and since carrying out some kind of poll is the only answer they know to any argument, perhaps some man did actually go knocking on doors in Cheltenham and interviewing retired colonels as to their artistic and sexual tastes. I should like to have been there.

I cannot recall – because I was back in Youghal at the time – just when Malcolm emitted his first Bronx cheer, his rallying-call to the frustrated lurkers in the underbrush who were going to emerge and say, 'this is what we've been waiting for'. Probably it took a little time to do that, while waiting for the heavy thinking to end.

I do recall a day when he came to visit me in Ireland and, as he sprang from the train at Limerick Junction, remarked with profound satisfaction, that the issue of the magazine he had just sent to the press was 'likely to get us all into a lot more hot water'. This piece of intelligence encouraged me a good deal as we bowled across the plains of south Tipperary and into the astringencies of County Cork where, unless you want to be made a comon fool of, you are on parade and on your toes all day and half the night too. Kitty Muggeridge, Malcolm's wife, received the news with less enthusiasm but with experienced calm. She was a niece of Mrs Sydney Webb, and had, in youth, had a close-up of Fabian politics and then of almost every other sort of politics. She and Malcolm recalled, for instance, that summer school in Surrey where H. G. Wells seduced the wife of a fellow-Fabian, who – the husband, I mean – forgave him, in a spirit of freedom and no-prejudice. It was assumed – it was part of the Fabian bargain – that as a result of this forgiveness Wells would see the error of his seductive ways and concentrate more on the lecture showing where Henry George was so wrong. What Wells actually did was to lure the girl-wife into the rhododendron bushes growing very lush in that part of Surrey, and seduce her all over again. A motion was brought in that evening at the meeting of the Society stating that 'in the opinion of this House Mr Wells is a cad'. Naturally it was passed. In the Fabian book a lot of people were cads.

Mrs Webb, Lady Passfield, I conceive to have been one of the most disagreeable women produced by the British race. Malcolm told me once that when he went to stay there – in the pursuit of love, I suppose – she used to order Sydney Webb to go for a walk before lunch because it would be good for his physique. (It was during that period when people still believed that exercise is good for other people. Just now the doctors say it can be nearly fatal.) The great economist and ex-cabinet minister used to set off, with Malcolm, at a quick jog, while Mrs Sydney Webb watched from the front door. Then Webb would dodge behind a barn, seize Malcolm by the arm, indicate a nice bundle of hay where reclining could be done, and the two of them would spend the next hour there, talking of communism and the future of the world. The only disagreeable feature of these expeditions was that the return to the house – a distance of a couple of hundred yards – had to be accomplished at the double, because when Sydney returned Mrs Webb was apt to assure herself that he was genuinely in a sweat – a sweat, she thought, poor woman, such as could only be worked up by the five-mile walk she supposed they had been taking while she was writing her assessment of something or other.

I met her once when I was very young. She and Sydney Webb had just returned from the Soviet Union. On their way back they had visited Trotsky, then in exile on the island of Prinkipo. The Webbs talked Fabianism to the exile. He for his part told them they were talking nonsense. There was no such thing as gradualism in revolution. He declared that Britain would be no exception to the general rule. There, too, the streets would run with blood and the exploiters would be hanged from lamp-posts. And what, someone asked, had the Webbs replied to these assertions? 'We told him *no*,' said Mrs Webb.

As I recall, the cartoon that was expected to heat the water for us that time was a singularly disobliging study of the ageing Winston Churchill, apparently sunk in senile reverie while the affairs of the country went to pot. It had, immediately, the desired effect. Leading Conservative publicists and politicians howled their rage, helping by their din to notify one and all that Britain had something a little new in the way of magazines. Inevitably a cartoon of this kind – a kind that, in relation to the Grand Old Man, had been taboo for years – produced a little friction and head-shaking even inside the office. (Equally inevitably we heard from a number of people in Fleet Street and Westminster that this act of bad taste, this stab in the back of the great Leader, had been suggested and promoted by ex-Red Cockburn. It was untrue – I had been hundreds of miles away at the time, and in any case had absolutely no influence on the choice of cartoons. But this rumour, too, was useful – it gave people something to talk about, and increased the amount of verbiage they issued on the subject of *Punch*.)

In the newspaper business compromise is always dangerous. And it was in the nature of the situation at *Punch* that Malcolm was frequently forced to make compromises between his own ideas of what was effective and permissible and the ideas other people had.

His own notions often enough appeared outrageous even to some of the members of the staff. For some people always think that by trying to get the best of both worlds they are playing it safe. Excite, they think, new possible readers, but do not unduly offend the old customers. In reality this is about the most dangerous thing you can do. You do not utter a shriek piercing enough to reach the inattentive ear of the new, and yet you give the old the impression that you are not quite as nice as they used to think you.

After working with him for only a month I had given it as my opinion that the only thing that could go seriously wrong with the new *Punch* was that he would become suddenly bored with it. 'With you,' I told him, ' the tendency to become bored has the quality of a vice.' Being not much subject to it myself – though there have been times now and then when I have suffered desperately – I find it difficult to understand. But I have seen enough of it in other people to conclude that boredom is a factor in life and behaviour which most people underestimate.

On this subject Edward Crankshaw makes, somewhere, an illuminating point about what might be called the role of boredom as a factor in international affairs. Discussing Russian political attitudes to the West, he suggested – and supported the suggestion with some convincing illustrations – that from time to time the men in the Kremlin get purely and simply bored with the whole business of pretending to think as though they were West Europeans. They find the strain tedious. And when boredom finally overcomes them we witness one of those disconcerting shifts of attitude which the diplomat commentators find so difficult to interpret. It is certainly, I should judge, part of the truth. And it is related to Professor Wright Mills's exposition, in *The Origins of World War III*, of how, whether in the Pentagon or the Kremlin, the eternal preparation for a war which does not actually happen, the endless preoccupation with an eventuality which is not realized, can produce a state of mind in which those responsible, though they know the war will be suicidal, may be subconsciously longing for war to break out.

Malcolm unreservedly agreed with my early prognostication about *Punch*, and, in a sense, I was astonished that this vice of boredom did not overcome him earlier. But after the Toronto fiasco, I noted that he became increasingly a prey to it. At that time I wrote for *Punch* almost every week – mostly from Youghal. I would telephone him every Monday morning to get from him some proposal for the subject of the article, or to make a proposal myself. We would mull over these proposals for twenty minutes or so, and I would mail him the article on Monday night or Tuesday morning. For a long time these conversations were, as they say, 'constructive' in the sense that I could feel the whole thing coming to life as we talked. Indeed, as often as not, it seemed to me that the piece in its final form owed at least as much to Malcolm as to me. Gradually, however, he showed less and less inclination to talk about material for *Punch*, entertaining me instead with scandalous gossip or Christianity or television. Often, particularly if the long-distance line from Ireland was in poor shape as a result of tempest or other interruption, I would suggest that since we might get abruptly cut off at any time, we ought perhaps to turn to practical discussion of my next article. 'Hell, my dear boy, I leave all that to you. Write anything you like.' Once, having mailed my weekly piece, I had a little *arrière pensée* and rang him up on a Thursday morning to suggest some small improvements. He sounded bewildered. It then transpired that it had become his habit simply to send the articles over to the printers without reading them. 'It's perfectly all right. I'll read it in galley proof.' Later still he once confessed to me that he found it nearly impossible to start reading any of the articles in *Punch* until the paper was actually in page proof. He had to postpone until the last possible moment paying attention to a matter which had come to bore him so cruelly.

23 Plague

ONE night in London I heard one of my children calling for help. My wife being out at the time I ran to his bedroom, and found that he was calling in his sleep; an effect of nightmare, no more. Yet the immediate impression was frightening. Although there was, as the saying goes, nothing to it, it was an incident which seemed to give a sharply horrid reality to the fears everyone has about children – fears that they will have to call for help and there will be no help one can give, or one will not think of the right help to give until it is too late.

The alarm and depression I then felt continued through some hours, as though it were I that had had the nightmare and, waking, could not erase its impression. Nobody knows quite enough about extra-sensory perception or precognition to be perfectly assured on the subject. But it is a fact that people do have what used to be called a 'premonition of disaster'. I did not think of this as a premonition of anything, but the state of seemingly unmotivated depression was as marked as it would have been if I had actually supposed myself to have received a warning of unpleasant things to come.

We were living at that time in Hampstead because *Punch* wanted me to be in London for a half year or so, available for production of topical articles and reportage such as could not be written from Youghal. The house was commodious enough and full of convenient mechanical gadgets, including two television sets and a labour-saving bar in a big semi-basement room at the back. For some reason I had taken an unreasoning dislike to the place on first seeing it from the street, and, once inside I was vexed by a meaningless sense of uneasiness. It was annoying, because I had looked forward to this time in London. I was eager to experiment with numerous projects for *Punch*, and I thought, too, that, being at close quarters, I could sell articles to other papers more easily than I could from Ireland, and should be able to shore up, even perhaps establish on sound foundations, our always tottering financial structure. Nevertheless, I was no sooner in that house than I felt mysteriously less happy than I had expected and intended to be, and this *malaise* continued right through the summer.

Despite the television which, living normally in the south of Ireland, they had never seen before, and other amusements of London life, the three boys either actively hated London or could make it tolerable for themselves only by spending money like drunken little sailors. My wife, too, though she briefly enjoyed a series of parties, and visits to the theatre, was irksomely cut off from all the creative activity involved in the development of farm and garden, the breeding of horses, the raising of sheep. Also her upbringing had been such that she instinctively imagined that to be in London in August was to indulge a perverse masochism. No one, she had always been led to believe, is in London in August, and although, rationally, she agreed that the statement is nonsense, she could not help feeling horror at the prospect, and a conviction that to stay there deliberately in that month woud be foolish and injurious to us all. For all these reasons we arranged that at the beginning of the school holidays – the eldest boy was at school in Perthshire, the second one at a preparatory school near Dublin, and the third (then six years old) at a day school beside Hampstead Heath – we should all go to Youghal, and that I, by agreement with *Punch* – would fly back to London for one week in three.

At the last moment we hesitated because of news that a somewhat abnormal number of cases of polio had been reported in Cork City. We reflected, however, that there were certainly a good many cases in London, too, and that whereas, if things got worse, we could, at home, virtually isolate the children on the farm, in London they must be daily exposed to whatever risks of infection might exist. There was no reason why things should get worse. We set off. It was true that on the boat I heard several conversations among people who were sailing to Cork with the sort of apprehensions you encountered among people travelling to London from the country during the bombing. I thought this the talk of people trying to make life more exciting. Men who always got drunk in the bar of the *Innisfallen* said, that night, that they were drinking as a prophylactic against polio.

The boat docked late, and it was mid-morning before we loaded all the luggage – mountains of it, as there always are when one travels with young children – into a van and packed ourselves into the hired car for the thirty-mile run to Youghal. We had to visit a shop in St Patrick Street, the centre of the city, and I was suddenly surprised – pleased, at first –by the ease with which we found parking space in a street where normally it is nearly impossible to park at all. The shop, too, was agreeably empty of pushers and jostlers. I remarked that we seemed to have hit on a lucky day. The driver of the car looked at me with astonishment. 'People are afraid,' he said. 'They're afraid to come into Cork. Business is going to hell. If the epidemic goes on, in a few weeks half the shops on this street will be bankrupt.' Not lingering to buy anything but essentials we drove out into the countryside and home.

Under our circumstances at Youghal that horrible summer, the boys could at least ride horses about, or bicycle in the neighbourhood. But here again I could note that there is perhaps a discrepancy between what the elders think the youth must be longing to do and the true facts of the case. The elder boys did like to ride, but they did not care to ride much. What they liked was to build hidden huts or tree houses, to lie motionless on their backs in their tents, or find a dangerous way to the roof and sit there reading, with emotion, *The Waste Land*.

In these pursuits the summer seemed to be passing away harmlessly enough. I went to London two or three times for a few days on each visit, motoring to Cork, travelling by train from there to Dublin and thence flying. Then, one day, I had a headache and the tips of my fingers pricked with pins and needles. I am unused to headaches and thus noticed this one. And the pricking in my fingertips was so queer that I made myself tedious about it, mentioned this pricking until everyone was much bored with the information. My eldest son also felt this pricking. We thought it was either meaningless, or else he had perhaps picked it up psychosomatically from me.

Much later, several doctors confirmed to me that this combination of unusual – baseless – headache with the prick of the finger-tips is a common, almost an infallible, sign of polio. At the time we knew nothing of that. In reality, it appears, I had picked up the bug somewhere along the line between London and Cork. Even then, inevitably, Cork people had to travel in trains on their business. I recall that on the last of those journeys there was a clearly perceptible atmosphere of fear, suspicion, or perhaps simply high-grade caution on the train. Already things were at the point where Dubliners returning from some necessary trip to Cork felt that they could at least lessen the risk they had been compelled to run by not associating with Cork people longer than was absolutely necessary. We Cork people found ourselves, without the slightest word being said – and perhaps with not much of a conscious thought being thought – sitting at one end of the bar and buffet car, with the Dubliners at the other.

As the situation deteriorated in Cork, the Cork people defensively spread terrifying stories about what was happening elsewhere. It was said, and absolutely believed by very many people, that in Dublin the epidemic was worse still than in Cork. People were dying like flies in every fever hospital in the city. But, due to the savage wiles and intrigues of the Dubliners, the newspapers had been, as the Irish saying goes, 'brought to see' that it would not be in their interests to report the state of affairs in Dublin. Instead they should concentrate on ruining poor Cork.

And in Cork itself the owners of some of the biggest stores in the city made a *démarche*. In deputation to the newspapers they threatened to withdraw advertising from such newspapers as might continue to report regularly and in detail on the polio epidemic there. They were intent on bringing the newspapers to see the justice of their viewpoint. As always, too, in the sordid backwaters of panic, there were people made to suffer by the frights of others. Some nearly bedridden people nearly died in various parts of the city because it was thought that all bedridden people must be polio victims, and in consequence nobody would go to their houses to deliver the milk and meat and vegetables they needed. The Gardai had to be called in to make the deliveries to those houses which were supposedly so dangerous but in reality – not that the delivery men had any means of knowing that – were no more dangerous than the air you breathed at the railway station or the General Post Office. And that was dangerous indeed.

Things were apparently going along well enough, and I was in London, at this increasingly hateful house in Hampstead, working fast to make enough money to take us all, I thought, to Mexico for a while; a place I much wanted to visit. I came down, one late summer night, the crooked road that led to this big squat house and heard the telephone ringing. It just chanced that I had dined early and alone, and was coming back to sleep at nine-thirty in the evening. No one with good news ever rings you at that hour. How could, or would they? They are eating and drinking, and if all your affairs were in proper order you would be eating and drinking too. A call at that time can only be an act of desperation, a signal of emergency.

This was such a call. My wife had been trying to call me from Youghal and finding me from home had telephoned Malcolm at his home in Sussex, and he had kept on calling me every ten minutes with a message.

The message was to say that the youngest child was ill. I had no doubt what the message meant. My wife is no alarmist. With Malcolm's help – there has never been a man on God's earth who would do more for you when the chips are down, and he has seen a number of chips down in his life – I flew free to Dublin and hired the needed car at three o'clock in the morning to go the couple of hundred miles to Youghal. The message had meant just what I had supposed. The youngest boy was in bed with suspected polio. In a couple of hours the doctor was coming to confirm or nullify the diagnosis. He confirmed it. Two hours later the child was in the ambulance on his way to St Finnbarr's fever hospital in Cork.

By a trick of the mind, when grief and anxiety are at, you think, their imaginable height, some factor intrudes itself to give the screw an extra turn, heighten the grief and anxiety a little more. In this case, in the agony of her distress, my poor wife conceived the idea that she, because of her love of Ireland and boredom of London, had selfishly overlooked the dangers to the children involved in a return to County Cork, and was thus actually responsible for what had happened. I recalled this, many months later, when I was talking with Kitty Muggeridge about the death of their youngest son – he was eighteen or nineteen years old – in an avalanche of snow in the French Alps. She herself had been a ski champion once, and it seemed to her, after the event, that when he had mentioned to her that he was going skiing in that particular place at that particular season of the year, she should have remembered, over all those years, enough about conditions there to warn or discourage him, saying that at such a season there was danger of avalanches. And from this, by afterthought, it had been only a small step to the conviction that she had not only not tried to dissuade him from making the trip but, by some kind of implication, had actually encouraged him. She knew, when she talked about it, that all this was untrue or irrelevant. The young man had made his plans, he knew all that anyone needed to know about the possi-bilities and risks, and he would have taken those risks whatever anyone might have said. Just possibly – it is at least a possibility

192

worth considering when grievous things happen to loved people –
some people experience a compulsive need to assume guilt for what
has happened, and this in reality is only an expression of a desire to
become closer to them by involving oneself in their fate, rather
than assume that they have been struck at by impersonal forces far
beyond one's control.

Other than a compulsive need of that kind, there was no reason
for Patricia to feel this bitterness of remorse, but she did feel it.
And – again just possibly, although it did not look to me like that at
the time – it may have been that what seemed to me an additional
affliction for her was in reality a kind of aid; it could be that a sense
of being in some way involved in the child's disaster, rather than a
passive spectator of it, provided in its tortuous way a kind of balm
in this gloomy Gilead. Yet in general remorse is both futile and
debilitating.

Immediately after they had taken Patrick away in the ambulance
I telephoned the school near Dublin where Andrew – then nine –
was at work. For this had all happened at the very end of the
holidays, and Andrew had been back at school for three or four
days. He returned. I really thought all might still be well up to the
very last moment when the diesel train pulled into the station and
Andrew got out. I then saw that his body was bowed slightly
forward in an awkward way and that he was moving his legs
sluggishly. But this was the more terrifying because I had learned,
by now, that the most dangerous period of polio is the period
between the incidence of the infection and the moment of its
diagnosis. The longer a person goes on leading a normally active
life after the infection has struck, the more probable it is that he will
quickly die of the disease or be permanently maimed by it.

By the following morning he, too, was in St Finnbarr's fever
hospital.

Patrick was the first home. And when finally he came, I feared
that, back in the surroundings in which he had spent almost all his
short life, he would be even more aware of his disabilities than he
had been in the strange world of the hospital. He had never run
across the hospital lawn, or climbed a tree there, or ridden a pony
on its driveway. I feared that at home the lawn, the trees, the pony
and a lot besides would savagely jog his memory of things past.
Nothing of the kind happened. First he was so happy to be at home
that his escape from the hospital, for he had – as he later admitted –
been convinced that the hospital was going on for ever, was seen by
him as in itself an exhilarating achievement. And then, being now

alert and eager again, he became preoccupied not with the big range of things he could no longer do, but with the tiny extension, day by day and week by week of things he was learning to do again. To crawl from the bed to the floor, to walk a few more steps today than he could yesterday – these were a continuous, ascending series of triumphs, as uplifting as a succession of victories leading to membership of the team for the Olympic Games.

In the first weeks after his return home I was merely astonished and relieved by his vigour, determination and evident happiness. In my own mind, the dominant fact was the blow that had struck him. Gradually, under the influence of his attitude to these facts of life, I was aware of a shift in my own. It became possible to see the present, and the future that was now being constructed, as being of greater importance than the past.

24   The Worst Possible Taste

A MAN came angrily back to Youghal from a trip to London in 1963 and stamped about the quays complaining that whether you wanted to talk about selling Irish lobsters, or the present and future state of the theatre, both subjects which interested him, nobody in London would talk about anything but the Profumo case. I agreed, it must get tedious, especially as forty per cent of the talkers were only quoting the newspapers, twenty per cent were drooling a dream fantasy, and of the rest twenty-five per cent were the most bare-faced, though clumsy, liars since Ananias, or at least Stanley Baldwin. All the same, I said, it was probably hard for the people on the Ark to stop talking about the weather.

Personally at that time I was temporarily letting myself off the British newspapers altogether. I read the Irish newspapers and the invaluable *Le Monde* of Paris. It was a practice which seemed to me to freshen the mind; shift, in a healthy way, one's angle of vision. This produced occasionally tricky situations. I was at that time writing a weekly column for the *Sunday Telegraph*. The editor, Donald McLachlan, had arranged with me that we should have, around noon on Wednesdays, a short telephonic consultation about the general lines of next Sunday's piece. Like most dwellers in the world's big conurbations, Londoners are somewhat provincial in outlook. They believe, for instance, that everyone within reach of London publications is reading what they are reading. Donald would say to me, 'Don't you think that first paragraph in the *New Statesman* Diary gives you an excellent peg upon which to hang a satirical comment?'

Not having seen the *New Statesman* for months, I had to think fast. 'Donald,' I said, 'the most appalling thing has happened.

There has been an almighty flood here and the van bringing the copies of the *New Statesman*, and, I may say, the *Spectator*, has been either held up on the Cork road or utterly submerged.'

'Oh bad luck. Look . . .'

Another day Donald remarked that obviously I would be doing something about a big, significant letter in *The Times* from some bishop whose name I was unable to catch. I had to tell him there had been a hurricane at Cork airport. Before its precious freight could be unloaded, the plane with *The Times* – and, I hastened to assure him, all the other British daily newspapers – aboard, had been blown off the tarmac to hellangone; no one knew whether and when they might be salvaged and delivered.

'Good God!'

Later, Donald was supposed to be coming to stay with me, but suddenly cancelled the trip. A mutual friend told me that Donald had explained that he had only a short holiday, and did not dare have it ruined by the climate of County Cork. 'Floods, hurricanes every other week – I can't risk it.'

Among the publications I had heard of but never read, was *Private Eye*. I was thus baffled to receive, that summer, an invitation to go over to London and, as 'guest editor', take over production of a single special issue of the magazine. Having informed myself as well as I could in the circumstances – *Private Eye*, one need hardly say, was not available in Ireland – I decided, for many good reasons, to decline. Just for a start, I was approximately twice the average age of the men who had conceived the paper, were running it, and were giving it its unique character. A person of my generation would probably, I thought, even in a single issue, seriously damage its 'image'. Also, England appeared to me, just at that time, as Czechoslovakia did to Neville Chamberlain – a far-off country of which I knew little. Also, when the invitation came, I was sitting on a hot rock by the blue water of Ardmore Bay in a rare, wonderful heatwave, and I wanted to go on doing that.

I sat there thinking about satire, and its functions. With the ruins and Celtic myths of Ardmore all around, I naturally reflected on that thing that happened to prehistoric Irish King Bres, whose father was a Formorian and mother one of the People of the Goddess Danu. He was elected King, and married one of the People of the Goddess Danu, in the expectation that peace would thus be brought about between these latter and the Formorians.

In those days nobody could be a King in Ireland who suffered from any physical blemish. Bres was in good physical shape, but he was arrogant, inefficient, and vexatious. So vexatious, indeed, that the people went to the Satirist Cairbre and begged him to do some Satires on Bres. Cairbre complied. Bres stood it for a while, but in the end these savage satires got, literally, under his skin. Boils burst out all over his face. As a result of this blemish he was forced to resign, and a war broke out between the Formorians and the People of the Goddess Danu which lasted seven years. I recalled, too, that the Celtic hero Cu Chulainn, who was so agile in battle that he could 'turn round in his skin so that his feet and knees were to the rear and his calves and buttocks to the front', was ultimately brought low by a poet who threatened to satirize him unless he complied with certain demands. Cu Chulainn did not dare face satire. He acceded to the demands and was ruined.

These were stimulating recollections.

I got off my rock and went home to write a letter to *Private Eye* saying 'Yes'. I did, fortunately, manage to come out of my exhilarating haze of thoughts about satire long enough to stipulate that I must be paid a sum – huge in relation to their tiny financial resources as they then stood – sufficient to assuage the fears of any Irish creditors who might be alarmed at my leaving the jurisdiction. I also made it a condition that I must have at least three weeks in London, before assuming the temporary editorship, in order to inform myself of the state of affairs: to see some men who knew some men. This was to be at the expense of *Private Eye*. But by a nice coincidence the *Sunday Telegraph* people got the idea they would like to have me within easy reach for a bit, so they paid these expenses instead, relieving *Private Eye* of quite a burden. It is always agreeable to see the rich helping the poor. Still, I could see I was going to be busy. For despite Donald McLachlan's eager anxiety to cut what he called the 'Umbilical Cord' supposed to be spiritually linking the *Sunday Telegraph* to the Tory orthodoxy of its rich Mama, the *Daily Telegraph*, it was still going to be quite a trip, involving sharpish changes of climate from the *Telegraph* office in Fleet Street to the bottom of Greek Street, Soho, where – between a strip-tease and a betting-shop, into which some gangster had recently thrown a more or less abortive bomb – was located the office of *Private Eye*.

The barker for that strip-tease has a claim to be classed with the top ten of the world's optimists. As I approached the office for the first time very early on a bright Friday afternoon he spoke to me urgently, begging me to view the naked women. Since I was a stranger, that was intelligible. I certainly hope that I am not the only man who looks as though he might want to spend a sunny afternoon in that way. But I have entered the *Private Eye* office several hundred times since then, and when I have been alone, the barker has never failed to look me in the face and repeat the invitation with the same hopeful urgency. On this first occasion, before going up to the office I stepped into the betting-shop and placed the type of bet known as a 'Yankee' on four of the races still to be run that day. By the evening I was able to collect a little over £72 for the twenty-two shillings I had bet. That was agreeable in itself, and could be deemed a good omen. That betting-shop was certainly an amenity. In the old days, a person briefly visiting London from Ireland with its very numerous legal betting-shops, had found it a frustrating, sometimes nearly agonizing, task to find a place to get his money on in a hurry. With betting now legalized in Britain, I used often, when editorial problems became harassing, to drop down to this place next door and enjoy, for a half-hour or so, the mingled excitement and relaxation of betting a little money, and listening to the races being broadcast from the course. Other *habitués* included many heavily razor-scarred but, for the most part, infectiously cheerful Maltese negroes. They were obviously poor, and I cannot imagine what they had to laugh about. Nor did I ever find out, because they were notably stand-offish with whites. But, as a tiny contribution to study of the Social Scene, I noted that their nerves seemed in better shape than were those of the white gamblers. These latter would often twitch and swear and even gnash their teeth as the loud-speaker reported the failure of their fancy. The negroes from Malta – who must have guessed wrong just as often as anyone else – smiled through it all, only occasionally letting go with a guttural sigh.

Greek Street, like so much of Soho, is soothing in its architectural charm. It is not always easy for a sane man to appreciate the charm because he is rightly nagged by the thought that there must be something perhaps dangerously wrong with a society which can daily produce enough customers to support so many strip-tease joints. Brothels are less unseemly. The best, though certainly not the 'peak' Viewing Time for Soho is a shining Sunday mid-morning. (At night the neon lights are pretty, though they could often be a lot prettier, but they obscure or distort the building structures.) On Sunday morning the streets are almost free of traffic. The poor strippers are at rest. So are the rich club owners and the protection racketeers. Behind a closed door here and there, the coshed and the burgled are for the most part still unaware of what happened to them in the dark early hours. There is so little noise that you can hear the church bells calling the faithful to prayer. Sunday is press day for *Private Eye*, and on the first such Sunday I was there I was standing on the doorstep of *Private Eye*, waiting for the Coach and Horses public house to open, when the customary hush was shattered by a rising roar of motor-cycle engines. From Soho Square, a cohort, led by a uniformed policeman, was coming slowly and rowdily down Greek Street. It just crossed my mind that we were being raided, possibly for seeking to raise boils on the already red faces of government men. Just as the leading policeman drew level with us, he turned to shout over his shoulder at the cohort behind.

'And that,' he said, with a big hand-signal, 'is *Private Eye*.'

We ascertained that the cohort was composed not of policemen but of aspirant taxi-drivers. On Sunday mornings Scotland Yard takes a score or so of them on conducted tours of London, teaching them the geography of the city and the location of the most notable buildings and institutions. It was gratifying to realize that we were up there among the worthwhile sights and tourist attractions along with St Paul's and the White City dog-track.

I taxied and telephoned for the stipulated three weeks, working at meeting – or re-meeting – the men who knew the men. The experience reminded me of the days of *The Week*. Under certain stimuli, the normally taciturn or discreet members of the British Establishment can become quite astonishingly talkative. The reek of the political mess of that year provided such a stimulus for many. A surprising number seemed to feel that the best way for all good men and true to come to the aid of the country was to spill whatever beans they might have to an uninhibited satirical magazine. (Naturally, a lot of the beans were mouldy, or phoney – made of plastic gossip. But, as I have said before, even the existence of a particular rumour can be a significant fact.)

Nevertheless, as the time approached when I was to take over sole editorial charge, while the regular editors took off for foreign parts, I was daunted, and often wished myself back on that sun-warmed, lonely rock. But the charm, the ebullient confidence, and the tireless assistance of all concerned in the enterprise reduced any natural alarms. Also the ululations against satire and satirists now to be heard on all sides seemed convincing evidence that the satirists were achieving something useful, and might achieve more.

In this belief I was notably encouraged by the personality of Richard Ingrams, editor. He had been a progenitor of the magazine – a bold notion in itself. Perhaps more important and remarkable was the fact that as editor he had kept the little boat afloat in storms – external and internal – which would certainly have wrecked a craft less ably skippered. (I speak of 'internal' storms because obviously people working enthusiastically for such a magazine are not likely to be the most placid of men.) Even Malcolm Muggeridge at *Punch* had no more tricky a job than Richard.

'"Daddy's on the engine",' says the old music-hall song, '"don't be afraid. Daddy knows what he is doing," said the little maid. "Daddy's on the engine, there's no need for fear. My Daddy's on the engine, and my Daddy's an engineer."' Such reassurances were being loudly voiced from Westminster, Whitehall and elsewhere, as always in Times of Crisis, whatever government chances to be in power. I have forgotten whether, in the song, the little maid's faith was justified, or whether the train was wrecked with carnage. In real life (and I am not speaking principally or even mainly, of the farcical, yet unpleasantly ominous, events of 'Profumo year', a year in which the Profumo affair can be seen by hindsight as one of the least of the nation's troubles), it is customarily hard to believe that more than a very few of the numerous people on the engine are engineers at all.

At this point we get one of the main divisions in political thinking. Granted that the man on the engine has very little idea what he is doing, ought we or ought we not to apprise the passengers? There are those on the one hand who say, 'Absolutely not. People would panic and start pulling the communication cord. They might even surge up the corridors and try to get on the engine themselves, whereupon the whole vehicle would be brought into greater peril than ever. Leave the men on the engine alone. With a large hatful of luck they might get us somewhere without a smash-up. And if not, well, that just goes to show that journeying through the world is a hazardous business and it is a mistake to look for too much security.' The people who take this view exist everywhere – in communist countries no less than in others. It was one of the reasons why Stalin got left on the engine a long time after he was visibly unfit to run the train. Others, and they, too, exist in millions everywhere, are all for spreading the dire news among the passengers as speedily as possible. They think these unfortunates have the right at least to know what is going on up there at the head of the train. Some of them think that just spreading that news, and pointing with derision at the way the driver is acting, is all that they can usefully do. They are satirical and unconstructive. They admit they probably could not operate the engine any better themselves, while claiming as credit to themselves that at least they are not even pretending to. Some others are firm in the belief that once the passengers know what is happening they will somehow find ways and means to avert the threatened catastrophe – perhaps, somewhere in the second-class coaches, there are some real engineers. These call themselves democrats, but as they have never yet got full control of the footplate, nobody knows what their large claims amount to.

What arouses the indignation of the honest satirist is not, unless the man is a prig, the fact that people in positions of power or influence behave idiotically, or even that they behave wickedly. It is that they conspire successfully to impose upon the public a picture of themselves as so very sagacious, honest and well-intentioned. You cannot satirize a man who says 'I'm in it for the money, and that's all there is to it.' You even feel no inclination to do so. In the 1930s it was easier, or perhaps simply more stimulating, to satirize the leaders of the British Government than to go to work on Hitler or Mussolini. For these latter, at least in the eyes of other peoples than their own, were creatures who roared out in public their bestial thoughts and intentions. Hitler in particular, because he had the enthusiastic support and spiritual concurrence of the vast majority of Germans, had no need of that hypocrisy which Wilde described as the tribute vice pays to virtue. He said he was going to persecute and murder the Jews, and no sooner was it said than it was done. He proclaimed his delinquent's contempt for civilization, and, to ensure that nobody misunderstood him, organized such fêtes and galas as the 'burning of the books'. He lied certainly – lied continuously. But his lying was of a special kind – it did not, and could not by him have been expected to, deceive anyone who did not secretly wish to be deceived. In this he resembled the great confidence tricksters.

The confidence tricksters consider it axiomatic that no wholly honest man can be regarded as a likely victim of the confidence trick. It is not the mere fools that the confidence men successfully delude. It is, in their pregnant phrase, the 'larceny in the blood' of the victim which results in his victimization. And that was how Hitler operated – exploiting and using as his leverage the 'larceny in the blood' of innumerable politicians in every country who wanted to believe that here was a man who really had found a way of making diamonds out of plastics; a way, that is to say, of making a quick profit out of an illicit sale of the Western soul. You cannot satirize a confidence trickster – the best you can do is expose him, or send for the police. But when you find a respectable citizen – the victim – who, beneath his air of solid good sense and goodwill is secretly hoping to turn a dishonest political profit by getting a flashy-looking collection of goods labelled 'peace' or 'security' or 'the end of Bolshevism' for some minimal down-payment in the way of a betrayal of the Jews, or the sacrifice of a couple of small nations, then you have a subject which invites and excites the attention of the satirist.

The satirist, as I have remarked, is certainly among those who cannot bear that the passengers should be left for a moment longer in ignorance of the incompetence or malignancy of the engine driver. He is also likely to feel that having done that much his particular function has been accomplished, and he is not apt to pay much heed to those who keep asking him for his 'solution'. He will reply that while he may, in some other capacity – as, say, a voter or a magistrate or trade union secretary – feel able and bound to propose and work towards 'solutions', as a satirist this is not his job.

With such thoughts in mind I started to get my special issue together. About lay-out I know scandalously little. Nothing, in fact, or just enough to be a nuisance to experts who do. (It is characteristic of our educational system that when I was young nobody told journalists just graduated from Oxford that it was their business to know at least the elements of all the processes of their trade, including some manual labour at the composing machines. By the time I had grasped that this was important, there never seemed to be a spare moment in which to learn. As in so many other areas of life, one regrets, too late, not anything one has done, but all the things one might have done but never got around to doing.)

Fortunately, I had the almost imperturbable Tony Rushton to take total charge of that part of our operation. I say 'almost' because at times my notions of the technically feasible must certainly have perturbed him to the point of madness. But he remained cheerfully sane, and helped to keep me sane, I think, too.

That press day was an unexpected strain, and sometimes a nightmare, for both myself and Tony Rushton. For Dr Stephen Ward, a key figure and victim in the Profumo case, having in fact attempted suicide, was still hanging between life and death in the hospital. We had to have two cartoons ready, one for use in case he seemed to be going to survive, the other in case of his death. We rang up the hospital every half-hour, and every half-hour the printers rang us to ask why the copy was so late, and warn us that if we hung on much longer the magazine would not appear that week at all. However, it did punctually appear, and the circulation shot up to a record

figure. This, of course, was in large part due to the special circumstances of that particular fortnight, the super-heated political
atmosphere. All we did – all any publication could have done – was
to make sure that we were giving the fullest possible expression to
the true mood of the period; were reflecting what a lot of people
who were inarticulate in public were muttering in the clubs and
pubs and on their way to church, or to university lectures.

I stayed on in London for a while in case of trouble. Men who
knew men kept ringing me up saying we were going to be arrested
for this or that vexing misdemeanour committed in the issue. They
said that, as was natural enough, MI5 and the Special Branch, on
learning that the ex-editor of *The Week* had suddenly appeared out
of the deep green yonder of Ireland to do this *Private Eye* job, were
keeping a particularly sharp lookout. There was, in fact, a bit of
trouble, because I had disclosed, as a matter of current interest, the
name and address of the head of MI5. This was supposed to be a
deep state secret. One could be, it seemed, heavily penalized –
presumably under the Official Secrets Act – for disclosing the
man's identity and function. Except that I thought one might have
been hustled off to jail after a trial of which the vital parts were
conducted *in camera*, with no chance to put one's case before the
general public – a danger never to be quite disregarded when
official secrets are involved – I would not have found such a case
wholly unwelcome. Since there was no doubt at all that the Russians,
the French, the Chinese and the Americans all were familiar with
the name of the official concerned, it seemed to me ludicrous that
the British public should be kept in ignorance.

A source I had good reason to consider well-informed arranged
to meet me in an agreeably open space without microphones – not
that I believed that there really were any in the *Private Eye* office –
and told me there was a terrible row going on about the naming of
this man. Some important people, it seemed, were insisting that I
must be arrested, not because they seriously supposed the name was
not known to every major embassy in London, but 'on principle'.
It might be well known to everyone who might possibly make
improper use of such knowledge, but it was still officially secret. To
let *Private Eye* get away with publishing it would create an evil
precedent. One big thinker had, too, taken the view that to disregard *Private Eye*'s behaviour would 'cause jealousy' in Fleet
Street and thus injure MI5's secret public relations. My informant
urged me to go back to Ireland, while the going was still, possibly,
good.

I was eager to get back to that rock beside the bay. But I thought that to slink away – it would be the phrase used – just then might make myself and the magazine appear either ridiculous or guilty of some genuine crime. Also it seemed to me that, provided I was allowed to make it, my defence was unanswerable. So I stayed on till the storm blew over.

25 The Loved One

W<small>HILE</small> I still loitered in London, Mr Donald McLachlan confided to a Mutual Friend that he felt the paper was not 'making enough use' of me.

'Send him,' said the Mutual Friend, 'to New York.'

Naturally enough, McLachlan demurred – not to say recoiled.

'But surely,' he said, 'with his left-wing opinions, his general attitude to what he calls capitalist society, he would hardly be inclined to ...'

'My dear fellow,' said the Mutual Friend, 'there are Europeans who fear and detest America. There are Europeans who rather like America. Claud is the only real European I know who for more than thirty years has been passionately – and often besottedly – in love with America. Send him to see how the loved one is getting on.'

The paradox was, nevertheless, a reasonable assessment. Perhaps it is nonsense to talk of being 'in love' with a country. (Albert Camus certainly did not think so. In his story *La Femme Adultère*, the chief character – Janine – falls so much in love with the North African desert that she, lying alone on the roof of the house, listening to the silence of the desert broken only by 'the muffled cracking of the stones which the cold was splitting up into sand', and watching the stars, has a complete orgasm.)

Personally, although I have never quite duplicated Janine's experience, I believe Camus was on the right track with that story. Certain places, certain scenes, do produce in some people reactions easily comparable to the experience of sexual love. The Danube valley has this effect upon me, and so does North America.

I thought it prudent not to attempt to explain this theory to

Donald McLachlan. Such ideas can easily be misunderstood. One could be classified as unbalanced. Or else an unseemly story could percolate through the office to the effect that 'they're sending Claud to New York to have an orgasm'.

Still less, naturally, did I seek to explain myself in these terms to the United States Consul-General. In view of my past and the American present, I had to explain a good deal else to him.

Without the assistance of McLachlan and the *Sunday Telegraph* I would hardly have got to first base. The Consul-General was exceedingly kindly and co-operative. But, the United States laws on the subject being what they were, it was quite impossible for him to grant a visa to a formerly prominent member of the Communist Party without careful interrogation. The results of the interrogation had to be sent by him to the State Department, and by the State Department to the Department of Justice. Then, if the Department of Justice was satisfied, it could issue a 'waiver', permitting the State Department to inform the Consul-General that a visa could be issued.

On the steps of the Embassy in Grosvenor Square, as I went in for my interview, Patricia had given me a last, percipient, warning. 'For God's sake,' she said, 'don't try to be funny. They won't like it.' I promised, but there were moments when it was a hard promise to keep. In fact I nearly broke it in the first quarter of an hour of the interview.

The Consul-General courteously explained to me that, had I been a more or less anonymous member of the Communist Party, sitting like a bump on a log with my mouth open through months and years of meetings, and then just checked out of the organization, the matter of the 'waiver' would be simple enough. But not, very regrettably, so. I had been diplomatic correspondent, foreign editor, political correspondent, of the *Daily Worker*. I had written hundreds of thousands of communist words. I had agitated on public platforms. I had fought in Spain. Therefore, what the Department of Justice would be looking for was some evidence of what was called 'commensurate counter-activity'.

I said, 'You mean like Arthur Koestler and Douglas Hyde?'

He maintained diplomatic silence and immobility.

Breaking my promise to Patricia I said, 'If there's still time, I might with your assistance, rush out and write an article for *Encounter*.' This was in the days – now past – when *Encounter* was supposed to benefit – directly or indirectly – from the special interest of the State Department and the C.I.A. As Patricia had predicted, the

Consul-General was not amused. But despite this he went right ahead doing his best for me.

Towards the end of the interview he asked, more or less perfunctorily, what 'front organizations' I had been a member of in my time. I said 'None', and then recalled that I had been, for a matter of two months, the press officer of an organization called the People's Convention. I told him that, and he said he knew that already. But what other 'front organizations' had I belonged to?

'None.'

He looked very grave. It was an answer, he conveyed to me as diplomatically as possible, that would not satisfy the Department of Justice. Indeed it would make them very suspicious. From his explanation emerged the fact that the American Establishment had become the prisoner of its own propaganda to the extent of believing that since the cunning commies are known to operate through front organizations, all genuine communists must have been members of a lot of these, and a communist – claiming to be ex-communist – who denies that he was a member of such, must still be a cunning commie, not 'ex' at all.

I racked my brains to think of some such organization, somewhere, that I might have at some time joined. Restrained by my promise to Patricia, I prevented myself listing a lot of impeccably Tory or Labouristic or religious organizations which, had I named them, would have found themselves under laborious surveillance by the F.B.I. and the subject of interesting reports from the C.I.A.

At length, I said, 'Sir, I can only tell you that being a full-time, hard core, all down the line, red Red, was a full-time job. I just did not have the time to go out and join anything else. Besides, I never got on very well with the front members of front organizations.'

He sighed resignedly and made some notes. But he must have been as honestly friendly as he seemed, for in a couple of weeks my visa came through.

If New York really resembled the image of itself it projects through the cinema and other media it would certainly be hell – or, at the best, Dortmund. A cliff-dwelling Megalopolis, smooth and shining, and whizzing around the clock with inhuman precision.

On the contrary, the essential quality of that city is that it simply refuses to tick over in that fashion. It is a rich museum of ramshackle inefficiency. Only those Europeans who have been willingly brain-washed by the films fail to notice its true, and truly endearing characteristics. It is, one must remember, a city created by fanatics and extremists: the original Dutch and English refugees from religious and political conformity; the German liberals on the run; the starving Irish; and the Jews who, even when they are most active and successful in their service of Mammon, never omit to remind themselves and everyone else of the pervasive existence of things unseen. In New York, a rich Anglo-Saxon can lull you into the belief that being rich and Anglo-Saxon is about as far as you can get. But the rich New York Jew almost always gives one the impression of a man with a mask that keeps slipping. The mask twitches and slips, and has the effect of caricaturing the whole set-up, the whole of the values according to which he purports to live.

And if the reader now thinks he is observing simply the effects of the love affair, let me say at once that if you take another close look at that haggard old bag, New York, you will not have to look or go far to see its casual cruelty, the callous wickedness of man's in-humanity to man. In fact, when you feel you may be falling fatuously in love with New York, the thing to do is to take a walk through Harlem, if you, as a white person, dare do that. The fact that a lot of white people would, quite rightly, not dare walk through much of Harlem is sufficient comment on the state of the city. It is a supreme example of social inefficiency triumphing, temporarily at least, over all the advantages provided by riches and technology.

This is the far from endearing aspect of New York's ramshackle way of life. On the other hand, that way of life – product of all those fanaticisms which New York fought and cherished turn by turn – has produced in large areas of New York life a kind of genial permissiveness, a shirt-sleeved *je m'en foutisme,* an acceptance of the fact that the next man may look mad to you but may seem sane to himself, which is the antithesis of everything that is meant by 'McCarthyism' or 'Goldwaterism'. It is no great wonder that Gold-water once expressed the view that it would be a good thing if New York just broke off from the continent and floated away into the Atlantic Ocean, joining, I suppose, the wrecked ships of the world in the Sargasso Sea.

You can relax in New York because people there freely and openly admit what is going on to an extent that the London people who know do, as I have said, only under special stimuli. You do not have to contend with either hypocrisy or complacency. In New York even a banker will tell you that, in his opinion, the 'system' makes less and less sense, and may have to be defended with the sub-machine-guns of the police. He may be wrong. But he says it. What London banker would allow such thoughts to pass the barrier of his lips? Only the newspapers even hope to be believed when

208

they claim that napalm versus peasant is 'democracy's last hope'.

But all this time, as everyone now sadly knows, a time bomb was ticking – and not in New York alone.

Adlai Stevenson went to Texas and was there spat upon and otherwise physically assaulted. And in the atmosphere of those days – electric with hatred – the episode was not regarded as a major national scandal. Naturally I had no notion of what was really going to happen next, but I did remark to a number of people that there was something dangerously sinister about the situation in which a man of Mr Stevenson's eminence – United States Ambassador to the United Nations – could be thus treated without the newspapers raising more than a perfunctory, routine-type outcry and protest.

Then Mr Stevenson came back to New York and did a thing which, in his position, was courageous. He warned President Kennedy that in his, Stevenson's, opinion, it would be a dangerous thing for the President to go to Texas – an intention of which Stevenson had just learned. I was told of this warning on the following day in the very greatest confidence. I have sometimes wondered since whether it was, perhaps, one of those confidences one is supposed to break. Just possibly someone had the idea that if the fact of such a warning were published somewhere (whereupon it would be likely to be picked up and published everywhere), the grim course of events might be changed.

But that was not what I thought at the time. What I thought then was that the story, though really creditable to Stevenson, could do him nothing but harm. He would be accused of trying to put his own scare into the President of the United States.

But with the confidential knowledge of that warning in mind, I began to be just aware, at the back of my mind, of the possibility of a tragedy moving as though written by Sophocles, an ineluctable conclusion. On the day I returned from the United States, I tried to explain some of these thoughts to people in Fleet Street, and elsewhere.

It was not easy. And the difficulties of so doing were expressive of the basic difficulties of Anglo-American relations. For in the United States people had been inclined to regard me as typically Anglo-tepid in my supposed underestimation of the power of the political dynamite that might at any moment this year, next, sometime, but not never – explode. In London I was treated as a sensationalist.

However, I am used to being so treated by English people, and I plugged ahead, seeking to set out my view. It was an error, I told them, to suppose – as most of them did at that time – that President

209

Kennedy was so universally popular and loudly acclaimed as to be politically omnipotent. On the contrary, his necessary effort to keep the South in line for his re-election of 1964 – and he absolutely needed the South – had at this time produced a mood of disappointed scepticism about him (and still more about his brother, the Attorney General) among many liberal and negro leaders. They were not by any means against the Kennedys. But the impetus of their enthusiasm for them was lagging and sagging.

All through a horrible November day in London I tried to clarify to myself and others – I had left New York only the night before – the atmosphere in which it seemed to me these things must be regarded as important. I was aware of boring a lot of people a lot of the time. Finally came that moment of defeat, so common in England, when the editor I was lunching with said, 'Well, well that's all terribly interesting, and I'd like to talk about it some more next week. There might be a piece in it. Meantime, you've been flying the Atlantic half the night, so why don't you go back to your hotel and have a nice rest? Relax.'

I did that. And around six the telephone was ringing and the editor was saying, 'Can you get down to the office right away? The President has been shot dead in Dallas.' The fact that you have had a feeling, as the old saying goes, 'in your bones' that a particular appalling thing might happen, makes it no easier to realize that it actually has happened. And there is, in all such circumstances, the odious sensation that someone is going to accuse you of saying 'I told you so.' When, in reality you did not – absolutely could not – have 'told them so'.

In the months after the assassination, veritable demons were working overtime in millions of hearts, and millions longed chiefly for the demons to be put under heavy sedation. After what seemed, in moments of depression, the nearly demonic world of New York and London, it was a relief to return to Ireland.

26 At Arlington House

I AM not sure – perhaps no one else is either – just when people began to choose decades as being the segments it is proper to hack time into. Did people in, say, 1580 refer to the spirit of the 1530s, or the attitudes of the 1560s, some of them thanking God that such spirits and attitudes were eschewed by their contemporaries of the eighties, others deploring their disappearance?

Such divisions and characterizations are neat for ready reference; and may sometimes help to light up a bit of truth. But when I read, as one so often does, sapient stuff about the spirit of the 1930s I get a buzzing in the head and wonder 'Was you there, Charlie?' Because whereas what I am reading may be a roughly accurate sketch of the spirit in which Tom squared up to the problems of that decade, it certainly is not true of the way Dick carried on, and as for Harry, my God I could tell you a thing or two about *his* attitude to and in the thirties. So how accurate, in terms of what you and I think and do, will twenty-first century generalizations about the 1970s and 1980s prove to be? Moreover, how is one to explain to the questioning grandchildren how the average person thought and acted in this decade or that, if the average person never existed, and the decades keep blurring into one another?

One answer is, by recalling and seeking to depict not some imaginary average man, woman or child, but quite to the contrary a real person who, so far from being average, may have been a rum customer, in some way outstanding, yet of whom you can say with confidence: that one could not have existed at any other time; he shed light upon his period; was in fact a period piece. Get a whiff of him and you have a whiff of the genuine *Zeitgeist*.

With this in mind, I think at once of Lord Beaverbrook.

As I mentioned early in this book, Lord Beaverbrook had been just out of sight on the fringe of my life when I was still a boy, charged by my Uncle Frank with concealing from my father Uncle Frank's unavowable intimacy with 'that fellow Aitken'. As the years wore on, the probability of my personally meeting Lord Beaverbrook lessened with each successive step in my career. I was thus considerably astonished when, on one of my occasional visits to London in the early sixties, I received – transmitted by some functionary at the *Daily Express* – an invitation to dine with Beaverbrook at Arlington House, the apartment block just behind the Ritz known as the Millionaires' Rookery. I thought this invitation particularly bizarre because I was at the moment staying with Malcolm Muggeridge, with whom, for reasons I was not clear about (I think Malcolm had insulted him in print or over the air), Beaverbrook had for some time been engaged in an implacable feud.

Malcolm explained to me that my astonishment was naïve. The invitation, he said – and he proved to be correct – had been extended not despite the feud but because of it. 'Just because,' said Malcolm, 'he knows that we have been closely associated, he cannot resist trying to do something to separate us – poison our relationship. That is the way his mind works.'

'But why the devil,' I said, 'should he *bother*?'

It really did puzzle me, and Malcolm had to read me another lecture on the subject of my naïvety. However rich, powerful and hugely able such tycoons as Beaverbrook may be, they are inexorably impelled, like similar jumped-up despots and tyrants in the ancient world, to take anxious notice of, and action against, every manifestation of hostility, however small. The action may take the form of trying to buy off the hostile elements, or of trying to ruin them. Certainly the tycoon will seek to create dissension among them. 'Probably,' Malcolm said, 'he will hope to inveigle you into making some small criticism of myself. Then he will cause an exaggerated version of this to be conveyed to me. "I hear Claud was speaking pretty coolly about you at Max Beaverbrook's the other night." You'd be surprised how often it works.'

'The way,' I said, 'that some women in bed try to lure one into saying something disobliging about one's wife.'

'Exactly.'

Arriving at Arlington House I was reminded that someone had once written of Lord Beaverbrook that his idea of the finest and grandest in the get-up of a dwelling place had been implanted long, long years ago when, as a poor boy from New Brunswick he had first been dazzled by the foyer of the Château Frontenac Hotel in Quebec. A thought full of pathos. In this spacious and depressing décor I found my host alone, and immediately learned that I had been asked early because he wished to have some private discussion with me. Seen at close range he was just a little more unsightly than I had imagined from his photographs. While champagne was poured, I remembered how, when a very young man, I had asked a young woman for whom I had calf love, and who, I knew, had been a mistress of Beaverbrook's, how in God's name she had managed to endure physical contact with him without nausea? In youthful jealousy and passion I described him as 'that warty toad'. I said I supposed she kept her eyes tightly shut and thought of his millions. She explained that I was the victim of a typically childish mistake. 'There was no question,' she said, 'of overcoming sexual repulsion for the sake of money and power. If you were just a little more experienced you would know that money and power are in themselves, and quite without detours, sexually attractive.'

Nevertheless it still seemed to me that it must be sad to have such a body, and seeing this body squatting in that melancholy expanse of apartment I felt a sort of sadness and pity for my little host. This absurd feeling was so strong that I accepted the champagne which I did not like much at any time and detest as a drink before dinner. But it was evident that my host believed it to be the finest, grandest drink on earth at all times, and in my ludicrously pitying mood I felt that to ask for a dry martini instead would have wounded the little fellow's feelings. And suppose, by some astounding mischance, there were no ingredients for a dry martini available? What an intolerable loss of face that would be. For I share the original Chinese understanding of 'loss of face'. In English it has come to mean that the person who makes some gaffe, or exposes himself in some way, is humiliated. But in its original sense it means that when anyone, including your enemy, exposes himself in such a way, not only he, but you too and the entire human race are thereby diminished. That is why it is wrong to pursue an argument to the point where your opponent suffers a visible and total defeat. One must always stop just short of that; must let him, in the later phrase, 'off the hook'.

Musing thus, gulping the unwelcome champagne, and longing for a really big slug of gin or vodka, I heard Lord Beaverbrook, seated by my side, saying:

'You are a good friend of Malcolm Muggeridge?'

I said that was so.

'Do you,' said Lord Beaverbrook, 'consider him a good man?'
'I do.'
'Do you consider him a truly great man?'
'I do.'

Recalling Malcolm's warning, I noted what seemed to be a flicker of annoyance cross Beaverbrook's face as I rapped out these unqualified responses. There was a small but noticeable hesitation before he produced what was clearly intended to be the clincher.

'Do you,' he said, 'regard him in the light of a latterday John the Baptist, sent among us with the mission to lead the peoples out of darkness into light?'

'Lord Beaverbrook,' I said, 'you take the very words out of my mouth.'

He was only briefly nonplussed by this counter-ploy. He jumped up from the sofa, went purposefully across the room and hopped up onto a small podium or dais upon which, incongruous with the other furnishings, stood a gnarled-looking wooden lectern. I was told later – but I am not sure whether it was true – that this was the lectern from which his father used to read the lessons in the church of his native place in New Brunswick. Laid out upon this in preparation for my visit were papers covered with figures and comparative statistics all designed to prove that Malcolm's period as editor of *Punch* had been disastrous for the circulation and advertising revenue of that paper.

These statistics Beaverbrook read aloud with a fervent intensity which would have been suited to a reading of some minatory passages from Jeremiah. But just as the prophet Jeremiah often treated his Israelite audience as nearly moronic in its awareness of truth and holiness, so Lord Beaverbrook, as I had sometimes heard from others, was inclined to regard anyone with my sort of un-businesslike educational background and accent as being ignorant to the point of total gullibility in matters of finance. He had therefore not taken the trouble to ensure that his figures and statistics, when read aloud with vehement conviction, should at least sound more or less genuine. In fact they were faked in the way statistics commonly are – that is, the individual figures were correct, but had been selected and juxtaposed in such a way as to give a grotesquely false impression.

The matter seemed not worth arguing about, and in any case I was saved from saying more than that it was all very interesting by the interruption of the first of my fellow guests, Randolph Churchill.

He said 'Good evening', shook hands with me in a perfunctory way and turning to our host said:

'I suppose I should know you well enough, and understand sufficiently the London of our day, not to feel any surprise when, on visiting a multi-millionaire and leading newspaper proprietor, I find him tête-à-tête with a former associate of the bloody dictator Stalin, a journalist who throughout his career has aided and abetted many of the vilest international political crimes in history and regularly exerted himself to instigate and foment dissension and subversion among the lowest and worst affected elements in our own country.'

This colourful tirade should have been stimulating. For although it was the kind of thing I had, naturally, often read about myself, and heard spouted by public orators, there was a novelty about these circumstances which should have been refreshing.

Unfortunately, except when drunk at mid-morning, and then preferably mixed about fifty-fifty with a half pint of Guinness in what is called either a Bismarck or a Black Velvet, champagne's effect upon myself is disagreeably sedative, producing a most unsocial torpor. In the forty minutes or so before Churchill's arrival I had drunk much of Lord Beaverbrook's fine vintage, swallowing each glass in the futile hope that it would have a more uplifting effect than the one before.

I even began to wonder whether there might be any way of calling the whole thing a day and getting away to have a sandwich and enlivening drink in a pub. Annoyingly, though not meaning to be annoying, I remarked to Churchill that although I had naturally heard it all before, I was quite happy to hear it all again, so well-phrased. Indeed it was a curious fact about Randolph Churchill that he could talk a whole lot better than he could write.

My dopey impassivity in turn annoyed Lord Beaverbrook, who said, 'I think you should be a little more aggressive, Mr Cockburn. Just a little more aggressive.'

This revealing remark really did shake me out of my lassitude. I realized that this dreary, bored little chap had brought about this encounter between Randolph and myself simply for the reason that some people go to watch a cock-fight.

It seemed an excellent opportunity to leave, telling our host that whatever Mr Churchill might feel about it I did not wish to act as a fighting-cock for his amusement. But before I could do so there began to arrive further guests of such macabre historical fascination that I could not possibly forgo the experience of their presence.

I think there were five of them. But since, with one exception, they all looked much alike I was not immediately sure which was which. The exception was Churchill's then wife, a youngish, pretty girl. The others had an air of having been exhumed: some seeming to be skulls with rouged lips and cheek-bones, others still having tatters of skin and shrunken flesh above their black ties or bare collar-bones. Two of them were introduced as Lord and Lady Margesson, and once again I experienced the sensation of living in several decades at once. For a great part of the thirties, David Margesson had been of powerful and sinister significance. As chief Tory Whip in the House of Commons, he had been a principal and indispensable operator of the cruel and ultimately disastrous policies of the National Government throughout that period. He had played, as I vividly recalled, a continuously more important role than many far better-known figures in that 'little moment between the crisis and the catastrophe'.

Lord Beaverbrook, with his incitement to aggression, had already disclosed his motive, discourteous if not downright shabby in a host, for getting Randolph Churchill and me simultaneously to dinner. But I found the presence of the Margessons inexplicable. Perhaps Beaverbrook recalled some particularly offensive remarks of mine about Margesson in *The Week*, or some other publication, and wished to lace the soup with a little more mutual hatred and disgust among his guests. But in that case, who were the other two barely resuscitated corpses at the board? Possibly relatives of Neville Chamberlain? Or of Nancy Astor?

Conversation with the woman member of the pair did not reveal their identity. Indeed it occurred to me as being not so much a conversation as some kind of invitation to necrophilia. It is just possible that had I not been rendered languid, and my brain addled by the champagne, which continued its fizzy flow throughout this dinner, this neighbour at the table might have proved to be a sparkling talker and woman of rare intelligence whom it was a privilege to meet. As things were, I turned as soon as I decently could to my neighbour on the other side, Mrs Randolph Churchill. I did not suppose we would find a great deal in common, but she was refreshingly easy on the eye and we exchanged a few civilities, not far above the 'cool for the time of year' level. Almost immediately an explosion occurred on the other side of the long, rather narrow table. Randolph erupted into a roar of unintelligible abuse.

Beaverbrook shouted down the table to him to shut up. He protested.

'Max,' he shouted, 'when I see my wife being fondled by the

bloodstained hands of one of the wickedest of international terror-
ists, when I see her virtually in the embrace of a notorious political
murderer, am I to make no protest? Am I to accept such a situation
in silent resignation?'

Listening to this tirade, I admired, not for the first time, Randolph
Churchill's capacity as a sensational journalist. He could have
reviewed *Pride and Prejudice* for the *Sunday Express* and made it
sound like Harold Robbins.

Despite shouts from Beaverbrook and disapproving murmurs all
around the table, Churchill continued to froth and roar until his
intrepid wife led him from the room, leaving the rest of us seated
amid the social debris of the dinner party. I felt sympathy with
Churchill. If what he saw as the enormity of my presence on such an
occasion had so much shocked and startled him as to bring on a
brainstorm of uncontrollable rage, that, though it could be classed
as over-reaction, was to my mind respectable. That is to say it was
respectable, assuming that he really believed all the nonsense he
talked. People do become the victims of their own propaganda,
and he possibly did see me as a mass-murdering terrorist, and
unsuitable company at dinner.

I, for my part, was obscurely depressed and even shocked by the
realization that Lord Beaverbrook, who had for so long played so
important a role, sometimes public, more importantly behind the
scenes, in British political life, should prove, on personal acquaintance, to be a person of such laboriously spiteful triviality as he had
this evening shown himself to be.

In particular, I thought of all the people – especially young people
of the left – whom he had at one time and another corrupted and
politically seduced. Even now it would be futile to print the names
of some of those who had taken his money, because nobody would
believe it. Some of them did not believe it themselves. I remember
saying to the wife of one prominent politician of the left that I
thought she should warn her husband against a habit of speaking
indiscreetly, especially when drunk, of his relations with Lord
Beaverbrook. As happens when one foolishly attempts to offer this
kind of advice, she flared up furiously. 'Never a penny in cash has
John ever had from Max,' she shouted. 'Hotel bills, hospital bills, a
holiday on the yacht, maybe. But never a penny in cash.'

Beaverbrook was a less corrupting influence at the top of the
Establishment than Lloyd George. That was for the sufficient
reason that he had so much less power. There was nothing astonishing in the extent and blatancy of the corruption which are no

greater in Britain than in France or the United States. What truly astonished me was the extent to which the British Establishment, including the corrupters and the corrupted, have, despite all, managed to keep alive for public circulation the legend that that sort of thing does not happen in England: or that when it happens it is an unusual phenomenon, swiftly dealt with and eliminated the moment there is any evidence of its existence. In the 1930s, when London was a secretive place and the press suffered from discretional lockjaw, it was not surprising that this façade could be maintained. It was more difficult to understand it in the supposedly, and sometimes genuinely, more open 1960s and 1970s. Yet it was so, despite, for example, the Poulson case, despite the behaviour of some of Harold Wilson's friends and acquaintances, despite the reek of his final Honours List.

But to return to the dinner party, or rather to its aftermath.

'You deserve a stiff Scotch,' said Malcolm, when I finally tottered back to his house. 'After all, you have been disillusioned, bored, and repeatedly insulted all in the course of a single evening.'

'Not exactly insulted.'

'Not by Randolph? He *is* a bit of a bully.'

'I don't find his sort of talk insulting. If that's the way he thinks, it's the way he thinks. I suppose I was a bit insulted by Beaverbrook thinking I would cock-fight for his entertainment.'

'He's so used to people dancing to his tune he's lost his sense of who'll dance and who won't. Not surprising when you think.'

'True. When you think.'

We both thought. I told him how I had once met Kingsley Martin, then editor of the *New Statesman*, in a state of shock after a visit – his first I gathered – to the Beaverbrook pleasure-manse at Leatherhead.

Kingsley had accepted the invitation on the assumption that his opinion was to be sought on some matter of national, or international, importance. This was a natural assumption for Kingsley to make. He was one of the most English Englishmen I have met. So that, for instance, it seemed to him reasonable, if not quite inevitable, that this Canadian flibbertigibbet twirling around for so many years like a bat out of hell in an England obviously alien to him, should at some point seek counsel of one who combined with rare political acumen a native and instinctive understanding of what makes the English tick; a man of the left certainly, a socialist indeed, but a socialist of the strictly English type, no doctrinaire, but a pragmatist of the kind who could without political rancour or *parti pris* offer impartial advice to such a one as Lord Beaverbrook.

He accordingly prepared to sacrifice a half day of his, and the *New Statesman*'s, time to this act of political ministry. And since he felt, as so many Englishmen have done before him, that he understood Lord Beaverbrook a lot better than Beaverbrook was likely to understand him, he was pretty confident that he would, with quiet subtlety, exploit Lord Beaverbrook just when Beaverbrook thought he was the one doing the exploiting.

He came back in a state of shock. Surprise and setback number one had been to find the place full of left-wing socialists, many of them younger than himself and, if possible, more left, more dedicatedly socialist, and all confident that they were in some way exploiting Lord Beaverbrook. It was pretty soon evident to Kingsley, from various scraps of conversation and from his general observation of their attitudes, that in this they were absurdly and naïvely mistaken. They were being, more or less subtly, more or less crudely, bribed. Kingsley knew theoretically that this sort of thing happened. He had read Belloc's line: 'It was as some preposterous thing, as when a rich man meets a politician.' But when he saw it happening right under his eyes – in, so to speak, the flesh – it gave him a jarring jolt.

This was an aspect of his Englishness which I had often encountered when I was running *The Week*. I would mention in connection with some story I had published or was about to publish that, obviously, the explanation for this or that turn of events was that this or that official, this or that political leader had been richly bribed by this or that interested party. Kingsley would look at me with his kindly indulgent smile which held at the same time a touch of pity for my continental-type ignorance of what is done and what is not done in England. Sometimes when my cool assumption about certain causes of certain effects struck him as peculiarly outrageous he would cry out in dismay – not dismay at such a thing happening, but dismay at the fact that I or anyone else should suppose that it possibly could have happened.

One occasion when he expressed more than usual horrified incredulity concerned an allegation of grave financial impropriety about a high official of the War Office. I had told him I was going to publish it, and did so. I had hoped, not at all confidently, that, the matter being of large public importance, the *New Statesman* might take it up. Not so. A week later *The Week* repeated the allegation in sharper terms, which were extensively quoted in the European and American press. From the British Establishment press silence was naturally to be expected. But surely the socialist *New Statesman*?

Still nothing. Then, learning that I had arranged for a courageous Labour M.P. to ask a question about the matter in the House of Commons, the official concerned abruptly resigned.

And at that, Kingsley wrote in his famous *Diary* column: 'For three weeks we have been waiting for the heavens to fall upon *The Week* as a result of its allegations.' It was now evident, said the *Diary* etc., etc. I was impelled to call on Kingsley and, finding him out, to leave a note on his desk saying, 'Thanks, pal.'

27   Fellow Passengers

I⊤ was long after midnight before Malcolm and I reluctantly ended
our talk. Early the next night, as I made my way towards the saloon
bar of the pocket liner *Innisfallen* plying between Fishguard and
Cork, a tall figure with a noble-looking head and face seemed to
materialize beside me, bowed with a somewhat old-fashioned elaboration and asked was I indeed Mr Claud Cockburn, of Youghal,
journalist and author of books? Yes? In that case, he would venture
to introduce himself. He gave me his name which, let us say for
convenience of reference was Malahyde. He lived, he explained,
not very far from Youghal, on the far side of the Blackwater. He
had read much that I had written. There were several topics he
would deem it a pleasure and privilege to discuss with me. Would it
be convenient for him to call upon me at some not too distant date?
I fixed a day early in the following week, and, with another, slightly
less elaborate bow, he began to turn away. Checking this movement,
he faced me again and said: 'Before we part for the moment, Mr
Cockburn, may I ask whether you would consider it advisable for
us to form a posse, as it were, of men of goodwill to go out to Chile
to assist progressive elements there against what I fear are not only
monstrous, but exceedingly powerful enemies?'

   A little taken aback, I said that perhaps we could consider the
question of a dash to Chile at our meeting next week. A slight
frown on his handsome face, and a momentary pursing of his fine
lips seemed to indicate some dismay at this dilatory attitude on my
part. But these expressions of unease almost instantly disappeared.
He nodded assent. 'If you think so,' he said, 'I am sure it will be all
right. I have great faith in your judgement.' With that he moved
away across the deck, walking very erect and dignified under the
harsh lights.

Entering the saloon bar I saw first a distinguished Swiss horse-trainer and international show-jumper and trainer of show-jumpers, an able, courageous and amusing man with a kind of *panache* about him which one is platitudinously inclined to attribute rather to Gascons or Marseillais than to the supposedly stolid Swiss. Just beyond him at the bar I noted the unusual appearance of a thickset man in early middle age seated upon a shooting-stick, the point of which, designed to be plunged into the turf of hillside or racecourse, had been driven between the planks of the *Innisfallen*'s deck.

He wore enormous knickerbockers of the shape called in the 1920s plus-fours and at that time much worn by golfers, shooters and other people who for their own purposes, innocent or malign, wished to be taken for golfers, shooters etc. Until I saw this man that night I think I had not seen anyone in that class of leg-cover for around thirty years. His were the more striking because they, and the jacket that went with them, were patterned in enormous blue and white checks – each square being approximately four inches across. His cap was of the same tweed and pattern.

I chatted briefly with my Swiss friend but, having some arduous show-jumping to do next morning he had to go to bed. His going left me and the man in plus-fours alone with the barman and two drunks who had just managed to get aboard at Fishguard, had swallowed a few glasses of whisky and passed quietly out.

His buttocks balanced on the shooting-stick, the knickerbockers overflowing it on either side, the man said in a thick German accent 'You are French, eh? Not true?' When I told him not he said 'So is good. I do not like the French.' His tone implied that not only did he not like the French but that in this he showed judgement superior to that of anyone who did. His tone was emphatic and his accent so marked, that I asked him in German why he felt the way he did. Fishing at random for an explanation, it occurred to me that his mother might have been one of those German girls who were so much raped by French colonial troops occupying the Rhineland after the First World War. If so, I was ready to say that I understood his feelings, and that though some of the rape stories had been exaggerated the French had certainly, in my opinion, behaved badly whether one looked at the matter from an ethical standpoint or in terms of mere expediency, *Realpolitik*.

My condolences on that possible score were not needed. His censorious opinion of the French was otherwise grounded, and he explained those grounds at length. He introduced himself – 'Von Apfel'. 'You see,' he said, 'I spent more than two years of the last war in Paris.' And after a pause he added, as though I might suspect him of selfish or unpatriotic behaviour, 'in an official capacity in the service of the Reich'. 'And that,' I asked him, 'was when you began to dislike the French?' 'No, no. Not then. The behaviour of most of the French towards me was entirely correct. They perfectly understood that they had been defeated. And the intelligent ones understood that the victors have certain requirements which must be fulfilled. That is war, my good Sir.'

Enormous numbers of people of every nationality have an urge to give lectures to other people, bringing light into darkness. In my experience this urge is more than ordinarily powerful among Germans, though I have known fell-Scotsmen who ran them close. I could see that within seconds this man on the shooting-stick was going to loose off a gas attack about the meaning of war. I moved quickly to head him off, telling how many people in the Channel Islands – the only sector of Great Britain occupied by the Germans – had also behaved with the utmost correctitude, co-operating, for example, with the Gestapo by providing lists of people with subversive views or Jewish antecedents.

He nodded brusquely in acknowledgement of the Channel Islanders' correct behaviour, and went on to give further instances of how a satisfactory number of Parisians had shown themselves good Europeans who understood the meaning of war. Since he had not been in the army, and yet, from the slightly swaggering tone of his Parisian reminiscences appeared to have occupied a position of some authority and power – including, it seemed, power to intimidate such French people as might fall short of full correctitude – I had to conclude that he had been a member either of a branch of the Gestapo or SS or of some other civilian department which could whistle up the Gestapo as required. This suspicion increased as his narrative continued. It transpired that as the Allies advanced on Paris after D-Day 'certain elements' among the French, *canaille* one might say, were more and more looking for opportunities to 'revenge themselves upon me for certain things which had happened to them. There were still people about with Jewish connections.'

Apparently – his story at this point became deliberately obscure – these threats and menaces had become so irksome that rather than await some general, organized withdrawal of whatever outfit he worked with, he and some equally notorious companions had decided to make good their retreat across eastern France on their own, crouching in an east-bound railway coal wagon. The train moved very slowly, often stopping for hours at a time at stations along the route. During these stoppages von Apfel would peer furiously out of the tiny window of the wagon, note the name of the station they were at, and try to calculate 'how much longer I must endure such dirt and discomfort'. 'Like,' I could not refrain from saying, 'a Jew in one of those east-bound trucks on the way to Auschwitz.' I thought this would terminate our conversation. Not so. He nodded, obviously appreciative of my understanding of the hideous indignities put upon him. 'Exactly,' he said. 'I was in a position no better than a deported Jew.'

Despite the rigours and deprivations of the journey – 'I tell you my friend during the last twenty-four hours we were really hungry and we had to eke out the wine we had brought from Paris by severe rationing' – the train dragged them at last on to German soil. There followed an account of the difficulties experienced by such a man as von Apfel in post-war Germany so lengthily piteous that it looked like lasting the whole width of the Irish Sea. The attitude of the British, he told me in a tone more of sorrow than anger, towards an energetic German businessman trying to re-establish himself in Düsseldorf at that period, had been 'not always quite correct'. Also, in the first months, it had often been lacking in *Realpolitik*: those known as having been active Nazis, members for instance of the Gestapo, were discriminated against, even legally penalized, although it was obvious to 'men of intelligence on both sides that what was most urgently needed was mutual trust and collaboration against the danger from the East'.

In the long run, the essential demands of life had indeed been *realpolitisch* assessed. What with massive American aid and the wise encouragement of Chancellor Ehrhard to free enterprise, not to mention the collaboration of prudent trade union leaders who knew which side their bread was buttered – 'not like some of your English, eh? Not true?' – the German economic miracle had taken place and von Apfel had been richly rewarded for all his efforts on behalf, he said, 'not of myself alone but of my country and, if I may say so my friend, of all of you in the West'.

Remembering how this conversation had started, I said, 'But you still do not like the French?'

'Not *still*,' he said, 'it was just at that time that I *started* to see into and despise the French character.'

'How so? How just then?'

Well, having become rich he married a beautiful Rhenish girl. He already had a big car, and now he bought a still bigger one. For his honeymoon trip he planned something quite original and delightful: he would take his bride in the great car along the exact route of that terrible freight train, journeying this time from east to west. He would stop at various of the points he had noted on that dire journey in the coal wagon and enjoy to the full the change in his fortunes.

They took the trip all right but, believe it or not, the damned French spoiled it. A mere fifty miles or so west of the frontier von Apfel and his spouse – 'dressed very fine, up-to-date chic you may be sure' – stopped for lunch in the principal restaurant of one of the towns he had espied from the coal truck. Overflowing with gratitude to the Almighty – 'after such experiences as mine a man must believe in some kind of divine power' – and hearty goodwill to fellow-beings, von Apfel had taken occasion to explain to the waiters and, raising his voice so that all those in the little restaurant might share in enjoyment of the tale, told of just how he happened to have chosen to revisit this locality: told how after years of the occupancy of Paris he had been forced – 'the chances of war, my friends' – to flee in the freight train and now, look, he was, he dared say, as prosperous and rich as any man in that French town. It was a wonderful example of what energy and intelligence plus a bit of luck could do, and it showed that just winning a war was not everything.

It was right then that he began to turn against the French. For instead of congratulating him on his achievements, the other clients of the restaurant first glared at him, and then continued their meal in hostile silence. The waiters first ignored the couple, then slammed down their last course and, instead of bringing the liqueurs they had ordered brought the bill instead.

All along the road to Paris von Apfel's efforts to create *bonhomie* and international understanding – though he modified them somewhat after that first experience – were more or less sharply rebuffed. And at one place two tyres of the great car were covertly slashed while its owner was lunching.

It all went to show, he said to me, that the French lacked generosity of nature; were incapable of forgiving and forgetting. The Germans were prepared to forget and forgive: why not the French? 'Obviously,' he said with a tolerant, understanding kind of shrug, 'it is the fault of the Jews. They keep alive disagreeable memories, things the rest of us understand it is better to forget.'

Some of the things it would be 'better to forget' flashed across my mind. Paris under the occupation, the round-up of the Jews, the torture of the death trains, the horror of those camps where, as the

225

psychiatrist Viktor Frankl noted, many people welcomed the gas chamber as an escape from intolerable suffering. One could spit in the face of this thug. But then he would appear as the aggrieved party. One might – I believed I knew the ship better than he – lure him out on deck to see the moon on the Wexford coast and guide him to a place where he could be tripped and sent overboard. But there was a high risk of failure, and in case of failure, once more this von Apfel would certainly gain public sympathy and the result would be notably counter-productive. In the couple of seconds it takes a person to appraise such matters I concluded that the best possibility of doing him some sort of mischief lay in keeping an eye on him and, at this moment, learning something of his plans.

After that unhappy honeymoon trip, what, I asked, had happened next? He had returned to Germany and continued to boom along with the German economic miracle. So now was he coming to Ireland on holiday? Not so. He had bought a country house and estate in the west of the country and proposed to settle there, taking occasional trips to keep an eye on his business in Düsseldorf.

I expressed genuine astonishment that a man of his position in such a booming city as Düsseldorf should take such a step. He looked at me sideways with an expression simultaneously knowing and contemptuous, the contempt being speedily shadowed with suspicion. After a little pause he said 'You don't read the papers? You are not informed of the political situation in Europe?'

'In a general way.'

He gave me another long look while he evidently tried to make up his mind as to whether I was a simple ignoramus or some sort of trickster. Then he said 'You are aware I suppose of the danger from the East? Or are you as ignorantly complacent as I am afraid many of your countrymen are?'

At that, the familiar fetid stench of the Cold War seeped along the bar. Yes, indeed, the barbarian Russian hordes were only biding their time: any year, any month, almost any day now those red-starred tanks would start to roll across Westphalia, engulfing West German civilization, including the industrious businessmen of Düsseldorf. Those of them who, like von Apfel, had 'played a certain role during the period of the Third Reich', would be placed in especial jeopardy. 'Self-preservation,' said von Apfel instructively, 'is an instinct shared by human beings and animals alike. You understand this? True?'

'Too true.'

Well then, in face of the mounting threat from the East and the incomprehensible, not to say criminal, failure of the West to take adequate steps to save civilization by a nuclear bombing of Minsk or some other action, what was such a one as von Apfel to do in order to preserve himself? Whither go? He had studied the question with care. He had taken soundings. And he had concluded that of all the countries of Western Europe within easy reach of Düsseldorf, only Ireland filled his specifications: for he had discovered, he told me for my information, that Ireland was above all a country un-infected by the disease of socialism; a country run on sound Christian principles such as respect for property; a country where subversives and other *canaille* were smartly and sharply dealt with.

'So I looked about,' he said, 'for a good gentlemanly house in Ireland having some extensive flat acreage.'

'Flat?'

'Naturally. For the helicopter landing. Let us say one day I am doing business in Düsseldorf and I get the tip-off that those swine are about to move. I have my helicopter always in readiness. I get aboard and, in the bloody nick, as you say, I skip over to that green isle beyond the Irish Sea, land on my flat acreage and shit on the Bolsheviki, laughing. Ha!'

In accordance with these considerations, and with this appraisal of the facts of life in the mid twentieth century, he now conducted himself partly as a businessman beside the Rhine, partly as, he said, 'landowner and good sportsman in so lovely Ireland'.

Becoming jovial and feeling, he said, a sense of comradeship with myself, he slapped the bar vigorously with his hairy little paw and invited me and the barman to join him in singing – 'it is your real national anthem, not true?' – *It's a long way to Tipperary*.

It was indeed in Tipperary that he had acquired his gentlemanly house and the flat acreage requisite to a bolt-hole. I kept tabs on him in a random way over a number of years, vaguely on the lookout for an opportunity to bring about his discomfiture. With some disgust, I came to realize that in a limited way, and so far as his personal situation was concerned, his assessment of Ireland as the paradise and safe haven of the predator, a land where socialists cease from troubling and the racketeer is at rest, was accurate enough. I asked a friend in Tipperary why local society – land-owners, guaranteed copper-bottomed aristocrats with pedigrees and ancestral portraits, masters of hounds, powerful prelates, not to mention rock-solid businessmen and farmers – should immedi-ately cast all decency, let alone dignity, to the winds and receive into their social embrace a man who was obviously a crude bore and guttersnipe and, if one examined his career, probably a murderer too? My frank friend's reply brought me astringently to my senses.

'We accept him,' he said, 'in the first place because he is stinking rich. Richer than many of us. Also, since he is trying to buy his way into "society" or whatever you like to call it, he is more lavish with his money than we are apt to be, giving splendid parties with no expense spared for our entertainment. Secondly, his views of socialism, his paranoid fear and hatred of the Russians, his mingled contempt of the working class and obsessional fear of it, are all shared, in greater or less degree, by the majority of us. We possibly don't express ourselves quite so openly as he does, because we feel that even in Ireland, though less so than in England, to come out flatly with such views is very slightly dangerous, or perhaps vulgar, and in any case may somehow, sometime expose us to some kind of reprisals. But that makes it all the more agreeable to hear such sentiments bawled and snarled aloud by von Apfel. Finally, by being a West German he has some of the prestige of, as it were, the front-line fighter. In fact if only he were unmarried half the girls in the area would be throwing themselves at him. As a matter of fact they do that already, jumping into bed with him one after the other because, as you know, riches are themselves a powerful sexual stimulant.'

In his determination to be, when in Ireland, the image and archetype of the jolly sporting squire, loved and respected by all whether of high or low degree, von Apfel realized that he needed something more than his plus-fours, shooting-stick and rustling Deutschmarks. He needed to cultivate the poor man at his gate who, he felt confident, would not in Ireland take advantage of mateyness on the part of the owner of the Big House to get ideas above his station. Once, sometimes twice, a week von Apfel would drive the mile and a half or so to the neighbouring village which had around four hundred inhabitants and seven bars.

Entering the first of these, a noisome shebeen which he liked to think 'typically Irish', he would loudly order drinks all round for the two or three drinkers on the premises. Soon, since his car was conspicuous in the village street, they would be joined by another half dozen. After twenty minutes or so of matey drink buying and jovial *camaraderie*, von Apfel would move on to the next bar and repeat the act. He reckoned that if there were an average of seven men in each of the seven bars visited, he had, in a single evening by this strategy, won or consolidated the warm affection and respectful loyalty of nearly fifty of these neighbouring peasants. Apart from other flaws in his estimate of the Irish character, there was one simple but fatal error in his calculation. He was, that is to say, at fault in supposing that the men he bought drinks for in the seven different bars were seven different men in each bar. Not so. The same drinkers simply followed him, at reasonably discreet intervals, from bar to bar, secure in their realization that von Apfel, from the complacent heights of his superiority, thought all Irish persons of the lower orders looked pretty much alike anyway.

For those drinkers von Apfel was a bonanza – a poor bloody damn fool, certainly, but a gift horse whose mouth no sensible man was going to peer into.

Naturally, by the time the seventh bar was reached, von Apfel himself who, like many Germans, thought his head was a lot stronger than it was, had usually become tipsy, maudlin and obfuscated. There came a night when his boozed condition was more than ordinarily notable. As he staggered to his car and drove off, waving drunken farewells with one hand and weaving back and forth across the roadway, his hardier drink-mates, savouring the last of his liquor, and buying another couple of rounds with the money he had saved them by his largesse, fell to wondering first, whether he was at all likely to reach his home without mishap, and then whether, considering all the drink they had got from him over the weeks, it might not be their Christian duty to go after him and see if he was in need of any help. By closing time they had decided that such was, indeed, the proper course for decent men. Those of them who were still capable of riding bicycles, mounted their machines and set off.

They had been right. For at the gates of the avenue to the Big House, they found von Apfel's car slewed awkwardly athwart the entrance and von Apfel himself slumped in alcoholic stupor in the driving seat.

Having come all this way and found there was no serious trouble, it occurred to the rescue party that it would be nice to end the evening with a merry jape. One of the party unshipped his bicycle lamp, while another sharply jerked open the door beside the driving seat. The man with the lamp shone it directly onto von Apfel's face, and, shaking him into consciousness shouted 'Get out! Israeli Secret Service here!'

The effect surpassed all expectation.

Von Apfel, they reported afterwards, seemed to suffer some sort of convulsion and they thought for a moment he was dead of a stroke. Then he reached out, slammed the door, got the car in gear, steered it somehow through the entrance, and disappeared up the half mile of avenue at amazing speed. It was like – one of the observers said – one of those advertisements of how a car can jump from zero to sixty miles per hour in five seconds.

He rushed into the house, shouted for servants to help him pack, and ran white-faced from room to room, carrying a pistol in one hand and with the other snatching up papers, account books and such, and jamming them into brief-cases and suitcases while the butler dealt with his clothes. By one in the morning he had five or six bags packed and loaded into the car, and went roaring off through the night on his way to Shannon airport, where he boarded the first early morning flight to the Continent – Paris, or Brussels I think.

No one in Ireland ever saw him again. But months later he wrote to acquaintances in Tipperary a cautiously worded letter stating that he was prosperously established on a coffee estate in Brazil which, it appeared, he had acquired years before in case of just such an emergency as had occurred. He wanted help from his Tipperary friends in realizing some valuable assets in Ireland, including his abandoned car, and getting the proceeds transferred to a bank account in Rio de Janeiro. And then, possibly a couple of months later, a series of strange things happened.

First one of his former acquaintances in Tipperary got a letter from him coolly announcing his imminent return to Ireland, and actually naming the ship in which he proposed to travel on a certain date. The vessel was not a regular liner but mainly a freighter – flying as I recall a Liberian flag of convenience – which could accommodate a few passengers. At about the same time a relative or relatives of von Apfel appeared at his house, and began to make preparations for his return.

Suddenly the relative or relatives received a cable from the London offices of the company which owned the ship, saying that during a stopover at Funchal, Madeira, Herr von Apfel had been taken ill, and might not be able to continue the journey immediately. Three or four days after that came another cable. It said that von Apfel's illness had been much more serious than at first supposed, and he had now died of it. He had, said this strange cable, been buried at sea.

No inquiry ever got any explanation of the mysterious circumstances of a man being buried at sea when, as the first cable had shown, the ship was in harbour at Funchal. And what had he died of? There had, apparently, been no full-time doctor aboard, the first or second mate rendering any medical services required. But the company said, or at least the relatives said the company said, that unfortunately this mate had left the ship at Lisbon and could not be traced. Had he left no record or log book? Apparently not. The ship's log only showed that a passenger by the name of Apfel had been buried at sea.

Whatever the truth might be, the story as told certainly was full of odd-looking holes. The only feature of it that seemed authentic was that somebody was anxious to prove to as many people as possible that von Apfel was dead. True, the intended 'proof' appeared to have been very clumsily manufactured. But it might quite naturally have been the best Apfel could do in the circumstances. I found rather to my surprise that those in Ireland who had known him best, accepted this 'conspiracy theory' as a matter of course.

If, they spelled it out, he was not something rather special in the way of a war criminal, why his panic flight when he thought, in an alcoholic daze, that the Israeli vengeance squads had caught up with him? Why, having fled and established himself in Brazil, should he suddenly venture back? Why indeed, unless there in Brazil he had suddenly found reason to believe that the Israelis were again getting close to him? To fake his own death might then have presented itself as an ideal solution.

It is, after all, a solution often sought, sometimes, one may opine, successfully, by men on the run from a wide variety of threats – the wrath of furious wives or mistresses, the long arm of the law, or the just vengeance of outraged fellow-beings.

Whichever way one looks at it, whether one imagines that von Apfel really did perish in mysterious circumstances at Funchal, or alternatively that he is alive and well and laughing Ha! on some Brazilian plantation, one must certainly feel that the story of his days and ways, told in simple language to the grandchildren, could do much to convey to them a taste of the somewhat acrid flavour of our times.

During the period when I was following with interest and malign intent the fortunes or misfortunes of von Apfel I had considerable converse with that other figure I had met on the same night aboard the *Innisfallen*, Mr Malahyde.

The Age had left its mark on this gentle and scholarly man by putting a bullet into his fine skull as he fought as an Irish officer in the British Army at the battle of Alamein. Some fragment of the bullet had remained there, lodged just in or under the skull.

Occasionally it disturbed his brain. 'I am,' he told me, smiling without shyness or affectation, 'a certified lunatic. As you may imagine, it is difficult for a certified lunatic to get any responsible sort of a job. On the other hand, this disability increases the size of one's pension. You probably disagree, but in my own view that sort of thing is arranged by God. For instance, if I had not been so long hospitalized or convalescent there I might never have grown to know and love Cairo, or learn Arabic.'

We were sitting in our walled garden on the afternoon arranged at our first brief meeting. In puffs there came to us across the lawn the delicious reek of the fifty-three varieties of roses planted and brought to glory by Patricia in this once shaggily barren acre, which now the roses shared with broad carpets of other flowers, beds of strawberries, bushes and canes of other fruits, and, beyond rows of peas and beans, spectacularly silhouetted against the western sky the monstrous heads of artichokes, nodding on their four-foot stalks like bizarre illustrations of a saga.

At that time and at other meetings in later years, I often found myself jolted or momentarily nonplussed by his mental processes, the movements of his trains of thought. Then I would grasp that what was confusing was not that these processes were complex or devious but were, on the contrary, disconcertingly simple and direct. I have sometimes remarked this same beautiful directness of simplicity in the conversation of Graham Greene. When Malahyde had startled me with his question about the desirability of organizing a posse to assist Allende he was quite simply asking my opinion on a matter which appeared to him serious. If direct action of that sort might have some kind of beneficial effect, however minimal, then surely it ought to be seriously and urgently considered.

It became apparent as we talked that this simplicity of thought – sometimes described as childlike by people who know little of children – combined with a habit of immediately translating, or trying to translate, thought into action, had got him into a lot of hot water in a lot of places. A fervent Roman Catholic, he offended an influential bishop by an address to some gathering convened by the bishop in which he pointed out aspects of Christian behaviour in the Middle East which were less Christian in spirit than the behaviour of the Moslems. A friend and pupil of numerous Mullahs, he irked some of them in turn by extolling the superiority of certain Christian attitudes. To Jews he preached the virtues of Arabs, to Arabs he tried to explain the many noble qualities of the Jews.

Explaining the failure of some self-imposed mission he mentioned casually that in Jordan he had been arrested and imprisoned twice.

'I was going about the country talking to different personalities about peace and asking questions about their attitudes, and they thought I was a British Intelligence agent. Naturally enough, I suppose. You see the British authorities were making delays about renewing my passport so, as I wanted to go quickly to Amman I travelled on a false one, and the Jordanians spotted it and you understand that being a certified lunatic I am not always welcome in one group or another.'

At some point he had received, I gathered, a tiny legacy and used it to buy, for a matter of thirty or forty pounds, a big, powerful fourth-hand car which he particularly valued because he could use it to drive out to the great Trappist monastery at Mount Melleray. Here, as is the rule of such monasteries, he got bed and board without question of payment, and, which was very important to him, religious conversation with other temporary residents and with the Guestmaster, the only inmate allowed to speak.

To drive through furious rain up into the foothills of the mountains with no windscreen was exhausting and hazardous but worthwhile. Children, finding his car unattended by the roadside, had smashed the windscreen with a great pelting of jagged stones. 'But,' he said, 'you know how it is. Those children don't have much to occupy them. It's natural for them to behave like that. I've invited a lot of them to my house and we can cook things on the fire and sing songs. It'll help them fill in the time.'

To ease his loneliness in the half-ruined house where he lived he had collected a curious assortment of pets. I never saw them all, but there were some pheasants, some special rabbits, or possibly Belgian hares, and other creatures I have forgotten of whom he spoke with affection. Again he went away for a week or so, to Dublin, or perhaps to England in connection with his Army pension, and on his return found that the children had broken into his place and killed or driven away all living creatures. This was clearly a shock to him, but he refused to express any kind of bitterness.

'Probably,' he said, 'I ought to have taught them more about those fellow-creatures – got them properly interested you know. Probably one spends too much time thinking about the state of the world instead of getting on with dealing with things right in front of one.'

There was, naturally, plenty in the state of the world to think about. There always is, but the urgency with which this or that grisly or uplifting event occupies a person's mind varies: there are times when it seems evident that now is the time for all good men and true to think unremittingly about what ought to be done, and how to do it, others when that sort of pressure seems to let up somewhat; there is a suggestion that the world is momentarily taking care of itself. Malahyde's exceptional sensitivities and human tenderness rarely permitted that sort of let-up. He had a wide range of acquaintances, mostly among ecclesiastics of the Christian and Moslem faiths, some of whom probably had some influence somewhere. He toiled for hours at his correspondence with them, sometimes consulting me as to how best to frame and phrase his letters so as to stir them to action.

When asking me to spend time in this way he would apologize saying 'I don't want you to think any of this is going to have much effect. Probably it'll have no effect at all. Still, it does seem to me that just in case, you know.' I agreed that a little time ought to be thus spent, just in case.

When he became discouraged, which was rare, at the supposed futility of his activities in these directions, I reminded him how often some action or agitation or protest which at the time seemed a more or less futile charade even to those taking part in it was seen by hindsight to have been, at the least, one of the drops that wore the stone away. I read recently an interview by a Western correspondent with a leader of the Vietcong. The Vietnamese showed the correspondent a section of the many miles of underground tunnel in which the Vietnamese, fighters and non-combatants, had lived for days and days on end under the seemingly endless, seemingly irresistible American bombing. The correspondent marvelled at the nerve, the sheer tenacity of those underground people. The Vietnamese told him 'We had our radios, and among the things that really kept us going were the news bulletins describing the marches and demonstrations against the war which were taking place all over the United States.' I hope that interview was read by some of those who must so often have returned from some wearying and possibly dangerous little demonstration with that sickening sense one often has on such occasions that the cynics are right, the whole thing has been at best a mere pissing in the wind, at worst some kind of self-indulgent, masochistic show-off.

At times when no specific crisis loomed, Mr Malahyde exerted himself to spread goodwill in general and more specifically goodwill between the West and the Soviet Union.

'It's truly horrifying,' he said, 'the extent to which people here are duped by the warmongers.'

I agreed that it was horrifying, though added that in my opinion and experience the Irish man and woman in the street was rather less often hoodwinked than the warmongers imagined.

'In any case,' said Malahyde, 'you agree that something ought to be done? Here's what I'm doing.'

What he was doing was to get up a fund to hire the town hall or the local ballroom for a gala entertainment at which the *pièce de résistance* would be a series of Russian songs and dances, preferably in suitable Slavic costume.

'But where,' I asked, 'are the performers to come from?'

He had thought of that. He had read in the paper that there were – I think – at that time seven, or possibly nine, male and female members of the staff of the Soviet Embassy in Dublin, including the Ambassador and the girl stenographers. Malahyde had written to the Ambassador inviting him to send as many of the staff as possible to sing, dance, and recite poetry. It would be desirable for them to bring such Russian instruments as balalaikas, and also anything they might possess in the way of characteristically Russian costume.

This letter must, I judge, have considerably astonished the Ambassador: or perhaps it was regarded as the kind of thing naturally to be expected in Ireland. Whichever way it was, Malahyde got a politely worded reply from the cultural attaché at the Embassy, thanking him for honouring him and the staff with such an invitation, but sadly regretting that none of them felt themselves to be sufficiently accomplished entertainers to venture upon such a performance.

Mr Malahyde blamed himself for having, he thought, phrased the invitation in such a way as to give a misleading and intimidating impression of the high standard of professionalism required. Should he, did I think, write again, stressing informality? I said I thought not: probably, given the state of international affairs, the Embassy people were really too busy to make the trip to Youghal.

There came the day when in Chile Allende really did fall victim to those 'monstrous and exceedingly powerful enemies' which included the C.I.A., the I.T.T. and the great American copper companies. As the news of mass murder and torture poured out of Santiago, I wondered whether Malahyde's active conscience would now reproach him for not, after all, having organized that 'posse of men of goodwill' which he had suggested to me at our first meeting. His reaction was, in fact, quite contrary.

'It shows,' he said, 'that I was naïve in my thinking. We could not have affected this tragic outcome. We may at least hope that it will have taught a lot of people to think more realistically.'

'In what sense?'

'In the sense of understanding that despite all the hypocritical talk about democracy, the other side will always use violence to prevent real reforms being carried out by peaceful democratic means. Strange that poor, poor Allende seems not to have understood that. His fate will be a lesson to everyone.'

I said we might certainly hope so.

28   Dangerous Border

A WOMAN who loved and much cherished her nearly new motor-cycle stood in the gallery at the Wexford Festival deeply longing to buy one of Patricia's pictures. But she did not have quite the price. She looked around at slightly cheaper pictures in Patricia's exhibition, but that was the one she desired. She asked that the picture be held for her for two hours. Patricia, observing the sincerity of her passion, agreed. Taking the motor-cycle for its last ride, the woman got it to the dealer, sold it, and came striding back with the price of the picture.

Such appreciation of art deserves success. And she had luck, arriving early. Very disparate people, some of whom could have sold a small oil-tanker or a chunk of a ranch in Texas, if they had been short of the price of one of the pictures they wanted, were circulating around Patricia's gallery that day. There were also some trawlermen, straight from the herring catch, and a group of nuns who had permission to use convent funds to buy at least one of these strange pictures. One of them took occasion to steal a bottle of superb whiskey, made for the directors of Jamesons exclusively and donated to Patricia by Shane Jameson. She knew the art-loving nun had taken it under her robe. But, as she said, 'You really can't frisk a nun.'

I used occasionally to sit in a corner of the gallery pretending to be absorbed and observing the reactions of the viewers. They were mysterious in the sense that they were mysteriously similar. Children would suddenly shout aloud, as at an exciting moment in the pantomime. Money-heavy picture-viewers from Hamburg and Minneapolis gave little gasps in the throat, indicating that they, like the children, had experienced a bit of a jolt. Once, in Cork, Patricia thought the place was being raided by the police. Dozens of men in blue were seen marching up. It was the drivers, conductors and inspectors from the bus depot who had been alerted by one of them who had originally looked into the gallery by accident. I had observed the same kind of reaction when she first exhibited in Dublin in 1972, and I observed it again later at her exhibitions in New York and London. In between exhibitions, I had the same stimulating reaction myself as the walls of the half-derelict room in our house which Patricia had turned into a studio glowed and sparkled and took on some peculiar, sometimes tricky or sinister looks as they finally began to crowd one another on the walls. A visitor said: 'Not content with displaying bits of the primeval ocean bed the way God made it, you've had the bloody nerve to get busy improving his handiwork.'

These pictures are partly the re-creation of an old art form, partly the creation of a new one. There was a time in the late seventeenth and the early eighteenth century when tropical shells were looked on in Europe as a kind of jewel. Good artists used them as a medium, and the resulting pictures were accorded much the same status as oil paintings. Later on, enterprising traders in London used to arrange with sailors on voyages to distant parts, such as the Caribbean, to collect shells. They provided them with boards, usually octagonal, with a pattern of holes in them, like a solitaire board. On the long return voyage the sailors devoted their spare time to fitting shells into the holes. Then the entrepreneurs bought the finished products and sold them to ladies who laid them about on drawing-room tables. Some of them that I have seen achieved an angular, Byzantine type of beauty. Others, as the critic and novelist David Hanley wrote, 'produced patterns that were cluttered and stiff, artefacts of loneliness or languor, having little artistic sympathy with the pictures that Mrs Cockburn produces today'.

As durable works of art, as heirlooms or investments, the lovely early pictures suffered from a fatal defect – the artists of the late eighteenth century had no gum which was not apt, indeed very likely, to perish within not much more than a hundred years. So that in, for instance, the Victoria and Albert Museum, you can see the frame and background of such a picture, with marks showing where the shells had been, but the shells themselves have fallen off and are lying at the bottom of the frame.

There followed a kind of Dark Age in this art, during which it was debased, at best, to the level of a cottage industry, and at worst to the sort of knicknackery which produced souvenirs of Margate in the form of basketwork encrusted round the edges with small coloured shells.

It was from this low condition that Patricia was impelled to revive and rescue the art. She had studied at the Westminster School of Art. She was a world traveller with a lifelong interest in conchology – and conchology in a double aspect; shells seen in their relation to marine biology in general, and shells seen as beautiful objects. 'The beauty,' she remarked, 'we casually crush under our feet into the sand.' And in the same way, she was equally interested in the chemistry of horticulture and the raising of flowers to make beautiful patterns.

Loving, as she did, to walk the Irish beaches she saw beautiful shells where most of us saw nothing but commonplace bluish and brownish little objects. She collected examples of every different type of shell there is in the official list of Irish shells. She went to work to make pictures of them, using combinations of acids to clean the scum off them so that they shone with their natural colours. And, unlike her eighteenth-century predecessors, she had gum that would hold as long as the oil of an oil-painting.

It was at the end of 1969 that Norah McGuinness, one of Ireland's leading painters, looked over Patricia's shoulder at the table where one of her pictures was being constructed, and said, 'If you don't go in for this professionally, you're a damn fool.'

By that day at Wexford in the seventies, I was still not much nearer finding out what it is about these pictures that has this singular appeal to children, mechanics and sophisticated connoisseurs. Talking volubly on that subject as we drove away I, supposed to be navigating, failed to read the map properly, and we had been going a long time before it was observed that we were headed approximately north-north-west instead of west. So, it occurred to me, looking in humiliation at the signpost, in about three hours' driving we could be on the frontier, in the middle of ugly civil war.

In his horrifyingly illuminating book *The Great War and Modern Memory*, Fussel, the American literary critic and historian, emphasizes as one of the major psychological factors in contemporary attitudes to the First World War that of 'propinquity': a man could be with his wife in a London theatre in the evening, and next afternoon in a world as unimaginably, inhumanly different as the far side of the moon, or hell. Nobody in, say, London could truly envisage the awful otherness of that unique world of desolation just across the Channel, though on the first day of the Battle of the

Somme, when 17,000 British troops were massacred within a few hours, there were people who boasted they had heard the noise as they walked on the front at Brighton.

Though there is no other element of valid comparison, this propinquity factor played an important role in Irish reactions to events in the north of the country. It often seemed to me that it was a factor underestimated by the British authorities. After all, there was not even a Channel between the areas of peace and the areas where the tanks and armoured cars dominated the scene, and numerous types of what were loosely called 'men of violence' murderously confronted one another. It is by no means surprising that there should have been times – for instance after the shootings in Derry on Bloody Sunday – when it seemed that popular pressures on the Irish Government to intervene – even militarily, even hopelessly – in the North might just possibly become such that a section of the Army would take matters into its own hands and confront Dublin with a *fait accompli*.

Those seriously, as distinct from merely emotionally, advocating such action did not suppose that the Army of the Republic, though it might not improbably achieve a swift, surprise tank penetration of Belfast, could for any length of time wage successful war against the British forces which would be immediately reinforced, if necessary, by the whole Army of the Rhine. They did argue that by forcibly 'internationalizing' the conflict they could explode the official British argument that the conflict in the North was a purely domestic British affair, not different from some civil commotion in Yorkshire. They would thus open the way to that intervention by the United Nations which Dr Hillery, Irish Foreign Minister, unsuccessfully sought to secure on a desperate dash to Washington immediately after Bloody Sunday.

We got our car headed homewards, in the direction of peace and civilized attitudes. Indeed it was truly striking how, despite the doings in the North, there was at no time, to my knowledge, more than a tiny, fanatical, minority displaying hostility towards Protestants. Many walls, it is true, were whitewashed with the words 'Brits Out' and other slogans of the Provisional I.R.A. For a time it was just a little risky to take a car with southern licence plates north of the border. Nervous British motorists thought they were in similar danger in the South. But in this they were mistaken. The common saying in the South was that the most dangerous road in the Irish Republic was that heading from Shannon airport to Limerick City. American tourists stepped off the transatlantic planes, jumped into their waiting drive-yourself cars, and roared off towards Limerick on the wrong side of the road. The feeling of Irish drivers was that they regretted the exceptional road hazard, but were glad to see the Americans still coming, undeceived by reports that when it came to sectarian violence and military commotion, the South was not much superior to the North.

Comically enough – and it is proof that there still exist some Englishmen who really are like Irish caricatures of the English – it was not uncommon for tourists from the United Kingdom actually to protest, to hoteliers or to the town council, about those 'Brits Out' slogans on the wall. Like Herr von Apfel during the occupation of Paris, they were looking for more correct behaviour on the part of the native inhabitants of the country of which they – for reasons which seemed to them self-evidently excusable and historically justified – were still occupying a big chunk.

These clownish harangues by the occasional Englishman, of the sort that ought never to be allowed out into any kind of modern political sun, raised some guffaws, and some gasps. And sometimes they had the effect of causing people who disagreed with the policies of the Provisional I.R.A. as much as I did to feel a brief throb of sympathy with those dangerously misguided men.

It was probably less difficult for an American to appreciate what was going on in the North than it was for even the most fair-minded Englishman who was rarely allowed to realize that from the viewpoint not simply of the Provisional I.R.A. but of very numerous people who regarded many of the Provisional's objectives as mistaken and their methods as wantonly, callously, and unnecessarily brutal, this was, in fact, a war.

If it was correct to speak of the Provisionals as 'men of violence' then how could one speak otherwise of the British soldiery? What, indeed, is a soldier paid and trained for except to be a man of violence? The British authorities treated the Provisionals as common criminals and repeatedly issued statements so describing them. The German occupiers of France took the same view of resisters there.

It would be fatuous to pretent that the analogy is historically accurate. It exists only in the sense that in both cases fighting men without uniforms are seen as in some way more violent than fighting men in uniforms provided by some government or other. This double standard has profound effects upon the way in which they can be, and are, presented to public opinion. And this form of distortion certainly does much to lessen the possibilities of any section of public opinion – in this case, say, British – understanding any other section – in this case, say, Irish.

Politicians, priests and pundits alike during the struggles in the North, repeatedly, lazily, wearisomely make incantation with this verbal mumbo jumbo to express their ritual shock, horror and disgust at events which certainly were shocking, horrifying and disgusting, but neither more nor less so than are the horrors ineluctably attendant upon any war. It is usually said that the horrors of civil war are worse than those of international war. Perhaps there was a time when that was true. But if you think of scenes in London during the blitz, think of the bodies melting in the flames of Hamburg or Dresden, think of children twisted in the womb after Hiroshima, then you doubt whether the relative degrees of savagery between the two sorts of war, civil and international, is at all easy to draw.

A number of my visitors at that time – American, British, European – would arrive asking, or obviously wanting to ask, one of two questions. One lot would be wondering how, and how long, a man like me could stand what they preconceived as the quiet (they meant stagnation) of rural Ireland. Wonderful for a holiday, of course, but surely I must be fretting to be where the action was? Or, a nasty thought, had a mixture of increasing age and country life got me so addled that I positively welcomed stagnation?

The other lot had a simpler, more earnest, and, in general, a more American approach.

Given, they reasoned, that we had an undeclared civil war in action nearly on the doorstep, given that this civil war in the North admittedly had huge repercussions in the Republic, was it possible for a person like myself to abstract himself sufficiently from the pressures and responsibilities of the immediate situation to get on with anything but very short-range writing – firing from the hip, so to say?

Both groups gave me the feeling that one is talking Swahili to a man who understands only Cantonese. I treid to explain to the first lot that so far from being stagnant, the Republic of Ireland – looked at economically, socially, artistically, religiously – was changing faster right in front of us than any country in Europe. My friends would assume I was kidding them. Not so. It was a fact. You could argue all day and night about whether this piece of change was for the better or that one for the worse. What you could not deny was that change was proceeding at a rate which was exhilarating to some, shocking to others, but in every sphere having mind-stirring effects greater, it seemed to me whenever I crossed the Irish Sea this way or that way, than any that were occurring in Britain.

To those others who thought that having a civil war on one's doorstep and a high degree of civil tension all around must be over-distractive, I tried to point out that there is reason to suppose that precisely that kind of situation stimulates, rather than inhibits, a general creativity. At least one can say that it does so in highly political animals. There is a lot of criticism of people in ivory towers turning out works of art when they might be better employed slugging it out down in the arena of everyday struggle. The flaw in this thought is the fact that in real life, and according to the literary and artistic form book, hardly anyone who immures himself in an ivory tower produces any creative work worth considering, so that the whole picture of a person achieving success by means of selfish withdrawal from mundane care and conflict is mainly nonsense.

At least, I should say that it seems nonsense to me. But that may be because I personally have never seen an ivory tower that I wanted to live in, and never esteemed any work obviously composed in one of them. To prove to my warmly well-wishing but apprehensive visitors that I was neither stagnating nor whipped into some sort of St Vitus' dance by the lash of current events, I could only point out that in addition to my regular weekly column for the *Irish Times* – certainly among the best and most civilized newspapers in Europe – and my column for *Private Eye*, I had, in the early 1970s, written a biggish book about the 1930s called *The Devil's Decade*, which aroused about equal enthusiasm and fury in all the right places in Britain and the United States; a rather small book called *Bestseller* which was, to put it pompously, a study of the social significance of selected bestsellers of the twentieth century from its beginning up to the outbreak of the Second World War; and two novels. In case they had read none of these books and wondered whether, given my circumstances, they could possibly be any good, I would, with coarsely shameless vanity, force them to read columns and columns of high praise by good people, columns of abuse by noted blackguards. No one was allowed to overlook the fact that Graham Greene in the *Observer* had chosen my novel *Ballantyne's Folly* as his 'novel of the year', and written of it that it was the funniest novel he had read since Evelyn Waugh's *Decline and Fall*.

The feature of the Irish scene which, I found then – and still find – most puzzling to the foreign observer is that successive governments (most notably the Fine Gael–Labour coalition) so often talked, behaved and legislated as though armed insurrection by the

Provisional I.R.A. was an ever-present probability, to be guarded against by what were usually called 'Draconian' ordinances of a blatantly undemocratic character.

I tried to save myself the trouble of answering separately innumerable persons' queries on this subject by writing for *Esquire* mazagine an article entitled 'Proper Thoughts on Ireland' and keeping copies of the magazine handy about the house.

In this I noted that it was natural, and to some extent correct, to assume that a lot of the governmental scare talk was to justify the government's seizure of the kind of powers every government would like to have but cannot get without producing some bogeymen to help the scare along. Bogeymen are certainly paraded often enough in the Republic. A former Minister for Justice, speaking to a visiting journalist, said: 'You have to remember that a great many of our laws are chiefly for guidance.' More recently, a member of the government, speaking much off the record said: 'Certainly it's quiet. But suppose you get what we call a doomsday situation in the North – and that can happen anytime. You know, we saw it after the shootings in Derry on Bloody Sunday, what the emotional reactions down here would be. In that situation you would just possibly see a get-together of both wings of Sinn Fein, in spite of the split and no matter what caused it. And with a united Sinn Fein and united I.R.A. as a magnet, you know and I know and everybody knows that a whole lot of old-style Republicans, young, middle-aged and old, the kind who say their uncles fought alongside Pearse and Connolly in 1916, would come rushing out of Fianna Fail, which is full of them and some out of Fine Gael too, to join with them.

'And in that case, my friend, you could get a running together of Catholic feeling, nationalist feeling, and more or less socialist feeling which, given the history and character of our people . . .'

The minister paused to leave a moment for appalled contemplation of this prospect. Like all generalizations about the supposed character of the Irish, his remarks were highly controversial. But their general tenor should command the closest attention. For no one can hope to think at all properly about Ireland, North and South, without taking into account the existence of three elements, normally more or less separate, which could be explosive if they fused.

Element number one is religious awareness, which is not the same as 'religion'. For it affects not only Catholics and Protestants, but also the relatively small but increasing number of freethinkers and pagans. Note here the remark of a British business executive after a year of monthly visits, North and South: 'I like the Irish all right, but I wish they wouldn't all of them keep bringing God into everything. My wife doesn't mind it. She plays golf all the time.'

This is the element in the Irish make-up which the more or less pagan British find hardest to understand. When an Irish Protestant shoots a Catholic or vice versa, British thinkers ask: 'How is it possible at this time of day for anyone to be so fervently Christian as to do a thing like that?' They conclude that the religious business is a more or less fraudulent façade, a disguise for more modern-seeming motivations, preferably economic. But it is no more a mere façade than are the religious beliefs of Hindus and Moslems, which also result in killings. It is at the very least the context within which all political activity must be conducted.

It is a fact that in the North the genuine beliefs of masses of Protestants are exploited by power-hungry politicians aiming to perpetuate their monopoly of power at Stormont. It is true that in the South the genuine beliefs of masses of Catholics are exploited by power-hungry politicians, supported by a section of the Hierarchy, aiming to consolidate conservative positions and interests against the perils of social change. None of this proves that the beliefs of those masses are not still genuine, passionate, and dominant in guiding their political behaviour.

Element number two is nationalism, born and bred during hundreds of years of British colonial rule before independence. It is less obvious in the North, among the Loyalists. But though the Loyalists, on religious grounds, are horrified at the notion of union with the supposedly priest-ridden South and proclaim attachment to the United Kingdom, they repeatedly startle and confuse the British and their governments by showing themselves totally alien to Britain in the Irishness of their attitude to life in general, and politics in particular.

The third element is an abnormally strong belief among active Irish people of all classes and religious adherence that the world is their oyster, or soon could be if they exerted themselves to prize it open. In the South, such beliefs were fuelled by the success – against all odds and the armed power of imperial Britain – of the War of Independence. In the North, people see themselves – once more against all the odds – as having successfully defended their territory and way of life against papist menaces and British betrayal.

This faith in their own capacity to open that oyster works in several directions. It causes young men starting in Irish business to believe, sometimes correctly, that they can become tycoons of international stature. It causes small farmers to believe, not often rightly, that with a big effort they may become big farmers. And if a man happens to be an industrial worker living in the slums or dreary housing estates of Dublin, he is apt to reflect that there is nothing in Irish history to prove that he cannot change an entire social system if he gets together with his fellow workers and tries hard enough to change the apparently invulnerable, established social system.

To throw light by factual example on some of these fusions and confusions of feeling, take the affair of the coaster *Claudia*. Flying the Cypriot flag and packed with arms and ammunition, the *Claudia* arrived in the spring of 1973 off Helvick Head on the south coast of Ireland. It was crewed by a number of Germans and Turks. But the most important man on board was a Mr Joe Cahill, one of the best-known and most active leaders of the Provisional branch of the Irish Republican Army.

The *Claudia* was met by an angling launch aboard which were a local printer, a headmaster of a school at Kilmacthomas, and an engineer specializing in plumbing. Since the security arrangements of the Provisionals are by no means up to normal international standards, the whole party was arrested. The Minister for Justice said that the arrests proved the success of the forces of law and order in suppressing the 'men of violence' and demonstrated to anybody, meaning in particular to the Northerners and the British, that the Irish Government was most actively engaged in suppressing this type of activity.

Publicly everybody quietly applauded that impeccable statement. But what a very large majority of the population actually felt was that it was perhaps a pity that, given the dire situation of the Catholics in the North, these arms had been denied them by the government of the Republic. Joe Cahill, it was true, was a political organizer, orator, and gun-fighter. At the same time, had he not done much to protect his co-religionists in the North? And from a national point of view had not the arms been destined after all to attack the British Army still occupying a section of this island?

An example of the third element in the make-up of the active Irishman was provided by numerous leading citizens in Dungarvan where the arrested engineering plumber had his business. They certainly were opposed to the activities of the Provisionals and they had very little interest in whatever might be happening in the Northern counties. But their factories were prospering, and the

246

arrested plumber was the only man available in the area who could keep the pipes going and the other technical apparatus working so as to enable them to continue uninterrupted production. Therefore, with no regard whatever to political considerations or political affiliations, they took to the wheels of their powerful automobiles and rushed to Dublin demanding the immediate release of the indispensable plumber. The demand was seen as justified and granted.

29   Days of Hope

KUANG-HSU, Emperor of China at the turn of the century, had bronchial catarrh and emphysema. It was noted that his voice had become 'light and thin like the hum of a mosquito'.

In 1974, during a visit to San Francisco, and later in New York and on Cape Cod, it began to be noted that my voice too, though not quite the hum of a mosquito, was certainly getting thinner and huskier, and became at moments, like that of the Kuang-Hsu Emperor, so feeble that 'those who were not in the habit of hearing him could not understand what he said'. Fortunately I, like the Emperor, had enough maladies to account for this condition without being forced to further inquiry. I say 'fortunately' because had cancer of the throat been diagnosed at that time the disclosure would have spoiled a delightful and stimulating trip. But as I was well known to have emphysema and intermittent bronchial catarrh, my voice trouble seemed satisfactorily accounted for.

One old friend said it was undoubtedly a punishment inflicted upon me by God for talking too much for about seventy years. Others added facetiously that it was a blessing for them, since they were able, at last, to get a word in edgeways.

The non-smokers, of course, said it was the result of too much smoking. The non-drinkers suggested that whisky was bound to erode the vocal chords at last. So we had a fine time unmarred by medical alarms, and it was not until after Christmas that the hoarseness and huskiness became so aggravating that I consulted the leading Cork throat specialist, Mr Michael O'Brien. He found a highly developed malignant cancer on a vocal chord, and shipped me off as a matter of urgency to the great surgeon Mr Harry Shaw in London.

There is necessarily a brief period of waiting between the surgeon's examination and the final diagnosis of the specimen cutting by the laboratory specialists.

That period, even though it may be only a few days long, is particularly trying to the nerves of the patient's relatives and friends. But for the patient himself, though worrying in its uncertainty, it is probably the time when he has the best opportunity to exert some influence on the course of events by the determined and concentrated exercise of what you may call either will-power, or strenuous wishful thinking, or an insistence that mind must have some authority over matter.

It is difficult to discuss this process without appearing to provide justification for some semi-mystical, perhaps quasi-religious mumbo jumbo. Yet it is a fact of existence as real as, say, a seemingly exhausted runner's capacity for a final sprint. Few people now deny the existence of psychosomatic illness: illness, that is, of which the symptoms may roughly be described as 'purely physical' but of which the causes, equally roughly, may be described as 'purely mental' or 'purely nervous'. It is not long since the victims in such cases were treated almost as malingerers, or frauds. But their symptoms and sufferings were real enough. And there is no reason why the process should not work in reverse: why the 'purely mental' should not play its part in curing as well as in causing disease. That this is so has, in point of fact, long been recognized in folklore, or common understanding expressed in common speech. How else did the expression 'the will to live' enter into use and become recognized by everyone as expressing a solid reality: a cause seen to be capable of producing tangible effects? (Admittedly folklore is inclined to look on the dark side. One reads more of people who lost all will to live, and so died, than of the other sort.)

Death from a broken heart is clearly the terminal stage of a psychosomatic illness. Old legends tell of very numerous persons who died in this way. The legend seems less interested in people who, at point of death, get such a powerful shot of heart-mending emotional balm that they spring to life again. I suppose many people who use the hoary phrase 'triumph of mind over matter' imagine they know what they mean by it. I think I know what people, including myself, imagine it means. But I am very hazy about it. Certainly it could mean something to a person who believed that there is a total dichotomy of mind and matter, very similar to the division expressed in the phrase 'body and soul'. In both phrases, about mind and matter, body and soul, there usually

249

remain traces of a more or less primitive religious view of the situation, in which mind or soul is morally and spiritually superior to matter or body. But if there is no such obvious distinction, or even contradiction, between them, if they are rather in the nature of co-operative elements in this or that human make-up, then it is hard to think convincingly of the one triumphing over the other. The notion of a sort of goody soul bringing law and order to baddy body has long been abandoned by thinkers of almost every school. But it may be noted that it is not much more absurd than the notion, which certainly is still popular with many philosophizers, that a person is simply the sum total of qualifiable chemical elements.

'To say that life is nothing but a property of certain peculiar combinations of atoms, is like saying that Shakespeare's *Hamlet* is nothing but a property of certain combinations of letters.' I do not pretend to have read all that was written by the former Economic Adviser of the National Coal Board, better known as the author of the best-selling *Small Is Beautiful*, the late Dr E. F. Schumacher. Nor do I agree with everything of his that I have read. But the passage I have just quoted from his book *A Guide for the Perplexed* is a brilliantly succinct reply to those described as 'reductionists' because they suggest that man can be reduced to, for instance, a bundle of atoms like the letters of *Hamlet*.

One good reason for the popularity of 'reductionism' among the philosophical outposts of the Western Establishment is that it can be, and is, used as a device for trying to take the wind, so to speak, out of the sails of Marxism.

For in so far as a reductionist philosophy influences the thought and action of an individual or group, it must do so in a negative manner, excluding any views of man's nature which would justify or make sense of man's mental and emotional aspirations towards improved life, new life; towards, ultimately, a human being superior to human beings as they exist under present conditions. In essence reductionism is a kind of anti-Marxist caricature of Marxist determinism. It is what anti-Marxists pretend that Marxist determinism is. A nonsensical pretence. Reductionist determinism implies, though it only occasionally asserts, the hopeless futility of man's effort to smash his way out of his limitations. Marxist determinism asserts only that people, as individuals or groups, can never be regarded as independent of the economic conditions in which they exist. But it asserts further that by taking thought, by exercise of his human skills, by correctly formulating his objectives, by audacious and dangerous action, man can limitlessly change those economic conditions. A Marxist declares that what happens to a sick man is determined by the physical and medical amenities available to him. It by no means denies that the effect of those amenities can be radically altered for better or worse by the individual's will to live, by his wishful thinking; by, if one wants to put it in such terms, the strength and judicious rationality of his hopes.

In an interview on Jean-Paul Sartre's seventieth birthday, the interviewer, Michel Contat, from the *Nouvel Observateur* suggested that Sartre's longing, as a child, to become famous had a lot to do with his actually becoming famous. Sartre replied: 'Yes, I think so. I think one becomes famous if one wants to, not through talent or innate disposition.' Contat did not further cross-question Sartre on the implications of a remark which, characteristically and no doubt intentionally, appears at the same time profound and teasingly smart-ass. Whatever Sartre may have meant, it is an observable fact that the construction, so to speak, of a hope certainly does contribute to the realization of that hope. Everyone recognizes this to be so (indeed it seems platitudinous to mention it) in connection with simple ambitions as, for instance, the desire to get a lot of money, or become Chief of Staff of some army, or be elected mayor and have a statue put up to you. Yet in less crude contexts, the notion of hope as a practical factor in a given situation strikes many people as mere whimsy.

It is easy to understand the nervous hesitation, or refusal, to accept a proposition which certainly does amount to an assertion that there is an important sense in which the present is determined not only by the past but by the future.

I have noticed that when I state this in bald terms as a fact of life people are apt to fidget and change the subject, as though I had advanced some idea not only annoyingly fanciful but novel too. This is the probably inevitable result of trying to talk intelligibly about time in spatial terms. But, as I have just said, in many contexts it is accepted as obvious. I have referred to the ambitions of individuals. The position is even more clearly evident when you look at groups or classes. Nobody, I suppose, is going to deny that mass actions, revolutions for instance, are affected both in their origins and their course by more or less well-defined hopes that not only is the change being brought about or at least attempted, with danger and sacrifice, going to be a change for the better, but also that the hoped-for better future will take a particular, more or less clearly pre-envisaged, shape. (This observation is not invalidated

251

by the existence of anarchist groups who, while believing that the dismantling of existing social orders is a prerequisite of any improvement in the human condition, consider that any advance definition of the shape society is thereafter to take must be some kind of betrayal of the spirit of revolution. To pin one's hopes on some deliberately indefined creative chaos is still to hope.)

While awaiting the report from the laboratory, and more vigorously still when it arrived and told the facts about my cancerous throat, I experimented with that 'do-it-yourself faith healing' which I had already practised many years before in a T.B. hospital, during an illness that lasted many months. It was certainly a lot too much to hope that this time round, with the tumour long established and flourishing, any amount of faith and hope was going to wish it away without major assistance from doctors and radiotherapy. But I did still believe on this later and rather more menacing occasion that wishful thinking, though it could not by itself effect a cure, must surely be able to contribute to it: perhaps, for example, this psychosomatic treatment, this mobilizing of mental and emotional power to affect the physical tissues, could help the cobalt rays to do the job without the necessity of a resort to surgery. If the ray treatment did in fact fail, surgery might still do the trick. But being then within a couple of months of my seventy-fourth birthday I had to admit to myself that 'tricky' was indeed what such an operation might be.

To my surprise and encouragement – surprise because I doubt if it could have happened twenty years earlier – two very experienced and hard-headed doctors mentioned, as a matter of course, that my obvious will to live was an important element in the case.

A peculiarly tiresome feature of the situation was the necessity to give up smoking. I had smoked an average of about sixty cigarettes daily for nearly fifty years. Before that I smoked fewer cigarettes because I was continuously smoking a pipe, as I had done since leaving school at the age of eighteen. Then one day, at around eleven o'clock in the morning, I suddenly fell down in a dead faint on the sidewalk of Fifth Avenue, New York. Finding no other discernible cause for this disconcerting mishap, my doctor decided, rightly I daresay, that the regular inhaling of strong pipe tobacco was probably respsonsible. I gave up smoking a pipe, and it is a fact that I never again fell down on Fifth Avenue, or any other New York street, at that hour in the morning. But I then took to cigarettes.

I expect, I almost wholly believe, the doctors are right in what they say about the ill effects of smoking and its connection with cancer. I certainly do not think that I myself or anyone else should take a chance on their being wrong. I do think, however, that the campaigns against smoking would be still more successful than they are if they were modified in two ways. First, the campaigners should talk more about, for instance, emphysema – which is more common, though perhaps less sensational, than cancer. Second, they should take somewhat more earnestly than they do the seriousness of the withdrawal symptoms and devote greater research to mitigating them. As things stand, any smoker who has learned from ex-smokers just how distressing those symptoms can be needs nothing less than the fear of certain death to make him face them and go on facing them without backsliding.

What, people used to ask, would have happened had Napoleon been in better physical shape at the battle of Waterloo? And long before there were jets and jet-lag, the Dover-Calais boat crossing by important statesmen and politicians did often exacerbate Franco-British relations. Similarly, every individual observer has a testing task when he tries to figure out how much his views, for instance, of a given country at a given time, his estimate of the way things seem to be going in those parts, are influenced by his personal state of health. The admirably perspicacious doctors at the Royal Marsden Hospital in London warned me at the outset that the cobalt ray treatment for cancer, though painless, is not only physically debilitating (the patient feels as weak as a kitten for weeks on end and may have to sleep around twelve to thirteen hours in the twenty-four). It also gets at the mind, producing more or less acute melancholia.

This is true – and in retrospect, though by no means at the time, it is an interesting experience. It is so particularly for persons like myself who are not normally of a melancholic or doleful disposition. Even such persons naturally experience occasions for depression several times a week. Your aeroplane has been delayed by fog; someone you love is taken seriously ill; you suddenly find you have even less money than you thought you had; the wrong people, a vile set, have triumphed in the elections to something or other; you realize too late that you failed to be as kind as you should have been to poor X, or as rude as you should have been to monstrous Y.

But all these are rationally comprehensible grounds for depression. If asked by jolly companions 'Why so blue, old boy?' you can respond as did the despondent-seeming American at the desolate coach station somewhere in the far Midwest when accosted by an ebullient Englishman.

'You seem,' said the Englishman with that touch of stern rebuke the stiff-lipped have ready for the whiners, 'a bit depressed, what?'

'Say, Britisher,' responded the lugubrious Iowan, 'my son is gaoled on a drug rap in Salt Lake. My daughter is a whore in Kansas City and writes to say life's fine. My wife is in yonder barn being fucked by a comparative stranger. Say, Britisher, would *you* be depressed?'

But the melancholia induced by the cobalt ray has no such firmly definable causes or even excuses. One minute you are sitting at your desk thinking of nothing more unusually depressing than the condition of Africa, your lack of money, or the platitudes in the morning paper's editorial; and from somewhere, as it seems, outside of yourself, like a cloud of tear gas loosed off at you by forces of invisible police, this melancholia, this murky despondency rolls up out of nowhere and envelops you. You try to identify its cause. You clutch at the doctor's last words: it is the cobalt ray. But of course it is of the essence of this kind of depression that such rationalization does not work. If it did, cobalt would be as feeble as a tiny devil confronted with a crucifix. On the contrary: it is of the essence of this radium-produced chemical gloom-maker that it is impervious to your reason: or rather it has infiltrated your physical apparatus, including your reasoning apparatus, and taken it over. A sad triumph of matter, one might say, over mind.

During that period, some of my principal contacts with the British public were the drivers of the mini-cabs I had to take to get each day across London to the hospital and back again. I thought that as a matter of principle one ought to find some way to employ the regular taxi-drivers, with their rigorous period of apprenticeship to the job, their solidarity and their useful trades union organization. I found that as a result of very complex factors, there were not enough of them available for my purpose. I was not strong enough to walk the streets hoping to pick one up, and the demand upon those that could be ordered by telephone repeatedly prevented any being reliably available to get me to my appointment with the ray machine. So twice daily I had a half-hour's drive with a mini-cab driver – thirty or forty different drivers over the period of my treatment. In one sense they were more illuminating than taxi-drivers, who are for the most part as totally, and, so to speak, regularly proletarian as dockers or railway-engine drivers. The background of these mini-cab drivers covered a much wider spectrum of British society. They included ex-army officers, some of whom were filling in time until someone offered them a job as mercenaries in some African state. They were eager to know what I thought were their chances. I was able to assure them that, in the light of such knowledge as I had of the facts of Africa, the opportunities for an able man to get fairly good money for that type of work there were good. I noted with interest that these would-be mercenaries were among the most hopeful of the drivers. So far as I could make out in the course of necessarily brief conversations, this hopefulness was in part due to barely conscious class feeling that society – like the public school system in Waugh's *Decline and Fall* – was not going to drop them altogether. More consciously and reasonably, it arose from an awareness of possessing special skills – specifically skills in the techniques of killing – which were bound to be in brisk demand somewhere sooner or later. A few others among the drivers had that mixture of faintly hostile taciturnity and sly braggadocio which often helps to identify the more feather-pated and disreputable sort of young criminal. They were the sort of people who, when I was their age, would have joined the Black and Tans and sought to terrorize Ireland. It is common to imagine that because such people are the product of our ill-made society, they are inevitably themselves enemies of that society. In my experience the second part of that supposition is false. Most of the young criminals I have known have been uncompromisingly, almost savagely, right-wing. For the more backward or brutal among them we have, today, no Black and Tans. We do have the National Front.

A large majority of the drivers were youngish men of, roughly, the lower-middle class, who had either been self-employed, or employed in small businesses as buyers or salesmen and had the business founder under them: mostly, it appeared, in the autumn of 1977. What all these unfortunate young men had in common was more notable than what differentiated them. They were articulate and quite without the reserve supposed to be general among the English. With one or two exceptions they appeared to be almost without ambition. One, indeed, went so far as to denounce ambition as a dangerously anti-social vice. He confided that his wife was tainted with this vice, and he expected he would have to leave her on that account. The drivers appeared, indeed, singularly content in their haphazard occupation, almost all being eager to point out how preferable it is to be one's own boss, able to take a couple of hours or even a couple of days off whenever it suited you rather than to earn more money at the cost of having to clock-in at a regular time, day after dreary day. (I saw an opinion poll some months later which seemed to show similar thinking among factory workers: a majority told the pollsters that if offered the choice between more money and longer holidays they would prefer the longer holidays.) About ninety per cent of the drivers who became known to me at all well were politically indifferent: many of them seemed quietly surprised that I should even wonder whether they had any political interests, let alone political preferences. (This, it should be said, was at a time when the newspapers were more than usually full of party politics, and there was much speculation about whether the outcome of some by-election then pending might not result in the Prime Minister going to the country in a general election.) In this total political indifference or apathy there was a mysterious, almost – it seemed to me – eerie absence of that fiercely expressed cynicism which I had so often encountered in the past: the loud demand to know what difference there was between any of the lousy, blabbermouthed, corrupt and incompetent political parties?

The mood of these men seemed to be one in which, since they expected nothing from the political system, they resented nothing either. They saw nothing much to look back on in more than mild indignation . One, who was currently on the run from the tax men, admitted that he had fiddled his taxes over a number of years. But it struck him as bloody silly, and a horrible waste of public money, that the tax people should have spent all the time and effort they clearly must have spent, in order to nail him. It certainly made you wonder. Another, a Greek by origin, had a mildly expressed grievance against the British apparatus of law enforcement. His trouble, he explained, was that he had until a few months ago been running a non-profit-making company of which the beneficiaries were foreign, and particularly coloured, students. The services rendered by this company were large, and largely appreciated by the students. Everything was swimming along very finely.

So what, I asked, happened to the non-profit-making company?

'All the time,' said the driver, 'my partner was stealing the profits and gambling them away at West End clubs. The law ought to have prevented that. And, then when I found out, the police said they were unable to do anything. So now I drive this mini-cab. Until the end of next month.'

'Why just then?'

Because then I shall have finished writing my novel, send it to a publisher and get an advance.'

'What's the novel about?'

'About the non-profit-making company, of course.'

'Why a novel for Gods sake? Much better write straight documentary.'

'No no. The English love novels. Look at John Galsworthy. You know about such things? Tell me a good publisher and I give you ten per cent.'

I met only one among the drivers who had voluntarily given up a well-salaried appointment with a financially sound enterprise. He had been one of a fairly large staff working for a pharmaceutical concern which was engaged, as part of its activities, in researching and testing sophisticated substances which might be useful to the police or the military when called upon to control crowds, subversive mobs and general rioting by dangerous elements. He and friends had noted that although the pay was good, the rate of labour turnover was strangely high. People would take a couple of weeks' sick leave, and then not return. He and others (all of them young married men) were sufficiently concerned to conduct a wide-ranging investigation. They made it their business to interview a large number of former employees of the concern. They found that some high percentage of them (I forget what he said was the exact figure but it was above seventy-five per cent) were suffering from unusual diseases – some not lethal, but disfiguring in their effects on the skin, others affecting the mind as well as the body. The victims were mentally deranged. I was peculiarly interested in this statement because I had recently read an account of similar symptoms, similarly discovered, after long delay, among workers at a plant manufacturing insecticide near Houston, Texas. I was aware also of how the police in California had turned down a similar method of 'anti-subversive crowd control' on the grounds that its effects made it, under present American conditions, politically too hot to touch. They passed it on to the Bolivians who used it successfully to quell student discontent and unrest.

The mini-cab driver I speak of was a well-brought up man with no subversive thoughts. He even wondered aloud whether he had not failed in his duty by quitting. I pointed out – claiming my privileges as a much older man – that he had his obligations to his family to consider. And, I said, there will be plenty of other chaps ready to do the job anyway.

This in turn gave him a further cheering thought. He said: 'I hear that now they're developing a really new crowd-control device. It doesn't leave any permanent scars, and it deranges the mind only temporarily.'

I said it sounded like a police chief's dream.

To my mystification, all these young and youngish men shared an attitude to cancer which one would suppose more appropriate to some believer in voodoo. I was mystified because I had come across this attitude before, but thought it simply a relic of the kind of thing one's aunts were taught to think in the Edwardian age. Not so. Politely, as a matter of routine, the drivers would occasionally inquire what was my business at the hospital. Apart from being polite, they simply wanted to know whether I could give them a time at which they might call for me, instead of my having – as was invariably the case – to call another mini-cab company.

I told them I had cancer of the throat, as I would have told them I had any other serious *malaise*. And here was where things became strange. Some of them sat rigid at the wheel, as though I had shown them some kind of Medusa's head, turning them to stone abaft the driving apparatus. Others, and this I found strange but touching, profoundly apologized for asking the question in the first place. Had they known, they said, they would never have ventured to pose such a question. They stammered in embarrassment and I could nearly hear their kind hearts stuttering too.

I nominate what *I* might call 'the Cancer Taboo' as a subject for a specialist thesis. The subject is, at least to me, of deep interest and must, I think, offer some kind of significant pointer to Western thinking. At a random guess one might suppose that this pother about cancer results from the belief that the disease is not only unspeakably painful but in many cases incurable. That this belief is too often justified by the facts still leaves a lot of questions unanswered. To mention just one: might one suppose that the existence of an incurable disease presents human beings with so humiliating a notion of their situation in what used to be called the Scheme of Things, that they would quite simply prefer not to talk about it? In that case, what needs to be changed is the fatalistic notion that the Scheme of Things is unalterable.

30 Envoi

I HAVE always believed firmly in luck. Considering what a lot of it I have had in my life I could hardly do otherwise. As the cancer treatment progressed, I reflected on my extraordinary luck in not being attacked by the disease a few years earlier. To judge by what doctors had so often said about my way of life, that might have easily happened. And now I understood from what I was told at the hospital that had that happened, had the tumour developed to the extent it had before the present ray treatment was discovered, my chances of survival would have been low indeed. That was the time when the X-ray suddenly indicated cancer as well as T.B. The doctors had to tell me – because I had asked them always to tell me truthfully how things looked – that they could not operate upon the cancer because of the already devastating extent of the tuberculosis.

At Heathrow airport on my way home from the cancer treatment, a man at a table near the bar asked why I was in a wheel-chair. What ailed me? I told him, and, referring to the recently developed wonders of the ray treatment, suggested that possibly if we could all hold on to life long enough, medical science would keep coming up with new cures, new methods of warding off senility itself, so that perhaps we already have a chance of living to, say, one hundred and fifty.

It was a sweaty day, some industrial dispute was in progress, the flight schedules were in chaos and I had already gathered that the man was missing appointment after profitable appointment in Dortmund.

Upon my offering this preview of possibilities he glared at me with weary contempt.

'What,' he snarled, 'makes you *want* to live to one hundred and fifty?'

I had no answer ready. I had foolishly taken it for granted that such a thing would be seen to be desirable. Before I could answer, he said: 'It won't happen, anyway, because they'll spend the money they might use for medical research on weapons of war; engines of ever-increasing destructive power, old boy.'

I admitted that seemed probable enough. 'And listen to me, old boy,' the stranger said, his face now absolutely aglow with gloom, 'Suppose, just for the sake of supposing, you survive the bloody holocaust? Y'know what you'll be doing? You'll be living like a caveman on the face of the devastated planet; you and all around you waiting to die a slow and agonizing death from leukaemia . . . watching women giving birth to babies hideously deformed.'

I said perhaps we could yet avert the imminent war. Perhaps, I said, the human race could show itself capable of facing changing conditions. Even animals can do this, sometimes surprisingly. Patricia had told me of three Australian hunters imported to Ireland. In the first year they grew heavy winter coats in summer, and nearly died of sweaty heat. In the winter they had only their thin coats, and nearly died of cold. But at the end of three years they started growing the right coats at the right time. I told the man this. Could not the human race, I asked, prove at least as adaptable as those Australian horses?

There was considerable uproar all around, and he may have thought I was calling him a horse's arse. More likely, for the phenomenon is becoming common enough among people of our day, he was simply outraged by a challenge to that conviction of the futility of everything which had become, for him, not only habitual but positively restful.

He looked at me with such fury that if I had not been in a wheel-chair he might actually have hit me. I could see the barman peering anxiously across at us. In the conditions prevailing at the airport, everyone's nerves were on edge and there could easily have been a nasty scene.

It would have made a suitably topical item in the newspapers. Men arrested for brawling about the future of the human race.

Index

Index